Yesterday's Papers
Volume 4.

Life on the Island 1935 to 1949.

*From the pages of
The Isle of Wight County Press*

by
Alan Stroud

Now and Then Books

ISBN 978-0-9565076-1-7
© Alan Stroud 2010.
Typeset by Alan Stroud.

Printed by
Short Run Press Limited
25 Bittern Road
Sowton Industrial Estate
EXETER
EX2 7LW

WITH WHICH IS INCORPORATED "THE ISLE OF WIGHT EXPRESS."

Acknowledgements.

As always I need to thank my wife, Sue, my son, Tom and friend, Richard Brimson for their proof reading skills and suggestions.

I'm grateful once again to the County Press Shop staff and Robin Freeman, Managing Director, all of whom could not be more helpful.

Thanks also to Charlie Taylor, Cowes historian, David of Isle of Wight Bacon and Maurice Leppard, who all kindly provided answers to my enquiries.

I am also especially indebted to Gay Baldwin who took the time and trouble to push me over the precipice of self-publishing.

Finally, thank you to Jane and Ian Kennedy of Oakwood Press who always said yes.

Please note the new publisher for this series:
Now and Then Books. Cowes, Isle of Wight .
E-mail: nowandthenbooksiw@googlemail.com

Volumes 1, 2 and 3 are published by The Oakwood Press, P.O.Box 13, Usk, Mon. NP15 1YS, from whom they are still available at www.oakwoodpress.co.uk or through local bookshops.

This fourth volume in the series 'Yesterday's Papers' covers the years 1935 to 1949, a period dominated by the Second World War. Once again the only intention is to provide what is hopefully an objective snapshot of life during these years using articles from the County Press archives, accompanied by some background information.

Happily the standard of those articles remains as high as in the previous three volumes in terms of variety and quirkiness, and it has once again been more a case of deciding what to leave out rather than what to include.

The paper, now 50 years old, was successful and confident; it was well received by its readers and especially well received by its shareholders who over the years had become accustomed to receiving regular and healthy dividends. As the only Island-wide newspaper it had now become *the* forum for airing opinions on the Island, especially through its letters column and during the war years its weekly appearance became a very important part of Island life.

For the County Press its reporting of the war was one of its finest hours, when overnight it came into its own as a trusted source of information and an unofficial rallying point for the Island. The wartime reporting is of the highest standard. Compelling, dignified and often touching, it deserves a book of its own.

The outbreak of war had been widely expected since the mid-1930s and when it did eventually come, history repeated itself as far as the County Press was concerned and almost immediately the supply of newsprint* dried up, just as it had done on the outbreak of the First World War. Luckily it was not a pressing problem this time because in early 1939 the management had made what were to prove very prudent purchases of newsprint, a board meeting of December 1939 noting that a gratifying total of 320 reels were held in store. This abundant supply, which on its own would produce more than a year's newspapers, did not guarantee the paper's physical size, however, and wartime restrictions meant that by July 1940 the number of pages in each edition had been drastically cut from 16 to only six. During the latter part of 1940 the number of pages per issue hovered between 8 and 12 and eventually the County Press settled down to become a 12 page edition for most of the war years.

Building up that store of newsprint had also been a wise financial move. In August 1939 the price of newsprint had stood at £11 per ton; six months later it had risen to £17 and by November 1940, just 12 months later, the price had soared to £28 per ton.

Life for the newspaper during the war was further complicated by a lack of manpower. Many of the younger staff were conscripted, leaving the production of the newspaper in the hands of the remaining more senior employees, not all of whom were used to working on the shop floor. However, through it all the paper never once failed to appear, not even on the occasion in April 1943 when their High Street office suffered severe bomb damage.

The six-page issues for the years 1941 and 1942 have left a lasting impression on today's microfilm archives. Ordinarily there is one reel of microfilm for each year but the reduced size of those two years' editions means that today, both years reside on the one same reel.

---

* The rolls of paper on which newspapers are printed.

Introduction

The Island in the 30s and 40s.

The Island was a pleasant place to live during the late 1930s. Like the rest of Britain it was beginning to cast off the depression; unemployment was falling, living standards were higher, personal income was rising and for the moment the future looked bright.

The Island was still a safe place to live. Between the years 1935 and 1949 there were no cases of murder at all, but there were three cases of manslaughter, two being crimes of passion which resulted in one conviction and one acquittal and the third manslaughter relating to an abortion. In each case, those involved were already known to each other.

The Island's courts were as busy as ever but the nature of the cases heard had changed out of all recognition over the last 50 years, motoring offences now taking up most of the court's time at the expense of the more interesting or quirky cases that had previously come to court. 70-year-old motoring offences are no more interesting than modern ones and the unfortunate consequence is that the number of court cases in this volume are considerably less than in previous ones.

The defining event of the period was the Second World War. Those Islanders who had lived through the first war and expected the second one to be much the same were to receive a harsh shock. Its effect on the Island and its inhabitants could not have been more different to that of World War I. This time they would need no letters home from the front, nor newsreel footage to appreciate the horrors of war; this time the Isle of Wight itself was to become a direct and intimate part of the frontline just as surely as soldiers on the battlefield. The war in all its horror was to visit them in an alarming manner and would soon threaten their very lives and those of their children.

For the next few years Islanders could expect to be bombed, and on occasions even machine-gunned, at any time of day or night just as if they were important military targets, for that, of course, was exactly what they had become.

Unfortunately for the Island it was just miles from a major port and an important naval harbour and was itself, home to a prolific shipbuilder, J.S. White of Cowes. In these circumstances the Island could hardly have expected to escape German bombs but the severity and duration of the attacks came as a terrible shock. The County Press accounts of the horrors of bombs falling on civilians are graphic and sometimes harrowing but are always restrained, even poignant. With terrible scenes being witnessed on a daily basis during the major bombing campaigns of 1941 it would have been understandable if the *County Press* columns had reflected the anger the public must have felt, but through it all, their reports remained professionally detached and unemotional which leant them a quiet dignity.

For those of us lucky enough not to have experienced the war at first hand mere imagination is not enough to understand what some of our parents and grandparents went through night after night and day after day. Due to wartime restrictions the County Press was not able to be as forthcoming about these events as it might have wished to be. Place names were strictly forbidden in accounts of bombing raids which lead to references simply to '*a south coast town*' or '*a south coast resort.*' Ironically, the practice was somewhat undermined by the next week's death announcements invariably giving the names and addresses of those who had recently died, stating they had met their end '*as a result of enemy action.*'

The end of the First World War had signalled the start of an economic boom which gave Britain's industries a kickstart but that was not the case when World War II ended. Instead, the first thing to hit Britain following the end of the war was a wave of austerity and the Island was to suffer its fair share. The wartime shortages, far from disappearing, continued and one of the most immediate and distressing of these post-war shortages was that of housing. On the Island house building remained at a virtual standstill for several years; the explanations offered being many and varied, ranging from stifling bureaucracy to a shortage of manpower in the brick yards. Whatever the reason, the end result was that many families on the Island suffered housing conditions as bad and as cramped as their ancestors had in Victorian times.

The Workhouse at Parkhurst was still in existence despite having undergone various name changes. In 1937 it was described in the County Press as '*Forest House, the oldest institution in the land*' while in 1939 an inmate was described as '*a pauper of the Public Assistance Institution, Parkhurst.*'

In 1948 the Poor Law system was abolished, which in plain English meant the end of what was left of the Workhouse. Since its beginnings it had been under the control of the local council in one form or another; by 1948 it had become known as 'Forest House' and now the old buildings of the workhouse were to be absorbed into the new NHS St Mary's Hospital. In what must have come as a major shock to many, the non-medical-case residents, numbering several hundred, were to be re-homed in 'guest houses' across the Island, but at their expense, rather than the state's.

Since the 1920s, the County Press had picked up 10,000 new readers and it is quite plain from the tone of letters to the editor during these years that not all of them shared the politics or social standing of the more traditional readers. The 'working classes' were becoming more vocal about their aspirations, more assertive about their expectations and their place in society; the status quo was changing and the pages of the post-war County Press demonstrate the point only too clearly.

The World in the 1930s and 40s.

War aside, the biggest domestic event of the 1930s was the abdication of King Edward VIII in November 1936 after a reign of just 10 months. The new king had charm and charisma but he also had a secret; he was in love, and unfortunately the object of his attentions, Mrs Wallis Simpson, had two insurmountable flaws; she was a divorcee and equally as horrifying in some eyes, she was an American.

When Edward became King only a handful of people in Britain were aware of the affair, not a word of it having so far appeared in the newspapers but through word of mouth it had slowly become an open secret. By contrast, in America the affair had long been public knowledge, with front pages given over to excited accounts of the King of England's infatuation with, and likely marriage to, one of their very own. In Britain the affair went unreported thanks to obliging newspaper editors until the Bishop of Bradford spoke, in a sermon, of the new King's responsibilities and in particular his marital duties as head of the Church. He later claimed that he had no knowledge of the King's affair but it was a moot point; the cat was out of the bag and British newspapers were at last free to run headlines declaring that their King wished to marry a twice-divorced American. Support for the marriage was thin on the ground, both here and in the Commonwealth, and within a few weeks the King had renounced his throne. The Coronation was cancelled, the spoons were melted down, and the books were pulped but the King's brief reign led to some interesting anomalies.

Millions of stamps bearing his portrait were already in circulation and were so numerous that they could still be found in stamp machines nearly two years after he had gone, but more interestingly, scattered across the country were permanent reminders of the un-crowned King, including one here on the Island. A handful of public buildings had been commissioned during his brief reign and as usual they had been designed to incorporate the King's crest but before the buildings could be opened, he had gone, and so it is that Newport telephone exchange in Crocker Street, commissioned in 1936, is one of the rare buildings in Britain to bear the crest of the King that never was. It can still be seen to this day in the brickwork above the front door.

The King disappeared just as Britain had seemed set fair for an economic boom. As the late 1930s approached, unemployment fell, wages rose modestly and the memories of the depression and mass unemployment began to recede but there was a cloud on the horizon. It was clear that some form of military action by the new government in Germany was inevitable but not even the gloomiest of forecasters could have predicted the scale of what was to become World War II.

Following the end of the war, the election of 1945 provided a surprise result when against all predictions, a radical Labour government came to power with a sizeable working majority. They promised the nationalisation of the iron, steel, coal, and fuel industries, the takeover of inland transport and the Bank of England, and the introduction of a National Health Service. During the next four years all these things became a reality.

During the war unemployment had dropped to its lowest level ever and this remained the case for the next five years, jobs being found for all the returning soldiers. For two years following the end of the war, 4 million troops were demobbed, amounting to 4000 to 5000 a day. According to government figures 31% of the population had been living in poverty in 1936 but by the end of 1949 that figure had dropped to just 3%, and 'National Assistance' soon became a major part of the Welfare State. When the National Health Service started it found there was a huge latent demand for glasses and false teeth, and £2 million worth of glasses, which in the past would have proved sufficient for nine month's supply, were dispensed in just six weeks. The NHS was an overnight success.

One problem facing the government after the war was Britain's relative poverty. Far from wartime shortages coming to an end they continued to grow; and in August 1947 the meat ration, still in place, was reduced even further and the basic petrol ration for domestic use was abolished completely which effectively brought about an end to motoring for pleasure until 1951. Travelling abroad for pleasure was banned and strikes, prohibited during the war years, remained illegal until 1951.

The national housing shortage was the worst frustration of the post-war years. Councils were encouraged to build 'council houses' and private builders were encouraged to build for councils rather than wealthy private owners. No building could take place without a licence from the local council and no licence was issued unless the building gave priority to homes, factories, and schools.

It was all to no avail. The housing shortage in 1951 was just as bad as ever.

Notes.

This volume starts where volume three ended, beginning with the first issue of 1935 and ends with the last issue of 1949.

As in previous volumes, the items headed 'The Week's News' and 'Town and County Notes' are compilations. They are undated for the most part as the date is usually superfluous but they are always placed within five or six weeks of their original appearance. On the odd occasion where the date of an item has been considered relevant it appears in brackets.

For the most part the items are in their entirety and appear just as they did when they were originally published. Some longer items have been edited and where this occurs it is indicated by dotted lines.

As in the previous three volumes contemporary spellings and printing conventions have been retained and are not misprints. The practice of spelling street names in the form 'High-street' or 'Castle-road' came to an end during this period, the change occurring in the late 1940s, correspondingly both forms appear here.

Throughout the book the titles used for the articles are those that accompanied them on the day they first appeared in the County Press; none have been altered or modified in any way. Photographs, previously relatively plentiful, are far and few between during this period. A weekly page of photographs had become a regular part of the County Press since 1924, but they immediately disappeared on the outbreak of war, not returning in any meaningful form until 1948, and even then only in very small numbers. Correspondingly, there are photo pages only for the years 1935 to 1939.

As in the previous volume the photographs in this book all originally appeared in the County Press and the reproductions have all been taken from the original photographs as they appeared in the paper at the time. Correspondingly, some of them show clear signs of their origin. Hopefully, their historical interest will outweigh these shortcomings.

The captions for each photograph are those that originally accompanied them when they first appeared, however, the dates shown alongside the photographs are the date of publication, not the date of the event.

CONTENTS

9

1935.

In 1813 tollgates were erected on the Island to raise revenue for the upkeep of the roads. Initially there were five at the approaches to Newport, two at Ryde and one each at Cowes, East Cowes, and Yarmouth. Others were added over the years and they all remained in service until 1889 when central government took over the funding of road construction.

The former keeper of the Debourne tollgate* in Cowes, now in her 91st year, told the County Press of her time collecting tolls there...

January 26th, 1935.

THE NONAGENARIAN OF THE COWES TOLL HOUSE

An interesting old lady is Mrs. Eliza Kavanagh, who resides at Sandown. She will celebrate her 91st birthday in October... She has a good memory and it is very interesting to listen to the stories she has to tell of years ago... For over 40 years she was toll-keeper at the Old-Toll-house at Cowes, situated at the corner of the four cross-roads, which still retains its old tiled roof. The deeds of the house date back 130 years, but it is probably much older than this. The upright oak pillars which support the roof are still in a fairly good state of preservation. The stone walls, which are over a foot thick, show how soundly the house was constructed in those days. In the garden is a well, some 20ft. deep; in Mrs. Kavanagh's time this was the only means of obtaining water for domestic purposes. Many Islanders remember this old Toll-house, with its two gates across the road, when they had to pay ¼d. a head for sheep and pigs, ½d. for a cow, 2d. for a horse, and 3d. for a carriage and horse. Pedestrians went through free. Asked how much a week she took, Mrs. Kavanagh replied '15s. to a £1.' She used to take the money to Northwood, where there was another toll-gate, and the money so collected from the two gates was sent to someone on the mainland. She received 5s. a week for the collection, but she states that 5s. in those days was a lot of money...

-------------◆-------------

THE WEEK' S NEWS.

COWES. — An interesting experiment is to be made by the Southampton, Isle of Wight, and South of England Royal Mail Steam Packet Company. They have decided that white is not a very satisfactory colour for the funnels of the leisure steamers and tugs, and they are therefore proposing to try dark red.

At a meeting of the League of Nations at Newport on Sunday, the Archdeacon of the Island (the Ven. Robert McKew, D.D.) said that on one of his visits to his native Ireland he hurried to a Dublin station to catch a train due to leave at 10.15 a.m. Two clocks were visible from the platform, one showing the time as 10.10 and the other as 10.20. He said to a porter: 'What's the use of having two clocks showing different times?' and the porter replied, 'And will ye tell me what's the use of having two clocks showing the same time?'

* The 'Round House' at the junction of Park and Place Road

LADY MOTORISTS VICTIMISED BY MYSTERIOUS MECHANIC. — Island motorists are warned against the activities of a young man, who, posing as a motor mechanic, has recently stopped several women drivers on the road, and after warning them that a wheel is wobbling and appears likely to come off, offers to carry out repairs on the spot. If he is allowed to attend to the alleged defect he demands exorbitant payment. We understand that several women motorists have met this individual on the Freshwater road and in the Cowes district... and in one instance he demanded 30s., which was paid.

A MONSTER HEN'S EGG. — An egg weighing 7 ½ oz. laid by a hen belonging to Mrs. Lance Barnes, of Blythe Cottage, Brook, has been exhibited in our head office window at Newport this week.

———————————————◆———————————————

The National Health Service was 13 years away and for the moment nearly all medical care had to be paid for. One exception was dental care, which on the Island was funded by the School and Child Welfare Authorites, but despite being free not everyone could be persuaded to take advantage of the service...

January 26th, 1935.

SCHOOL DENTAL TREATMENT REFUSALS.
'OVER INDULGENCE OF CHILDISH WHIMS.'

'Until dental treatment is made compulsory a good deal of the time of the school dentists will be wasted' says the County Medical Officer Dr. J. Fairley, in his annual report as school medical officer, who suggests the need for 'a stricter discipline and less consideration for the 'fads and fancies' of many schoolchildren in regard to dental treatment and the serving of milk in schools.'

'It is difficult to understand,' writes Dr. Fairley, 'why half the children who need dental treatment are allowed by their parents to refuse it when this is not only advised but provided practically free of cost. Nowadays it is surely a matter of common knowledge that a person cannot enjoy good health if he does not possess a sound digestion... In spite of these elementary facts which must be known to nearly everybody, half the children needing dental treatment are allowed to refuse it. What is the explanation? It cannot be entirely due to parental ignorance, although that is one of the causes. It is probable that this is another instance of the tendency to over-indulge young children and their childish whims. It is the experience of most teachers that in the matter of the school milk ration some children must have it heated, some can only take it cold, and others won't take it at all; some must have it as Horlicks or flavoured with cocoa and so on. Can it be doubted that a stricter discipline and less consideration for the fads and fancies of these infants would be to their advantage? ... Out of every three children one did not require dental treatment, one needed treatment and had it, and one needed treatment but refused it.

———————————————◆———————————————

TOWN AND COUNTY NOTES.

NEWPORT — THE NEW FIRE ENGINE, was delivered to the brigade on Thursday. Unfortunately it was found that there is barely room to get it between the pillars of the Town-hall into the fire-station. There is not sufficient margin of safety for quick exit in case of a call, and either the entrance will have to be widened or a garage provided elsewhere.

YARMOUTH — TRAFFIC CONTROL ON YAR BRIDGE. - The first traffic light signals to be installed in the Island were put into operation at Yar Bridge, near Yarmouth, yesterday afternoon... Special arrangements for the working of the signals had to be made, owing to the fact that on the bridge itself there is only room for one vehicle...

The BBC Advisory Committee in its most recent list of pronunciations approves the use of the word 'televiewer' to describe the receiver of a broadcast television programme.

SEAVIEW. — Speaking at a League of Nations meeting at Seaview last night, a German who refused to give his name, but described himself as an anti-Nazi, said he did not agree with the views of a speaker that the old military class had returned to power in Germany and were dictating to the people. In Germany there were a large number of peace-loving people (applause)... He said he refused to give his name because he was shortly returning to Germany and things might be made very unpleasant for him if his name were known.

NEWPORT — THE RINK THEATRE TO BE DEMOLISHED. - In a speech at the close of the final performance of 'The Rebel Maid' at the Rink Theatre on Saturday, Mr. Challen said it would be rather sad to think that that would probably be the last entertainment given in that building as they understood that it was to be pulled down. It was a great pity that Newport should be without a theatre. Mr. A. Hill, the lessee, states that the demolition will begin on Monday ... A condition of rental was that the landlord should have full possession of the building for the holding of a wool fair one week in each year free of charge. This necessitated the removal of the whole of the seats, the cost of which was equal to half of the yearly rental. (Feb 23)

◆

Britain was on its way to becoming a nation of car owners and as early as 1935 nearly 10,000 cars had been registered on the Island. For the moment there was no driving test to pass and no national speed limit to obey and both of these factors were being blamed for the large numbers of road deaths.

In 1934 over 7,000 people had been killed on the road in Britain* and the County Press had sometimes needed to use the headline 'Motoring Fatality' three times in the same issue. The government was eventually forced to act...

---

* In 2007, 3000 people were killed on Britain's roads.

March 16th, 1935.
THE 30 MILE SPEED LIMIT.
IN FORCE ON MONDAY.

The 30-mile speed limit for cars in built-up areas (where there are public lamps) comes into operation throughout the country on Monday. During the last two days the County Council highways staff have erected 60 notices indicating built-up areas in the Island on which the 30-mile speed limit will be in force on and from Monday... Perhaps the most notable local effect of this restriction is that it will apply to the greater part of the roads between Newport and Ryde and Newport and Cowes. For the time being the unlighted villages are not affected. The signs indicating the commencement of a built-up area are circular plates 18in. in diameter with the figures '30' on a white background inside a red circle... It may be as well to remind drivers that the 30-mile limit does not absolve them from prosecution for dangerous or careless driving when proceeding at slower speeds, and they will be well advised not to attempt to overtake any car travelling at a speed approaching the limit in a built-up area, as this is the method the police are likely to adopt to catch offenders.

◆

THE WEEK'S NEWS.

On Thursday the Southern Vectis Omnibus Company took over the services of Brown's Buses which for 10 years have been a popular means of public transport between Newport and the West Wight and in the West Wight area... The Company have asked for authority to vary timetables to increase the number of pick-up places, and to reduce fares over a number of stages in the West Wight area.

NEW AIR SERVICE BETWEEN THE ISLAND AND LIVERPOOL. — The Isle of Wight ... has been further honoured by the introduction of a daily express return air service with the north of England by Railway Air Services. The service was inaugurated last summer from Cowes to Bristol, Birmingham, and Liverpool. The opening of the new aerodrome at Sandown enables the journey to be made direct from thence. By this excellent service passengers leaving the Island shortly after 9 a.m. can reach Liverpool by midday. (June 29)

BITTEN BY AN ADDER — MOTTISTONE BOY'S LIFE ENDANGERED. — Raymond Ryall, the 5-year-old son of Mr. and Mrs. F. Ryall, of Mottistone Farm-cottages, is now recovering in the County Hospital after being critically ill during the week-end as a result of an adder bite. The boy was playing in the backyard and he apparently trod on the adder, which bit him in the calf of the left leg ... By the evening the poison had so seriously affected him that he was taken to hospital by Mr. Jackman of Mottistone Farm.... Mr. Jackman and his sons kept watch at the spot where the boy was bitten and on Monday they shot a pair of fully grown adders.

A great deal of Britain's housing stock was sub-standard and needed replacement or repair and in 1930, legislation was introduced which allowed local councils to take matters into their own hands. On the Island many houses were owned by private landlords who now found their properties the subject of compulsory slum clearance schemes...

June 29th, 1935.

SLUM CLEARANCE SCHEME AT COWES.

An inquiry into the application by the Cowes District Council for confirmation of four Clearance Orders was held at Northwood house on Tuesday.... In the case of Order No. 2, 1 to 9, Felpham Place*, and Sussex House, Mr. Groundsell objected on behalf of the owner, Mr. A. A. Soper.... With the exception of No.1., which had a flank wall onto the street, and Sussex House, which fronted onto the street, all the houses opened onto a narrow court yard between the two rows. That passage was approximately 61ft.6in. long and 12ft.2in. wide, tapering to 8ft. Except for the end houses there was no through ventilation. With the exception of Sussex House the cottages had only three rooms on three floors. The rooms were small and dark. The floors, walls, and ceilings were generally defective, the windows too small, and in many cases in bad repair. The roofs were not sound and the tiles looked insecure. The gutters and stackpipes were defective, as also was the brickwork in places. The chimney stacks were unsound. There was no evidence of a damp course and the walls were 9in. solid. Five W.C.'s served the 10 houses and these were 75ft. from Sussex House and No.1. Three houses had coppers and the other seven used one wash-house. There were only two taps for the area, one at each end of the passage.... Sussex House was the largest of the cottages... No damp course was discernible and the side and front walls were bulging. There were no adequate facilities for washing or storage of food. The house had been well looked after by the tenants and appeared better than it really was.

Questioned by Mr. Groundsell, Dr. Wallace (medical officer of health to the District Council) replied that he did not agree that even if half the houses were pulled down there would be sufficient air-space... Mr Watkins stated that the Council had considered the whole matter dispassionately and impartially, and trusted that the minister would see his way to confirm the Orders.

◆

TOWN AND COUNTY NOTES.

NEW AUTOMATIC TELEPHONE EXCHANGE AT RYDE. — The new telephone exchange, which it is hoped will be opened before the end of the year, will mark an important stage in the development of telephonic services in the Island. The building is being erected at the corner of St. James's-street and Spencer-Road. The automatic exchange will replace the present manual one at the head Post-office.... Engineers will visit each subscriber to replace the present apparatus with new telephones of the dial type with which some people are now acquainted.

---

* Cottages located opposite the junction of Union Road and Sun Hill, with Sussex House cottage adjacent.

The picturesque old toll-house on the Ryde-Sandown Road, near the Ryde Airport, a relic of old-time travel close to a centre of the newest phase of transport. (July 27th, 1935.)

A corner of Old Newport which is being demolished to make way for the new Odeon Cinema, photographed from the church tower. Front right is the old Wesleyan Church, in which John Wesley preached, now Harding's workshop. The old court which used to lie in the centre of this block of buildings in the "good old days" was the scene of many fierce battles with the military piquets. (July 13th, 1935.)   *[Photo, Stevens.]*

YARMOUTH - A RECORD CATCH. — While fishing with a conger line off Bouldnor on Wednesday Messrs. C. Lansdowne and R. May landed an exceptionally large lobster. The crustacean weighed 11 ½ lb. and measured 2ft. 6in. from end to end.

OF INTEREST TO LADIES. — With regard to the colour of clothing … if you choose the wrong colouring it may easily get on your nerves … The general rules are simple to remember. People who are easily depressed should choose cheery colours like green and cream. People who are retiring and cold are best in warm colours like orange-yellow. Moody people should avoid mauve and red at all costs.

THE I.W. COUNTY PRESS COMPANY, LTD. — At the annual meeting of this company the Directors congratulated the shareholders on the continued prosperity of the company. The operations of the company resulted in a net profit for the year of £5906 14s. 9d… The directors recommended the payment of a final dividend of 10 per cent. (making 15 per cent. for the year) and a bonus of 5 per cent., both free of tax … The Chairman said they had had a most successful year. The success of the paper had been absolutely phenomenal.

———————————◆———————————

'Cameos From History' was a semi-regular feature looking at the Island's history through the personal recollections and notes of invited contributors. Miss Katherine Hearn*, a well-known local historian, had been a frequent contributor to the series and even after her death in 1932, her unpublished notes continued to appear...

September 7th, 1935.

HARVEST HOME.

Farms were very busy places at harvest time in the Island a century ago. Hard work demanded good food, and the industrious labourers were well fed from the farmhouse during haymaking and harvest time. Usually at harvest time extra hands were employed throughout the Island. They came from Somersetshire and Dorsetshire and had their quarters in the 'west countrymens' loft' for sleeping. Many Irish were likewise engaged, and they built a shelter for themselves with wheatsheaves and slept in the fields. Mottiston and other western manors had a full supply of 'men in the house.'

The eastern manors also employed their 'overners,' according to the acreage of the harvest fields. A century ago at Heasley Manor, according to Miss Katherine Hearn, who is descended from an old and highly esteemed Island family, 30 men had their sleeping quarters in the south-east wing of the house

---

* 12 weeks later the County Press appeared in the High Court in London to be jointly charged with breach of copyright regarding some other notes of Miss Hearn. It was alleged that Mr. Fred Mew, author of 'Back of the Wight' recently published by the County Press, had copied word for word Miss Hearn's notes on smuggling at Bembridge and had included them in his book without acknowledgement. Despite denying this, Mew halted the case midway, agreeing to pay an undisclosed sum to Miss Hearn's executors. The County Press was acknowledged to be free of blame in the matter.

during the harvest month. The household consisted of master, mistress, and children, nine serving maids, and then the carters, mates, and boys comprising the usual labourers, brought up the number to 60 persons who were daily fed from the manor during that busy month, and the mistress, assisted by her maids had the ordering and cooking for this big family.

The preparations really began in the previous October, when the strong ale and small beer were brewed in the huge coppers, and then conveyed to the hogsheads or tubs in the cellar. When brewing days were over, the pig killing commenced, and then the salting down in the powdering tubs. It was no unusual occurrence for 12 fat pigs to be slaughtered in October, the animals averaging from 25 score to 30 score each. The work of killing and salting was done by the expert village butcher and the resident farm labourers, and then for many a day the manor family and villagers feasted on liver and scraps. The mistress and her maids melted down the lard, of which there was a huge quantity, and that was used later for pasties, cakes, and doughnuts.

During the harvest month the men began work at 4 a.m. with a pint of small beer*, called a 'dewlip.' At 7 a.m. breakfast was served, consisting of cold fat pork, Isle of Wight cheese, home-made bread, and a pint or a quart of small beer for each man. At 11 a.m. another pint of small beer was served out, and at 12 noon the dinner cart arrived in the field where the men were at work. This meal consisted of hot mutton or beef, beans, potatoes, cabbage and hard puddings, made of flour and water and boiled with the meat. These last were called dumplings, or if flat, like pancakes, their name was 'skimmers.' There was a liberal amount of small beer for all the men.

The 'nammet' at 4 p.m. was also sent out into the field, and consisted of bread and cheese and beer. According to some authorities 'nammet' derived its name from there being 'no meat' at the meal. Others say it is a corruption of the words 'noon meat,' and was used generally to describe any form of light luncheon taken in lieu of a more formal meal. When the men came home after their day's work at 8 or 9 o'clock they gathered round the trestle board, and each one had a quart basin of mutton broth and a hunk of bread, after which they went to their sleeping loft and turned in for the night.

It was usual at Heasley Manor a century ago to kill a sheep every day and an ox once a week for the hungry household; they were all good trenchermen in those days. The sheep were cut up into joints, which were all boiled in the copper, the cooks afterwards adding marigold leaves for flavouring, with pepper and salt. The coarse salt came from Newtown Salterns and cost a guinea a bushel... The beer was taken out in puncheons or tin cans, and served in tin pint cups... Tea and coffee were very expensive luxuries in those days, and small beer was the ordinary beverage of the people... Finally came the Harvest Home supper, held probably in the largest barn on the farm, with floors swept as clean as a new pin, long tables heavily laden with suitable delicacies, and walls decorated with flags and evergreens. The squire presided, supported by

---

* 'Small beer' contained little or no alcohol. It was usually the product of flushing previously used brewing mash with water a second time. It owed its popularity to the fact that the water in it had been boiled and so, in the days of bad water supplies, was known to be safe to drink.

his bailiff, the vicar of the parish, and perhaps some of the neighbouring gentry, who delighted to take part in the rustic merrymaking. After a generous supper the tables were cleared and churchwarden pipes and packets of shag tobacco were placed before the guests...

--------◆--------

In the previous 100 years there had only ever been sporadic sightings of otters on the Island but in 1935 a number were said to have set up home in the waters of Brading Marsh. The Courtenay Tracy Otter Hounds of Marlborough were invited to the Island to investigate just how large a number was involved. For two days the pack of nearly 30 hounds explored not only the streams of Brading Marsh but also the waters of Alverstone Mill...

October 5th, 1935.

OTTER HUNTING IN THE ISLAND.
COURTNAY TRACY HOUNDS IN THE EAST WIGHT.

For the first time on record otters were hunted in the Island on Wednesday and Thursday, when the Courtenay Tracy Otter Hounds from Wilton Kennels, near Salisbury, met at St. Helens and Brading. The event aroused widespread interest, and the sport proved well up to the average of that in the mainland otter counties. The Hounds' visit was at the invitation of several Island gentleman, who during the past few years have been eager for the pack to come over... The venue of the hunt was across Brading Marshes where otters have of late been troublesome, not only in destroying fish, but in damaging the drainage system. Last year an otter was killed here by Mr. Peter Adams, of Bembridge.

The two days' hunt was in the nature of an experiment, and if considered satisfactory the hounds are to spend a whole week in the Island next season.

The opening meet on Wednesday was at St. Helens Floodgates, where some 200 people gathered, including many Island farmers. The hounds hunted over the Thornycroft estate after being inspected by Lady Thornycroft. The hounds ... turned towards Brading and ran along the stream by St Helens station, and found near the concrete bridge. The scent was none too good, but they worked for nearly an hour until 2 o'clock, and the otter then left the water and was killed on the Bembridge bank about 300 yards from the floodgates. It was an old bitch weighing 15lb. The head was presented to Mrs. Francis Mew by the master (Mr. Simpson) ... When opposite Centurion's Copse they found again but they eventually lost it ... The day's hunting ended at about 4.30 p.m.... Mr. Percy Wadham, of Newport, has sent us some further notes on the subject ... The notes read as follows: It is interesting to place on record the establishment of a colony of otters at Brading during the last 30 years which has been under the protection of the late Sir John and the present Lady Thornycroft. In the opinion of Sir John's keeper, now retired (Mr. Albert Meade), otters have bred pretty regularly for many years at Brading ... He has seen as many as six at one time. They have become so numerous on the Brading Marshes that they have done a considerable amount of damage to the banks and undermined many trees on the river Yar, causing them to fall ... It is a wonder that so small a stream as the

Yar can supply so many otters with food especially in the lower reaches, where the stock of fish must have been almost annihilated by the 'devil water' allowed to escape from the gasworks... From the above it would appear that there are plenty of otters to hunt in the Island. On Thursday the hounds met at Anglers Inn, Yarbridge ... At the bottom of Marshcombe Copse they found a bitch with two cubs in the water and ran them into the bushes ... The pack was then taken by van to Alverstone Mill, but could find no scent.

THE WEEK'S NEWS.

BALLAST TRAIN RUNS AWAY. — At about 3 a.m. yesterday 14 trucks laden with 10 tons of ballast moved off of their own accord from Wroxall and ran as far as Brading. They ran through Brading station until they reached the incline towards Ryde at Rowborough, where they came to a halt and started on the return journey. They passed through Brading again and eventually stopped near Yarbridge.

COWES — Fishing single-handed in the River Medina on Saturday Mr. Gordon Jones, of High-street, had an exceptional afternoon's sport as he caught no fewer than 80 bass and mullett, all of an eatable size.

COWES — A VERY UNUSUAL INCIDENT, which caused no little excitement, took place in the High-street on Saturday afternoon. A herd of cattle were being driven to the Pontoon, when one animal entered the Fountain Hotel. Squeezing itself through the swing door, only one side of which was open, it proceeded along the main passage of the hotel. After looking in at the kitchen door it entered the large dining-room. After remaining in possession of the room for a short time the beast made its exit by way of the side entrance.

DL TO ADL. — The number of motor vehicles registered in the Island passed the 10,000 mark this week and consequently the additional index letter 'A' preceding the familiar 'DL' is now being displayed, the object of this regulation being to avoid having five figures on registration plates. Number 9999 was the last 'DL' registration and the next one issued was 'ADL 1.' The distinction of having first 'ADL' plate fell to Lady Rowbotham of Brook Hill House, and the last 'DL' licence was issued to Mr. M. Wavell, of Yarmouth.

ANOTHER FORD ACHIEVEMENT - POPULAR MODEL AT £100. —The £100 car, dreamed of by motor car designers for many years, has at length arrived. This week, at the Ford Motor Exhibition in London it was announced that the price of the Popular Ford Saloon was reduced to £100. The announcement is undoubtedly the sensation of the 1935 motor show... The Popular Ford has been in large-scale production for three years, and has established itself as one of the most successful light cars ever produced. The tax is £6.

IS THERE OIL UNDER THE ISLAND? PROSPECTING LICENCE GRANTED. ... The Board of Trade has issued prospectors' licences to the Anglo-Iranian Oil Company ... Borings may be made anywhere in the Island except around Bembridge Harbour, the area covered by the licence being 150 square miles... The discovery of oil in the Island would be a serious matter as the countryside in the region of the wells would immediately become industrialised ... The vast majority of Vectensians will hope that the prospectors will draw a blank here.

———————◆———————

It was a story with the potential to be a heart-warming account of hands across the water. Out of the blue Mr Hayes of Ventnor had received a postcard from the German soldier he had captured 21 years earlier during World War I, when their paths had crossed on the battlefields of France. The postcard had started so well...

November 2nd, 1935.

FORMER GERMAN PRISONER WRITES TO HIS CAPTOR.

In August, 1914, Mr. H. Hayes (manager of the Prince of Wales Hotel, Ventnor), then a non-commissioned officer in the Dragoon Guards, took a German prisoner at Mons and handed him over to the French Army. Before doing so he wrote his name and address on a postcard and handed it to the German with the request that he would let him know how he got on. The postcard, which has now reached Mr. Hayes after 21 years, bears the following message: 'This postcard which you gave to me when you took me prisoner has been in my trunk for many years. Are you alive? I was a prisoner of war in France for four years. Heil Hitler. – Hans Studge, Eckernforde.

———————◆———————

1936.

When King George V died just before midnight on Monday the 20th of January, it was a moment that made history in more than one sense. For the first time ever, the public were to learn of the death of their monarch not by word of mouth or by telegraphs and newspapers as in the past, but instead, from their radios.

As the King's life ebbed away during the evening BBC listeners both here and abroad tuned in to hear hourly news reports of the King's condition ...

January 25th, 1936.

DEATH OF H.M. KING GEORGE V.

When in the early hours of Saturday morning last it was our regretful duty to record the first bulletins from Sandringham announcing that signs of His Majesty's heart weakness must be regarded with some disquiet, great anxiety was naturally aroused, but everyone entertained the fervent hope that the King's invaluable life might be spared.... Anxiety gave place to despair on Monday evening, when, following an ominous silence at 9.30 p.m. at which time the news should have been broadcast, the following bulletin was radiated: 'The King's life is moving peacefully towards its close,' thus conveying the sorrowful realisation to the Empire that there was no hope for the life of its

beloved Monarch. All the BBC stations ceased their advertised programmes and the announcer in London invited listeners to join in prayer that consolation might be given to the King in his last moments. A short but deeply moving religious service then came from the studio - the 23rd Psalm ... and the hymn ' O God, my Father, make me strong,' and then silence save for the melancholy ticking of the clock signal and the repetition of the warning bulletin each quarter of an hour, preceded by the booming chimes of Big Ben until at 12.15 a.m. came the fateful news: 'It is with deep sorrow that we announce that His Majesty the King passed peacefully away a few minutes before midnight.'...

... Islanders will have the happiest memories of a beloved King enjoying a well-earned respite from the cares of State when participating in yachting, one of his favourite recreations.... It is a pleasant thought that his annual holidays at Cowes may have lengthened his life; it is melancholy to think of Cowes Week without his presence and that of his charming and gracious Queen, and to reflect that never again will they motor to Carisbrooke on Sunday afternoons to take tea with the late King's aunt, our beloved Royal Governor H.R.H Princess Beatrice.

THE DEATH OF THE KING.

All theatres and cinemas were closed on Tuesday night and racing fixtures were cancelled for the week.

There will be no further hunting in the Island until after the funeral.

For the first time since broadcasting began, wireless programmes were not radiated on Tuesday... What a difference it made in homes used to wireless music! It certainly emphasised the depth of the national mourning.

TOTAL SUSPENSION OF BUSINESS NOT DESIRED. — The following official announcement with regard to the King's funeral was made on Thursday: It is His Majesty's wish that the people of this country should on Tuesday mark the King's funeral in such manner as each may think proper, according to the circumstances in which he finds himself... It is left to local associations and individuals to decide as to closing of business premises.

Mr. W. K. Baker, secretary of the I.W. Licensed Victuallers Society informs us ... that as a mark of respect and sorrow all licensed houses shall remain closed until the usual evening opening hour on Tuesday.

◆

Ryde telephone subscribers were used to lifting their telephone and hearing the words "Number please" from a switchboard operator. It came to an end as a new automatic telephone exchange in Spencer Road was brought into service ...

February 1st, 1936.

DEVELOPMENT IN ISLAND TELEPHONE SYSTEM.
NEW AUTOMATIC EXCHANGE OPENED AT RYDE.

An important telephone development took place on Saturday, when the telephone system serving the Ryde area was 'cut over' to the automatic system....The switching over involved 769 lines and so perfect was the organisation that it was completed by four men in three minutes. In that time the old Ryde exchange, which had been worked by hand, was cut off, and every subscriber's telephone was temporarily placed out of order. Immediately the 'cut-in' was made the selectors could be heard as subscribers were dialling the new system in....With the new system calls between Ryde subscribers will be completed without an operator, the subscribers being able to dial the required number... The invited guests were able to see the first telephone directory for the country issued in 1897. It contained 89 subscribers in the Island, contrasting with 3000 this year. Another exhibit was the list of subscribers in Ryde when the National Telephone Company made their first installation 40 years ago. Two of those original subscribers are still users. They are Mr. J. H. Johncox, of High-street, and Mr W. C. Pearce, of Union-street.

——————————◆——————————

The last section of the reconstructed Military Road was finished. It had taken five years but it was now open throughout its entire length...

February 22nd, 1936.

THE ISLAND'S 20-MILE COASTAL DRIVE.
COMPLETION OF LAST PORTION OF MILITARY ROAD.

A magnificent marine drive ... became an accomplished fact this week when the remaining portion of the old Military-road to be restored, just over a mile length between Compton and Afton Down, was opened to traffic. Thus it is now possible to travel from Shanklin to Freshwater Bay over an excellent road, with the English Channel and the ever-changing beauties of the coastline almost constantly in view. Travelling from east to west one enjoys the following
SUCCESSION OF WONDERFUL VIEWS,
which for beauty and variety are unequalled in this country, and possibly anywhere in the world on such a short journey; the wooded undulations of the Landslip; Ventnor, with its unique beauty; the Undercliff and Blackgang, with its rocky crags and sylvan glades; the golden beach from Chale to Compton; the glorious line of downs inland; and, finally, Freshwater Bay... The County Council are to be congratulated on a splendid achievement. The main portion of the work, the widening and reconditioning of the old Military-road from Chale to Freshwater had only just started five years ago when the national financial crisis caused delays, and since then the task could only be proceeded with as Government grants became available. These restrictions led to a modification of the original plan to provide a 20-foot carriageway throughout, and some five miles between Atherfield and Compton have had to remain at the old width of nine feet ... It is, however, the Council's intention to widen the remaining 5 miles within the next two or three years. 29,000 tons of chalk have been removed ... This huge quantity has been utilised for filling up depressions at the side of the narrow portion of the road between Compton and Brook, and for road foundations in many other parts of the Island... The surfacing with 3½ inches of tarviated slag gives the highway a fine non-skid finish...

TOWN AND COUNTY NOTES.

Frogs migrating from their winter quarters to ponds for spawning held up traffic on the Hampshire Road on Tuesday. The warmth of that day seems to have caused a general awakening of frogs, as a correspondent informs us that the dew pond on Gatcombe Newbarn down and its surroundings were covered with thousands of frogs on Tuesday afternoon. (March 14)

With regard to the re-arming of Germany, Major Hannington, speaking at the Cowes meeting of the I.W. Conservative Union said ... it was not very wise to give burglars a new set of housebreaking tools or the key to the safe. Germany had given quite conclusive proof that she was quite unrepentant, that she still regarded treaties as scraps of paper and that she hoped to be more successful next time. Now was the time to come to an agreement with Germany ...

THE QUEEN MARY — is to be prepared for speed trials to take place off the Firth of Forth... Passengers on the Cowes-Southampton steamers now get a close view of the monster liner as she lies in dock near the pontoon at Southampton. In a comment on her furnishings a writer in a contemporary says: 'The Queen Mary carries over two acres of British tanned leather on her furnishings, and all the upholstery has springs made in Birmingham and hair from Empire horses.'

Mr. H. Prosser Chanter, writing on salmon disappearing from the Island, says: 'Never again will the salmon come up the Medina and knock at Mr. Percy Wadham's door, asking to be caught by his special fishing tackle. Mr. Wadham undoubtedly is right as to the ravages caused by pollution, but another contributory cause is the weirs and the absence of salmon passes. One can imagine what a splendid haven of solitude the Medina must have been before such things as 'Free Trade' wharves made the passage to Blackwater unendurable.'

NEWPORT MAN'S SHORTWAVE EXPERIMENTS. — Mr. W. G. Sherratt, of Messrs. Sherratt and Son, of Newport, informs us that recently conditions for shortwave transmission and reception have been excellent. On Sunday he was in communication by Morse code with enthusiasts in America, Canada, Australia, Egypt, and Iceland.

———————————◆———————————

The newly finished Military Road still needed a name. Various suggestions had appeared in the County Press over the years and now members of the public were invited to formally submit them to the Council's Roads Committee...

April 4th, 1936.

THE NEW COASTAL ROAD.
MORE NAME SUGGESTIONS.

Although we requested last week that suggested names for the new coastal road should be sent to Major Dennis, Chairman of the Roads Committee, a number have been sent to us by readers. We give them below so that Major Dennis can include them with those he has received, but in spite of the originality of some of them we do not think that they include anything more concisely expressive of the character of the Road than our suggestions last week, viz., 'Wightcliff Way' or 'Vectis Marine Drive.'

The names include the following: 'Wight Coast Road', 'South Coast Road', 'Drizzle Drive' (as it has been sometimes of late), 'Channel Chaseway', 'Waverley Road' and 'Avenado Isle o' Wighto.' Mrs. M. Barton, of Camp-road, Freshwater, whose father, Daniel Grist, now aged 92, helped to construct the Freshwater-Compton part of the old road in the autumn of 1865, supports Sir Godfrey Baring's suggestion 'Sunshine Way' and 'An Old Islander' at Cowes, who was old enough to remember the last conviction of smugglers caught along the southern coasts of the Island favours the novel title of 'The Old Smugglers' Way.'

After lengthy deliberations the Council announced the new name of the old military road ...

THE MILITARY ROAD.

... We understand that after considering no fewer than 64 different names the County Council have decided the coastal road will continue to be described as The Military-road.

Some things never change...

May 30th, 1936.

THE FLOATING BRIDGE.

To the Editor of the I.W. County Press.

Sir, — When first I made the acquaintance of the floating bridge I regarded it as a joke. It is a joke, but an expensive one, both in time and money. The money is paid largely by the people in East Cowes, who in return gain, so they say, one third of what are termed 'the profits.' But the time wasted is the important thing... The floating bridge is a relic of the past. It is high time it gave place to something better and more up to date. Such an improvement would benefit not only Cowes and East Cowes but the Island generally and add to the pleasure of residents and visitors alike.

The fact that last year the floating bridge was a hindrance to over one million two hundred thousand foot passengers and twenty thousand vehicles deserves some attention, particularly as it affects traffic on an Island highway of some importance.

Yours faithfully, JOHN NAYLER. East Cowes.

The storks being fed by Mr. Frampton's family at Bembridge, which they seem to prefer at present to migration, thus demonstrating their liking for an extended Island season.   *[Photo, Andrews.]*

The Jubilee Fleet Illuminations, photographed from a house on Ryde Esplanade, showing Ryde Pier-gates and the Esplanade Gardens in the foreground.   *[Photo, Nicholson.]*

The Hindenberg over Cowes on Sunday evening. (July 11th)
[Photo Mrs. Turf.]

Landing bogie coaches and engines for Island railways at Medina Wharf.
[Photo, The Topical Press Agency.]

THE WEEK'S NEWS.

DOUBLE-DECKER BUSES FOR THE ISLAND. – The first two of six double-decker buses ordered by the Southern Vectis Omnibus Company were landed at Yarmouth Quay yesterday (Friday) morning. They will be put into commission immediately. These double-decker vehicles and the others to follow will be used only on the Ryde-Newport-Cowes route. (May 30.)

BOULDNOR ESTATE MYSTERY. – Representatives of the War Office asked the Court at Newport to appoint a surveyor to fix the value of 165 acres of cliff top land at Bouldnor, which are apparently without an owner, in order that they might be used for national defence purposes... It appears that the land at one time belonged to the De Morgan family but all efforts to trace descendants have proved ineffectual. It is very strange that so large a holding should lack an owner ... It is even stranger that a local farmer should have been paying rent for 29 years for land without an owner.

GERMANY'S GIANT AIRSHIP OVER THE ISLAND.* – A remarkably fine close-up view of the Hindenburg, Germany's giant Zeppelin, was obtained on Sunday night, when she approached Cowes from the direction of Southampton... The huge airship, whose passengers and markings could be clearly discerned, followed the course of the River Medina to Medham and then passed over Wootton and Ryde, where large numbers of people watched her progress with great interest... The sun, shining from an almost cloudless sky, illumined her silver body and her name in black letters was easily discernible with the naked eye. When about off Puckpool Park she swung her nose seawards and her majestic flight across Spithead to Selsey Bill was followed by thousands of visitors until her outline was lost in the horizon after 15 minutes.

ALBANY BARRACKS OPEN TO THE PUBLIC. – On Thursday evening the 2nd Battalion of the Queen's Royal Regiment were 'at home' to civilian visitors... The event proved highly popular in spite of very inclement weather, as some thousands visited the barracks during the evening. Over 100 private cars were in the park on the barracks square at any one time and some 80 motor-coaches conveyed visitors from all parts of the Island.

————————◆————————

In a letter to the editor the previous week, a correspondent had questioned whether the Island's motorists were as considerate as they might be. The answers came in the following issue...

July 4th, 1936.

HOOTING MOTORISTS.

To the Editor of the I.W. County Press.

Sir, — I was interested in the letter in your last issue, re noise in the Island. I have travelled a good deal and I must say that the Island is the noisiest place for its size and population that I have ever come across. Whether it is that the

---

* See photograph, page 31.

visitors throw off all restraint in their delight in getting away on holiday, or whether the permanent inhabitants are exceptionally strong in limbs and lungs I cannot say, but the result is pandemonium. Buses do not hoot in the ordinary way, they go screaming down the roads, although the noise they make in any case is not inconsiderable. Private cars lose all sense of proportion and hoot when it is quite unnecessary. Wireless is put on as loud as possible; people shout to one another instead of speaking in ordinary voices, and all this goes on till well after the time when most visitors would like to go to bed to sleep, and forget the tumult of the day. The visitors who used to visit the Island and stay for long periods are going elsewhere and their place is being taken by day trippers and holiday camps. — I am, Sir, yours faithfully, 'NERVE-RACKED.'

To the Editor of the I.W. County Press.
Sir, — Your correspondent, 'A member,' writing as to the manners of Island motorists, is hardly fair. We have had considerable motoring experience in many lands and frankly the good manners of the average Island motorists surprised us. Where will you see such courtesy, such well timed hand signals, or such neat parking? Again, taking the drivers of commercial vehicles, all keeping to their proper side of the road, driving quietly without exceeding their legal speed. At the slightest demand from a private car they speed you on. As to your cyclists they are superb. No sir, we 'Overners' must hand it to the Islanders. — I am, Sir, yours faithfully, BXQ 485.

———————————◆———————————

The late King had been a keen sailor. He had also been a successful one, winning many races over the years on board his racing yacht Britannia. In his will the King left instructions that Britannia was to be scuttled after his death.
The preparations were put in hand at the East Cowes yard that had looked after the yacht for over 50 years...

July 4th, 1936.
THE SINKING OF THE BRITANNIA.
Preparations for the scuttling at sea of the hull of King George's famous cutter Britannia have been made at East Cowes during the week... The Britannia will be towed into the Roadstead and will take up the moorings she has used when in commission for so many years. She will there await the arrival of the Admiralty vessel which is to tow her out into the deep waters of the English Channel, where she will be scuttled. It is believed that the sinking operations will be carried out without ceremony of any kind and that the Royal cutter will be spirited away, either late at night or in the early hours of the morning, from the Roads where she has been such familiar figure....

July 11th, 1936.
THE LAST OF THE BRITANNIA
SUNK OFF ST. CATHERINE'S POINT YESTERDAY.
The late King George's famous 43-year-old cutter Britannia was launched for the last time at Mr. George Marvin's Minerva yacht yard at East Cowes on

AUTOMATIC TELEPHONE EXCHANGE FOR RYDE...

Ryde is now served by the new Automatic telephone system. At your command the dial sets in motion a wonderful mechanism, ready to serve you day and night at a minimum of cost.

YOUR FRIENDS ARE ON THE TELEPHONE ...ARE YOU?

The District Manager, Post Office Telephones, Southampton, will gladly furnish full particulars to all enquirers.

Lost and Found, Inquiries, &c.

FOUND in Spencer-road, Ryde, young dark tabby Cat, long haired. — Apply Cats' Home, Ryde. Tel. 2587.

LOST, in River Medina fields, lady's gold Watch, initials "E.T."—Reward on return Spence, Albany Barracks, Parkhurst.

LOST, very young Jackdaw, ring on right leg; finder will be rewarded.—Yarbridge House, Brading.

LOST, Tuesday, at Compton Cliff top or School-lane, Calbourne, horn-rimmed Spectacles.—Reward, Witham, Pyle House.

LOST, young Terrier Bitch, answers to the name of "Pat."—Anyone returning same to Salter, Pound Farm, Sandford, will be rewarded.

PLEASE note that lost cats advertised for, with a request to return them to Ryde Cats' Home, have strayed from their owners' homes, not from the Cats' Home.

Wednesday afternoon. On the vessel's bow was a wreath which had been placed there by Mr. E. Woodland, the yard Foreman, who has had charge of the hauling up and launching of the Britannia throughout her life of nearly half a century. The launching, which was without ceremony, was witnessed by a party of interested Greenwich schoolchildren who are staying at the East Cowes Holiday Camp. As the Royal cutter was towed down the Medina to the Roadstead by the tug Irishman, spectators on the pier head gave her a farewell cheer ... and as she was about to pick up her moorings in the Roads people on the Esplanade doffed their hats as a silent tribute... Shortly after 9 p.m. on Thursday two destroyers, the Amazon and Winchester from Portsmouth, steamed into the Roadstead and stood by the Royal cutter. As soon as darkness descended the necessary preparations were made and just before midnight the vessels which were to carry out the sinking operations proceeded down the eastern Solent with the Britannia in tow. It was subsequently learnt that the Britannia was scuttled in the early hours of the morning off St Catherine's. The sinking was carried out by means of the explosion of a timed charge, which rent a large hole in the Royal cutter and she quickly sank. Among those who witnessed the Britannia's doom were Captain Turner (skipper), Mr. Turner (mate), and Mr. Mason (steward). When the destroyers arrived there were a number of people watching from the parade, but a heavy rain squall quickly dispersed them and very few spectators saw the Britannia's departure.

———————————◆———————————

Well-known locals invariably received an obituary in the County Press. As a 20 stone 83 year old, sporting bushy white hair, Mr. Orchard of Newport could hardly have failed to be anything else but well-known...

August 15th, 1936.

THE LATE MR. W.H. ORCHARD OF NEWPORT

A fine figure of a man, standing 6 feet in height and weighing nearly 20 stones, with bushy white hair and a ruddy complexion, Mr. William Henry Orchard, licensee of the Robin Hood Inn, Newport, died at his residence on Friday week. He would have been 83 on August 11th.

Universally known as 'Captain' Orchard by reason of the round peaked cap he always wore, Mr. Orchard had held the licence of the Robin Hood for about 40 years. Before him the licensee was a Mr. Drudge, whose daughter he married as a young man. The first wife died 24 years ago and Mr. Orchard was married again, his second wife being Miss Alice Sweetman, also of Newport. At one time Capt. Orchard kept several cows, but he abandoned the dairying business some time ago.

As owner of a threshing machine, 'Skylark,' Mr. Orchard travelled all over the Island, stopping at farms en route to deal with the season's crops. In consequence he was known to farmers in every district and was always a welcome visitor. The Skylark lifted half of the new Coppins railway bridge in 1920.

Despite his varied business interests, Mr Orchard could neither read nor write and signed documents with his mark...

For several weeks in the autumn of 1936 the villagers of St. Helens and Bembridge played host to a group of storks who had stopped off on their way to Africa*....

August 22nd, 1936.

STORKS VISIT ST HELENS.

The arrival of 13 storks about dusk on Wednesday at St. Helens aroused a great deal of interest. The ringed birds were some of the 18 which started on their migration to Africa on August 12th. from Haslemere Educational Museum, Kent... The birds were first sighted coming from the direction of Bembridge and alighted on the chimneys of the Council houses in Station-road One, unfortunately, had to be destroyed. After colliding with the telephone wires above the railway station it was seen to fall into a field. Mr. Albert Mead, a retired gamekeeper, went to the bird's aid, but it had broken both legs, and was screeching with pain. The humane course was to shoot it and Mr. Meade did this. The remaining birds flew to the roofs of three cottages at the top of Station-road ... Messrs. Jack Wade and Collis caught two of them and they were fed with fresh herrings and released the next morning... Yesterday morning they alighted in Mr. A. Jordan's field. Water was provided for them and they immediately became objects of great curiosity. Some three or four hundred people visited them during the afternoon and they were fed with fish. The demand at the local fish shop was at one time so great that supplies became exhausted. They are very tame and allow themselves to be touched. A gentleman lifted a bird over a barbed wire fence that it was trying to negotiate...

On Saturday 13 of the 14 storks from Haslemere, Kent, made their departure. During the night they had roosted on the Vicarage, and on Mr. A Frampton's house in Love-lane, Bembridge. They visited Mr Jordan's field in the morning for food and water and took off shortly after 10 o'clock. After flying round the village and gaining a great height they made their way westwards and on Monday it was reported that they had arrived in Devonshire. One stork, however, remained at Bembridge, where it has been well fed, and is an object of much interest.†

———————————◆———————————

The days of horse-drawn traffic were almost over and the number of blacksmiths on the Island could now be counted on the fingers of one hand. George Arnold, one-time blacksmith to the Queen, had been retired for 15 years but was still sufficiently well-known for a brief account of his life to appear on the occasion of his 91st birthday...

November 12th, 1936

QUEEN VICTORIA'S BLACKSMITH.
NEWPORT NONAGENARIAN'S INTERESTING LIFE STORY.

Mr. George Arnold, of 34 Barton-road, Newport, who celebrated his 91st birthday on Sunday, has a very interesting life story. He was born in 1844 in the

---

* See photograph page 31.

† The remaining stork was named Eustace by the villagers and over the next few weeks became a local celebrity, being hand fed by the local children each day. He eventually left Bembridge on October 3rd but on November 28th the County Press reported that Eustace had been found dead in Normandy four days after leaving the Island.

house adjoining the Porchfield Congregational Church. He learnt the trade of general and agricultural smith at the old smithy at Stone Steps, Calbourne and at the age of 22 went to the Lock's Green smithy, which was in the Arnold family for some 200 years. After working there for 4 years he took the Blacksmith's Arms, better known as "Ye Olde Betty's Aunt," Carisbrooke, where he did the agricultural work of the district for 17 years, in addition to being the licensee. From there he went to East Cowes. Here he often shod ponies from the Royal stables at Osborne and roughed the shoes of the horses if they found the ascent to Osborne too slippery. His shop was on the land where the East Cowes Post Office now stands, and among others for whom he executed jobs were Trinity House, the Steam Packet Company and the local council At the time of the Queen's death he erected a stand on his property from which a large number of viewed the Royal funeral procession. After spending 18 years at South Fairlee Farm in the employ of the late Mr. Thomas Knighton, Mr. Arnold concluded his working life in the employ of Messrs. Smith and Whitehead of Newport, retiring some 15 years ago at the age of 76. Twice married, the first time by the Rev. Thomas Mann at the Sun-Hill Congregational Church, Cowes, Mr. Arnold had 10 children of his first marriage, and 10 by his second wife, formerly Miss Derham of East Cowes and 6 of each family survive. The eldest is 69 and the youngest 52. Mr. Arnold tells an interesting story of an old farmer named Cross whose lease of Alverstone Farm was bought by the Prince Consort, who pensioned him off. The old man, who lived at Pound, near Calbourne, employed Mr. Arnold as a lad in the garden, and he can remember two occasions when Mr. Cross spread out a bag full of Spade guineas in front of him telling him that some of them would be his one day. Mr. Cross and his wife and daughter, when they retired to bed, pulled up the ladder giving access to the upper rooms and kept a loaded blunderbuss trained on the door through a hole in the ceiling. When Mr. and Mrs. Cross died the guineas passed to their only daughter, but when she died a few years later no trace could be found of the hoard of gold and Mr. Arnold never received his share.

————————————◆————————————

The new King's secret affair had so far remained a secret but travellers returning from America, where the story was literally front page news, had ensured that by word of mouth the story had now become an open secret in Britain. Eventually Fleet Street could be restrained no longer...

December 5th, 1936.

THE KING AND HIS CABINET.
CRISIS OVER MARRIAGE PROPOSAL.

That a critical state of disagreement exists between HM the King and the Government as the result of His Majesty's desire to contract a marriage with an American woman was the news that startled the Empire on Thursday morning.

The lady His Majesty desires to marry is an American, Mrs. Ernest Simpson, who, it is stated, was recently divorced from her second husband, and has been a friend of the King for some years. The matter has been occupying the serious attention of the Cabinet for some time, as it involves the vital principle of whether His Majesty shall be guided by his Ministers in matters of national and Imperial concern, but British newspapers had tactfully refrained until Thursday from referring to the matter in the hope that some way out of this difficulty would be found, although rumour had been rife in this country, and many references to the subject had appeared in American, European, and even in Dominion newspapers...

Within a week the matter was settled...

December 12th, 1936.

KING EDWARD VIII ABDICATES.
SUCCEEDED BY THE DUKE OF YORK.

The grave anxiety existing throughout the Empire for a week as the result of the critical situation which arose owing to King Edward's desire to marry Mrs. Ernest Simpson, a native of the U.S.A., who has twice been divorced, was to a great extent relieved on Thursday afternoon, when the King announced his determination to renounce the throne in favour of his brother, the Duke of York. It was an unprecedented happening in British history for a monarch voluntarily to give up the Crown, yet it would appear to be accepted with sorrowful relief by the majority of his people as the best way out of a most unfortunate impasse...

The Abdication Bill passed quickly through both Houses of Parliament yesterday. It includes a clause that the ex-King is exempt from the law requiring members of the Royal house to have the permission of the King to marry. The Bill received King Edward's assent by Royal Commission just before two o'clock yesterday afternoon, and from that moment King Edward ceased to be the King...

It is authoritatively stated that the Coronation will take place as arranged, on May 12th.

December 12th, 1936.

VIVE LE ROI.

A few short months ago King Edward VIII ascended the throne with the loyal welcome of his subjects throughout the Empire... He was blessed with the conspicuous example set him by his beloved father as a constitutional monarch. Yet the citizens of the Empire have lately been profoundly stirred by most disturbing rumours, which have now been proved to have a very substantial basis, and have culminated in the abdication of King Edward VIII. Mr. Baldwin's account of the conversations with his Sovereign shows that, in spite of the arguments of love, duty, chivalry, and interest, the Sovereign came to the irrevocable decision which ... the Archbishop of Canterbury described as 'a stab in the heart,' and a capable journalist as 'a renunciation which has astounded the world.'

1937.

TOWN AND COUNTY NOTES.

RAM RAMBLES HOME.— About a month ago a stock ram from Street Place Farm, Calbourne, was sold in Newport Market to Mr. Biles, of Park Green Farm, Forest Side. Its new owner placed it in a field with an old cow, and the two became very friendly. A few days ago the cow was slaughtered, and the ram, feeling lonely, decided to seek its former companions at Street Place. It succeeded in making its way there, about 5 miles, and a notable point about its journey is that inquiries have elicited the fact that it travelled by road along the same route by which it was brought to the market.

The first motor licence with the index letters BDL was issued by the County Council this week... The change to ADL took place in October, 1935, so there have been 1000 new cars licensed locally in 15 months, or an average of just over two a day.

There was a gratifying reduction in the number of road fatalities in the Island last year. The deaths numbered only five, against the 11 in 1935... Several reasons can be given for this more satisfactory state of affairs, notably the tests new drivers have to undergo, the progressive policy of the County Council in dealing with blind corners and other dangerous places by schemes of improvement, and the introduction of the 'Halt at major road ahead' signs. These signs have undoubtedly prevented many accidents...

Herr von Ribbentrop, whose original behaviour since he arrived in London as German Ambassador has already made him conspicuous, created another precedent on Thursday on presenting his credentials to the King at Buckingham Palace... Instead of making the usual bow to His Majesty, he drew himself to his full height, clicked his heels, thrust out his arm in the Nazi salute, and rapped out the words: 'Heil Hitler.'

THE WORK OF THE BORSTAL INSTITUTION. — Mr. C. A. Joyce, Governor of the Borstal Institution, speaking on 'What is crime?' ... said they acknowledged the hunger of the body, but they so often denied the hunger of the spirit. There was a pseudo-psychology, the most fearful rubbish ever talked about, such as if they repressed a child by physical means they would hurt its immortal soul. Unfortunately to-day children grew up without parental control. It was often admitted in juvenile courts by parents that they had no control over their children. All he could say to that was that it was about time parents realised that if they proposed to have the pleasure of producing children they must also accept the responsibility for their training. Unemployment was admittedly a contributory cause of crime, although there were thousands of people who were unemployed and remained honest. The chief difficulty was with young men who had been unemployed since leaving school. Their state of mind was such that they were open to any suggestion by which they could earn

money. The young car bandit was often paid £20 for 20 minutes' work, and such men loved the thrill of the escapades...

◆

There is nothing that can usefully be added to this report...
February 13th, 1937.
THE GULL AND THE RAT.
On Sunday Station Officer Hawkes heard a bird hovering in the vicinity of the Blackgang Coastguard-station, making a strange croaking noise. On Monday a large bird was found dead entangled in the top of a tree near the hotel. On Tuesday, assisted by Mr. G. Dyer, Mr. Hawkes got it down. It proved to be a Royal gull, with a rat fixed in its throat, its tail protruding some 4 inches. From the amount of blood on the bird it looked as if the rat had been swallowed alive, and had then bitten through the bird's throat, which had fallen dead into the tree. It was a fine specimen, standing 2ft.3in. high, with a wingspan of 5ft.2in., and weighing nearly 6lb.

◆

THE WEEK'S NEWS.
HISTORIC GUNS AT WOODY BAY - REMOVAL OF A CENTURY-OLD LANDMARK. — Residents of Ventnor and the Undercliff will learn with regret of the removal of the ancient cannon from the battery near Woody Bay. The guns, which are all engraved 'Paris 1793,' were the property of Major Cecil Pelham, who recently disposed of them to Mr. D. Valvona, of High-street, Oakfield, Ryde, who has since resold them to an armament firm to be melted down. The total weight was over 4 tons. They were removed from their iron and wooden trucks at Woody Bay by Messrs. Westmore, of Newport, and taken to Ryde.

ISLAND MINSTREL'S CORONATION SONG ACCEPTED BY THE KING. — Mr. Melvyn E. Upright, of Ryde, well-known throughout the Island as 'Uncle Winkle' the minstrel, has composed a Coronation song, which has been accepted by His Majesty the King. The song which commences with the words 'We're going to have a Coronation' has been set by him in a lilting melody, and Mr. Upright has received a letter from the King's private secretary expressing His Majesty's thanks for his contribution...

NO CLEMENCY FOR PRISONERS. — The Coronation is not to be made an occasion for granting special clemency to prisoners. The Home Secretary announced this week that the suggestion had been made to him from several quarters, but he could not see his way to make any recommendation to His Majesty. We understand that prisoners, at least those at Parkhurst, are to have special fare on Coronation Day, including extra rations of meat and a Coronation pudding - like Christmas pudding.

AIR RAID PRECAUTIONS. — In a meeting held at Ryde Town-hall... the Mayor said that because they were discussing air raid precautions it did not follow that war was imminent. It was necessary that everyone in the country should know what to do in the event of their ever being involved in a war... Precautions should be taken now, because it would be useless to wait until war was upon them... If they had the nation educated against gas attacks no enemy country was going to waste its aircraft on dropping gas bombs if they knew that that country was properly prepared. At the present time they had a factory in Lancashire turning out 60,000 gas masks a week, and in the London area they had about ten million gas masks stored. There was absolutely no truth in the statement that these respirators were useless; he assured them that they were absolutely perfect.

◆

TOWN AND COUNTY NOTES.

A NEST IN A CAP. — Wrens have built their nest and hatched out a lusty family of youngsters in a disused cloth cap belonging to one of the employees at Churchill's Farm, Shalfleet, which he left hanging on a nail in the cow-stable.

THE SOUTHERN RAILWAY AND THE ISLAND. — The new electrified train service between London and Portsmouth will be inaugurated on Thursday next. The Mayors of Newport and Ryde ... will be among the invited guests of the Southern Railway who will be at Portsmouth Harbour station to see the first electric train arrive from Waterloo.

ISLE OF WIGHT PLACE NAMES. — Dr. H. Kokeritz, a lecturer at Uppsala University, Sweden, is in the Island carrying on topographical studies of our place-names with a view to bringing out a book on the subject, probably next year*... Dr. Kokeritz would greatly appreciate it if readers who possess old maps of their grounds and similar documents would allow him to inspect these... Even the smallest list of names of fields, pastures, meadows, paths, streams, etc is very welcome.

Betty : 'Mummy, what happens to a motor-car when it is too old to run?' Mother : 'Someone sells it to your father.'

Miss Merle Oberon, the film star, spent the week-end with Mr. David Niven and his family at Rose Cottage, Bembridge.

Mr. and Mrs. J. B. Priestley and their family came to Billingham Manor on Wednesday, and will stay until their departure to Arizona in September. Mr. Priestley has decided to sell Billingham Manor, though he does this with regret, as he never expects to find such a study as he had built for himself in the roof of the house.

---

* "The Place Names of the Isle of Wight" by Helge Kokeritz was published in 1940.

The Sunday Entertainments Act of 1932 decreed that variety acts, comedy sketches, the use of stage props, and the wearing of stage clothes other than evening dress were all strictly prohibited on a Sunday. Entertainments not involving comedy, such as poetry readings and opera were felt to be more appropriate and were permitted.

The management of Shanklin Pier were prosecuted under the Act after an off-duty policeman, P.C. Lewis, had attended one of the regular Sunday night concerts held during the summer months. He told the court that he had attended the concert 'by accident' and was so shocked by the performance (featuring a young Tommy Trinder) that he went straight to the police station afterwards to make out a report.

In court the performance was dissected line by line and the merits or otherwise of chamberpots and nudists were put under the dry legal microscope...

August 14th, 1937.

SUNDAY CONCERTS AT SHANKLIN.
POLICE CONSTABLE AGGRIEVED AT TYPE OF ENTERTAINMENT.

Horace Terry Wood, managing director of the Shanklin Pier Company, was summoned under Section 3 of the Sunday Entertainments Act, 1932, for using the Pier Casino at Shanklin Pier for a public musical entertainment which was not of a type suitable for the day. He was further summoned for using the same premises for a public musical entertainment in which properties and stage costumes were used, also in connection with which, dancing was given, and, lastly, in which a play or sketch was given. He was defended by Mr. Odgers and pleaded not guilty to all four summonses. Mr. Palmer prosecuted for the police... The complainant, P.C. Lewis, went to the concert on June 27th, and as a result of his attendance those proceedings were taken... Particular objection was taken to the entertainment given by

Messrs. Clapham and Dwyer,

who appeared in both halves of the programme, as being offensive. The entertainment by them was what was known as back chat, a prepared repartee, which was neither music nor recitation. In particular, objection was taken to the tone of the jokes that he made. One of the men was supposed to be a

Porter at a Nudist Colony,

and he spoke of what took place there. One joke was that there was a fancy dress ball and that one gentleman attended with rings painted round his 'tummy' to represent a naval officer. That, said Mr. Palmer, to say the least, was vulgar, and represented the type of jokes which took place... In another part of the performance two persons came home apparently from a dance. They sang and then danced for a second or two, when one of them remarked 'Oh no, this won't do, it is a Sun—-,' and then stopped, which showed that the terms of their operating licence were known. Another of the party, Mr. Tommy Trinder, made a joke about his being able to wear a buttonhole. In regard to the summons as to the sketch, two of the men performers came in front of the curtain and in an assumed state of intoxication talked about the unfaithfulness of the wife of one of them. The curtain was then drawn, showing the unfaithful wife with her lover. The drunken husband entered and the lover was hidden in a bed. There was some play about the feet sticking out of the bed... Mr. Palmer suggested that such a sketch,

Based on Drunkenness and Immorality,

was very objectionable.

P.C. Lewis said... the performance of Clapham and Dwyer, who were in evening dress, lasted about 10 minutes. He did not take notes of the jokes, but afterwards went to the Police-station and made out a report. P.C. Lewis said Clapham came on as a commissionaire at a nudist colony and put on a peaked cap instead of an opera hat. He was asked by Dwyer if there was much work to do and he replied that there was heaps and as a matter of fact he had to sit on the seats to keep them warm for the others. Clapham also said they held concerts and dances at the nudist colony and gave prizes for fancy dresses. One lady had so many varicose veins that she went as a roadmap, and a man painted rings round his 'tummy' and went as a naval officer. Mr. Clapham said they had a game in which the ladies were kept on one side of the hedge and the men on the other and he had to stand by to see there was

No Beating about the Bush.

There was talk about weddings and Clapham said he was looking forward to Friday as a chambermaid from their hotel was getting married and that all the big pots would be there. Mention was made of a couple who had married in October and the wife had a child in March... In another sketch Ashmoor Birch and Tommy Trinder appeared before the curtain in an intoxicated condition and one spoke to the other concerning the unfaithfulness of his wife. When the curtain was drawn, the wife was seated at a table with the lover. Eventually the drunken husband came into the room and there was some talk about there being four feet in the bed, the lover having hidden there before the husband got into bed. Another member of the party wore a green baize apron and at the commencement of the show Mr. Trinder said he thought it would be all right to wear a buttonhole. — Cross-examined by Mr. Odgers P.C. Lewis said he went there by accident and paid 2s. 6d. for his seat. He did not take his wife with him, but had a female friend. - Mr. Odgers: I hope she liked the show. - She did not like the jokes. - Mr. Odgers: Is she here today? - No. - Mr. Odgers: You have told us you objected to these jokes of Clapham and Dwyer. I should have thought they sounded the feeblest things anyone could have mentioned. Did anyone laugh? - Yes, some people laughed. - Q. You are supposed to be the person aggrieved by this performance, did you feel aggrieved? - I did. - Q. Did you complain to the management? - No. - Q. Did you stay to the end of the show? - Yes. - Q. You knew that Clapham and Dwyer performed twice? - Yes. - Q. Then why did you stop till the second half? - I thought they might improve... Mr. Odgers: For the reputation of the Force at Shanklin you can't say you are aggrieved at a lot of silly nonsense. You're not so touchy as all that in Shanklin? - I knew that according to the conditions of the licence it was wrong... Mr. Terry Wood, in the witness box, said he was managing director of the Shanklin Pier, Ltd., with 20 departments, employing a large staff. He had run those concerts for 10 years without complaint... Clapham and Dwyer had been playing for him for 10 seasons. They did not submit any script and they were instructed that they must comply with the conditions of the licence. Clapham and Dwyer ... were doing exactly what they had done on other Sundays... He was in competition with the Shanklin Theatre and the Sandown Pavilion who

A neat job. Thatched ricks at Sheat Farm by Mr. Jones (October 2nd.)   *[Photo, Stevens.]*

A SAD END TO A GOOD DINNER.
This mouse found a jug of rice in the larder at the Red Lion, Freshwater. In the top of the jug was a funnel, providing a slippery downward path. The bottom of the funnel was just big enough for a hungry little mouse to slip it's head through and reach that attractive rice, but the chances of recovery for a satiated, bloated glutton were nil.

A 1910 Veteran Taxi.   Mr. W. Orchard, of Yarmouth, with his old 1910 Sunbeam, which will now have to go out of service, owing to the new motor regulations. (Jan 2nd)   *[Photo, Andrews.]*

The tug Marion and the Portsmouth ferry boat Queen high and dry on Baxter's Ledge, near Thorness Bay. Inset, the crew. (June 12th)
[Photo, White and Son.]

provided a similar type of concert... Questioned by Mr. Palmer for the police, he said he thought the programme was in accordance with his licence... William Mann said he had been with Mr. Terry Wood for five years, and had been in control of the concerts for two years. Clapham and Dwyer's jokes were a lot of nonsensical talk. He did not agree that the sketch was based on drunkenness and adultery, although it did arise in a very mild sort of way... They had performed at Shanklin ten times in eight seasons with the same jokes. Mr. Odgers: I wish our legal jokes would last as long as that. (Laughter). The Chairman: I hope not. (Laughter)... He thought the joke about the naval officer was good fun in the way Clapham and Dwyer said it but not as the policeman said it in the witness box; so much depended on the working of one's mind. All the jokes as said by the constable sounded bad, but when put over on the stage by Clapham and Dwyer they were quite different, and they were so much nonsense... Thomas Trinder, comedian, said he had been in the entertainment business 17 years. He wrote the sketch referred to... As the author, he hoped it was not based on drunkenness and immorality. The whole thing led up to the point of the four feet... It was based on the joke of a man seeing double when there were actually four feet sticking out of the divan.

(*Evidence was then heard from several witnesses who all agreed that they had seen nothing objectionable in the concert.*)

Mr. Odgers, in summing up for the defence, said it was a most tremendous storm in a tea cup over a little silly fooling on a Sunday evening about a joke as old as the hills. As to the entertainment not being of a type suitable to the day, he said Messrs. Clapham and Dwyer were well-known BBC artistes... The condition that the concert should be suitable to the day should mean according to modern conditions. They were not trying to impose in the summer holidays of 1937 a condition which would have applied in the days of 1887. There were many comparisons in regard to decency, modesty, and morals between to-day and those of the naughty 'nineties in which he did not think those of to-day suffered by comparison. They had to remember that the character of Sunday had changed. They could not get away from the fact that games were played everywhere, and that Sunday was no longer a day of rest in the sense that it used to be. Things were done openly on Sundays and passed as being right and proper... The person aggrieved was a police constable, who took with him a young lady who was shocked, but who was not called before them. They had the evidence that the hall was packed and during the interval the doors were thrown open yet no one left and not a single complaint was made to the management...

After the Bench had retired the Chairman informed Mr. Wood that they had given the matter careful consideration, as it was a matter of great importance to him. They dismissed the summonses with regard to properties and stage costumes but there would be a conviction on the summons dealing with a type of entertainment not suitable for the day, and he would be fined £10. There would also be convictions in regard to dancing and the performance of the sketch... The Chairman informed Mr. Wood that they knew it was very difficult to keep supervision of entertainments of that sort, but they were sure he would redouble his efforts in future.

ISLAND NOTES.

'SEMI-NUDISTS' WALKING IN THE STREETS OF SHANKLIN. - A discussion on what was described as the semi-nude condition in which some visitors are walking in the streets of Sandown and Shanklin took place at Tuesday's meeting of the Council... Mr. W. Russell said the time had come when a protest should be entered against it. No one objected to this on the shore, but he objected to the condition in which men and women were walking about the streets. Some hairy men, with a lot of whiskers, lead one to imagine he was at the Zoo. It was really disgusting... They should pass some bylaw to keep these people out of the streets. People don't know how to behave themselves. They try to be as rude as they can...It would be unfortunate if it went forth to the world that Shanklin was full of indecent people.

What are claimed to be the world's biggest pig (length 8ft. 8in., girth 7ft. 4in., weight half a ton) the world's smallest racehorse (weight 52lb.), and the world's biggest dog, will be exhibited at a fair at Portsmouth next week.

BURGUNDY ASHORE AT ST. HELENS. — Yesterday (Friday) a vat of burgundy, weighing 1000lbs., was washed ashore at St. Helens. It was taken charge of by the Customs officials.

CAPT P. D. MACDONALD, MP - 'NO DANGER OF WAR'. — At the annual dinner of the Sandown Conservative and Unionist Club last Friday Capt Macdonald, the Island's member of Parliament, said he was convinced that there was no danger of immediate war in Europe...

◆

RURAL NOTES.

THE ISLE OF WIGHT CEMENT TRAIN. — 'If a prize were presented for the neatest train on the Southern Railway it would be won by the Isle of Wight cement train,' says an article in the current issue of the Southern Railway Magazine. 'With its little green 'Terrier' locomotive and string of yellow and blue trucks this train is the most pleasing sight in the Island... The Terrier is spotlessly clean, and the wagons no less so, their contents of chalk, seen in the midday sun, are as white as a newly washed sheet. This little train confines itself to the two miles between the pits at Shide and the mills on the Medina river and shows its exclusiveness in travelling backwards through Newport station on its way to the mills for there is no run-round there. The mill consumes 50,000 tons of chalk each month, conveyed in some 6000 wagon loads, working three trips each day.'

THE ISLAND LOSING WEALTHIER RESIDENTS DUE TO HIGH CAR FERRY CHARGES. — The alleged declining popularity of the Island, especially of Totland Bay, as a residential district for the more well-to-do persons was attributed to the high cost of conveying motor-cars across the Solent at the meeting of the Freshwater Advancement Association. Persons who had cars wished to use them to keep in touch with friends and relatives, and to be able to travel farther afield than the 20 miles limit imposed on them in the Island. They would not keep on paying the prohibitive charges made for the ferry service... There was no doubt that the Solent offered a more expensive and time-wasting obstacle to the happiness of retired people than they would put up with.

FISHY BUT TRUE. — Mr. H. Barber when fishing from Shanklin Pier caught a 12½lb. skate. Inside the fish was discovered a Danzig five pfennig coin which, strange to say, bears a representation of a flat fish above the date 1932..

1938.

During the last 50 years the lot of Britain's animals had improved dramatically. Legislation regarding the treatment and care of animals and livestock had long been in place and in theory, systematic animal cruelty was a thing of the past; even Britain's wildlife and birds were now covered by Acts of Parliament.

That was the theory, but it was still not a good time to be an animal at Newport market...

January 22nd, 1938

CATTLE BRANDING AT NEWPORT MARKET.

An Island butcher writes calling attention to what, in his opinion, is an unnecessary cruelty in the branding of cattle by ear-piercing at Newport market. He says: 'On Tuesday night, I and many others who have had to slaughter cattle in the course of our business, were distressed to see a bullock bleeding profusely and obviously in great pain. If I were caught killing a lamb or pig in the old way with a knife I should be heavily fined for cruelty, yet the killing would be a far less painful business for the animal than is the ear-piercing as I saw it at Newport market. It is a Government regulation under the Beef Subsidy Act that this piercing should be done to graded cattle, but it should be done by a veterinary surgeon or someone properly instructed. In the case in point the ear had been pierced in the wrong place; in the thicker fleshy part, thus severing large veins, instead of in the thin part where the bleeding and pain would be much reduced.'

Many of the things that upset Islanders in the 1930s still upset some today; the number of tourists, the building of 'modern eyesores', the perceived loss of countryside and the price of car-ferry tickets, to name but a few.

Also a subject for heated debate was the number of holiday camps that were springing up across the Island and the effect they were allegedly having on Island life...

January 29th, 1938.
HOLIDAY CAMPS IN THE ISLAND
To the Editor of the I.W. County Press.

Sir, — With reference to the holiday camps in the Isle of Wight, there are two points which I do not think have been mentioned. One is the size of the Island, which is so small that any undesirable visitors make themselves heard, seen, and felt in a way which might not be the case where they could have a larger area in which to disport themselves, without annoying decent-minded people. The other point is the deterioration of the youthful native population, who very naturally are inclined to copy the strange behaviour of these temporary immigrants. The Islanders used to be remarkable for their courtesy and good manners — inherent from one generation to another. Now, alas, this pleasing trait is fast disappearing, owing to corruption from outside. Rudeness is mistaken for wit, warmth of clothing for fashionable freedom, and screaming and shouting for genuine enjoyment. Prevention is better than cure, and it would be wiser to stem this invasion quickly before the better class of residents are driven out of the Island, as must inevitably be the case if it continues.

I am, Sir, yours faithfully, CLARA M. ROSS. Green Gables, Freshwater Bay.

To the Editor of the I.W. County Press.

Sir, — With reference to the excellent letter from your correspondent on holiday camps in the Isle of Wight, we write to endorse heartily every word he says. These camps are a menace in every way to all the decent, orderly residents who have chosen to make their homes in the Island. The best part of the year is ruined during the nowadays prolonged season by this hostile invasion of campers who infest every bathing beach with their undesirable presence, and pervade our quiet streets and lanes with their raucous shouts and so-called 'singing.' Their manners are negligible, and they have no consideration whatever for others. One cannot get away from them anywhere. It is high time the authorities in our towns and villages woke up to their responsibilities and took measures to suppress any further depredations by the promoters of these camps in our midst.

I am, Sir, yours faithfully, FELLOW ISLAND RESIDENTS.

To the Editor of the I.W. County Press.

Sir, — I have read with interest a lot of disparaging remarks in your paper about holiday camps. I can only say that your correspondents are greatly biased. The holiday camps on the Island have mostly taken over derelict mansions, their owners having died, and their descendants not wishing to keep them up. The camps are large employers of labour and contribute heavily to local taxes, and their clients, about 20,000 last year, spend a lot of money with the local tradesmen... The visitors are not 'strange hordes,' but mostly teachers, civil servants, office workers, etc. I can assure him that he will not be attacked by strange hordes with battleaxes — they may be armed with nothing more than 'cheap' cosmetics.

I am, Sir, yours truly, FRANK BOYCE, 20 Cleveland Road, S.W.13

A DEBATABLE SUBJECT.

FOR OR AGAINST HOLIDAY CAMPS? —
THAT IS THE QUESTION!
THERE ARE ABOUT 10 IN THE ISLAND,
WHERE THOUSANDS OF CITY WORKERS
CAST OFF THE YEAR'S WORRIES AND DUST,

BUT THE RESULTANT NOISE DEMANDS AN ISOLATED POSITION FOR THE CHALETS.

WE DON'T MIND THEM WANDERING ABROAD IN THE WIGHT IF THEY ARE ORDERLY — AND IF THEY SPEND MONEY SO MUCH THE BETTER.

BUT THERE CAN BE TOO MUCH OF A GOOD THING!

THE MAIN ATTRACTION OF THE ISLAND IS ITS BEAUTIFUL SCENERY AND RUSTICITY.

THE GOOSE THAT LAYS THE GOLDEN EGG MAY DECAMP IF CAMPS INCREASE.

OUR PICTURESQUE OLDEST INHABITANT MIGHT EVEN BE OUSTED

BY THIS, COMPLETE WITH HAIRY CHEST "A LA SHANKLIN VISITOR!

The County Press was now regularly making use of the work of Tom Smitch, a print room employee who was also a cartoonist.

The 1930s saw the start of the decline of the country estates. The reasons were many and varied and would fill a book of their own but prominent among them were changes in agriculture, the new demand for building land, (ironically, including the building of holiday camps) and perhaps more importantly, soaring wage bills. The late 1930s was a prosperous time for Britain and wages of four to five pounds a week were not uncommon. People were no longer prepared to sell a year's labour to an employer for just 25 shillings a week, terms still being offered in many small ads in the County Press as recently as 1932, and by the early 1950s, intact working estates had become few and far between. On the Island the Swainston Manor estate, owned by Sir Barrington Simeon, typified their downfall (although in Swainston's case matters were not helped by major bomb damage during the war).

In an effort to make ends meet most of the estate was sold off to neighbouring farms in 1932 and the house would eventually pass into private hands in the 1950s, but for the moment life carried on as normal ...

February 12th, 1938.

OVER 50 YEARS A KEEPER.

RETIREMENT OF MR F. FALLICK OF SWAINSTON.

Mr. Frederick Fallick, of St. Hubert's Lodge, Porchfield, who for 30 years has been the esteemed head-keeper to Sir Barrington Simeon, Bt., on the Swainston Estate, retires from that position to-day after 52 years service, during which time he estimates that he has reared at least 100,000 pheasants. Mr. Fallick, who is 67, is a native of Porchfield and has spent his life in the woods extending from that village over the large Swainston Estate. He is a familiar figure to and is held in high regard by every gentleman who has shot over the estate, a long succession of employers, the tenants and his staff... Mr. Fallick became head-keeper at Swainston in 1906...

The largest 'bag' he remembers was during Sir Barrington Simeon's time, when 1100 birds were accounted for by six guns in three days... The pheasant rearing record referred to above has meant many day and night spells of duty in watching the young birds and keeping off marauding kestrels, sparrow hawks, and little owls. The inclusion of the last-named bird in the enemies of young chicks is interesting in view of the controversy which has recently raged over their depredations, but Mr. Fallick has no doubt about their character, as he has caught them in the act of carrying off pheasant chicks. He has seen a sparrow hawk kill a pheasant twice its own size...

Mr. Fallick's skill with the gun has often been envied by sportsmen and, strange to say, he has been regarded as an even more deadly marksman been ever since he had the misfortune to lose his left eye by a wood-chopping incident in 1919... Naturally, during such a long working life, Mr. Fallick has had many clashes with poachers, but apart from remarking that he once had the unpleasant experience of looking down the barrels of a gun held by a poacher who threatened to shoot him, he preferred to be silent on the subject. He did, however, venture the opinion that night poaching has almost died out in favour of day-time poaching by raiders in motor-cars.

THE WEEK'S NEWS.

AN EXTRAORDINARY MONTH. — According to the old saying ' A peck of March dust is worth a king's ransom.' 1938 should prove a year of bumper harvests, as it is doubtful if ever within living memory the third month of the year has been drier. Until Thursday night when rain, which was badly needed, came and continued yesterday (Friday) there has been no measurable rainfall at Newport since March 2nd. To have 23 days of drought in March is probably unprecedented. The mild conditions have led to unusually free growth.

ANOTHER AIR-RAID 'BLACK-OUT.' — The importance which the Government attaches to the protection from air attack of the area which includes the Isle of Wight is indicated by the fact that another 'black-out,' to act as a test of air raid and gas precautions, has been arranged for the night of March 23rd. It may be regarded as very significant that this area has been chosen for a second test. Its importance, including as it does the country's premier Naval and passenger ports, is obvious.* (Feb 19)

WAITING FOR THE FLEET. — Mr. Adams, of Southampton, possesses a pre-Trafalgar letter which has an Island interest. It is written by Phineas Board, on the Victory, to his mother, addressed to the Sign of the Millwright Inn at Newport. This inn was in Orchard-street and the building is now the corner premises between that Street and the new car park. It was later known as the Millwright's Arms. Mr. W.C. Smith of Newport, who was working nearby as a lad, informs me that it was the haunt of bogus beggars, who quickly relinquished their various 'ailments' once inside its hospitable doors. Phineas writes to his mother on August 25, when the British fleet were waiting for the French, who did not appear until the battle took place on October 21st, 1805. The letter, exactly as written, runs as follows : Dear Mother. This comes with my fond love to you, hoping these few lines to you will find you all well, as it leaves me at present, thank God. This is the third letter hi wrought to you, and hi am very oneasey because hi don't know wether you get my half pay because hi sent my will and power to you and hi shant be happy untill hi knowe. So send me an answer as quick as possable. We expect the French fleet out every day. Dear Mother, hi think hi made my fortune with the rich prisner we have taken, so hi shall be able to do something for you all very shortley. God bless you all.'

---

* Three weeks later the German Army invaded Austria. It was now widely accepted that war with Germany was inevitable and regular reports now began to appear in the County Press detailing the training of air raid personnel, the construction of air raid shelters and the distribution of gas masks.

TOWN AND COUNTY NOTES.

WELL KNOWN ISLAND HOUSE DESTROYED. — Fernhill House, Wootton was completely burnt out in a few hours on Thursday. The house was unoccupied...The fire was due to roofing material being ignited by a spark from a bonfire made by workmen engaged in clearing timber from the grounds... In spite of very zealous work by firemen on the roofs, it became obvious that the whole main building was doomed ... Lead in the guttering and piping ran like water and in the smaller ornamental windows glass melted and twisted into fantastic shapes... by 8 o'clock the flames were on the wane ...and in a little over an hour only a smoking ruin remained...*(See photograph opposite page)*

A SHILLING CALF. — A calf was sold in Newport Market on Tuesday for a shilling and there was nothing wrong with it except that it was a midget, only about the size of a terrier, although it was a week old. Among those who saw it sold the opinion was expressed that this must be a low-price record, but just to show how dangerous it is to claim any thing as a record, a farmer said that some years ago his father sent a much bigger calf to the old market in St James's-square and it made the same amount.

An incident strikingly demonstrating the speed and convenience of air travel was brought to our notice this week. A Croydon specialist has two patients in the Newport district. On Thursday morning he flew from Croydon to Ryde, motored to Newport, saw his patients, returned to Ryde Airport, and was back in Croydon to open his surgery at the usual time, 10.45 a.m. He commenced his early-morning trip to the Island at 7.10 a.m.

THE CRISIS. THE PREMIER'S RETURN. — On arrival at Heston at 5.30 p.m. on Friday the Prime Minister said 'Yesterday afternoon I had a long talk with Herr Hitler. It was a frank talk but it was a friendly one, and I feel satisfied now that each of us fully understands what is in the mind of the other.

IOW COUNCIL. RATS AND MICE DESTRUCTION. — The Minister of Agriculture has suggested that a NATIONAL RAT WEEK should be held commencing on the seventh of November 1938. All persons interested are asked to make an intensive and united effort for the destruction of rats during such a week. Any person desiring information on the subject is invited to apply to MR. TERTIOUS NOBBS, Superintendent of Rats and Mice Destruction, County Hall, Newport.

———————————◆———————————

In November 1936 the BBC started regular television broadcasts for viewers in the London area. Although it was to be 1954 before the Rowridge transmitter brought BBC television to the Isle of Wight, Mr Sherratt, the Newport radio dealer, was able to receive the new London transmissions by using a powerful aerial situated on high ground at Northwood.

He arranged a demonstration...

The fire-ravaged ruins of Fernhill, Wootton. (June 11)   *[Photo, Stevens.]*

THE WOOL FAIR IS COMING!!
Sheep being washed at the well known Calbourne beauty spot, Winkle-street. (June 11th)
[Photo, Andrews.]

Selecting timber for the stem of a lifeboat. On right, Mr. B. Maskell, timber convertor to the RNLI at East Cowes, who has retired after 22 years service; with his successor, Mr. P. Fenn   *[Photo, White and Son.]*

Photo of Jasmine Bligh, one of the BBC Alexandra Palace announcers, taken from the screen of a television set at Newport last week. (July 20)

July 23rd, 1938.
TELEVISION IN THE ISLAND.
DEMONSTRATIONS AT NEWPORT.

On Thursday the latest wireless wonder of the many which have resulted from the lifework of Marconi - television - was demonstrated near Newport under circumstances which enabled the Island once more to play a notable part in the history of radio.

Mr. W. G. Sherratt, of Messrs. Sherratt and Son, Newport, the well-known radio experimenter and dealer, organised the demonstrations in association with the Marconiphone Company, one of whose latest television sets, priced at 60 gns. was used. For some time, with apparatus of his own construction, Mr. Sherrat has been getting excellent results on the sound side of television, and at his suggestion the Marconiphone Co. agreed to carry out local tests of viewing. The tests proved so surprisingly satisfactory that public demonstrations were arranged. They took place at Bella Vista, a residence on the Newport-road near the turning down to Northwood Church. Mr. Godfrey, of the Marconiphone Company, collaborated with Mr. Sherratt in the demonstration... Hitherto, television reception has not been considered satisfactory at over 25 miles distance from the studios in London, and it has never previously been received over the sea, so the Island experiments are doubly interesting... Among those attending the first public viewing of a televised programme in the Island, were the Mayor and Mayoress of Newport, the Mayor of Ryde and the Chief Constable. Several London and Island Pressmen were also at the demonstration.

The pictures were remarkably clear. At times the definition was quite as good as that of a film, but at others there was some interference due to the sparks of ignition from passing traffic. The evening programmes sent out from the Alexandra Palace studios, consisted of a number of variety items, the latest Gaumont-British news film and a series of interviews with people distinguished in various walks of life and sport. Both viewing and speech were excellent.

In a talk after the demonstration Mr. Godfrey emphasised that although the experiments had proved to a surprising degree that television gave sound entertainment in the Island, nearly 90 miles from the studios, people should not purchase sets before they had sought expert advice as to the results which might be expected in their particular localities as there were numerous factors to be considered, such as height, surrounding objects, and traffic interference.

------------------------◆------------------------

THE WEEK'S NEWS.

A BLANK DAY AT THE POLICE COURT. — There were no cases for hearing at the Borough Petty Sessions on Monday. The Magistrates present merely had to deal with a licencing application.

A FOOLISH PRANK. — *Franklin Ratsey Woodroffe*, a 19 year old sailmaker of Cowes, was fined £5 on each of two charges for driving his car from The Parade, Cowes, up Watch House-lane into the High-street, and his licence was suspended for three months... Gladys Ward said that on October 21st she saw two men get into a car outside the Globe, and as she started up Watch House-lane she found that the car was following her. As they went down the street the occupants of the car gave a shout as if they had accomplished something brave...When asked by P.C. Humphreys if he would give any explanation Woodroffe said 'No, I don't think so. Those are the sort of things I do.'

BEMBRIDGE - BIRD PETS. — A dove belonging to Mrs. F. Griffin, of 2 Woodclose, Hillway, has just died, aged 24 years. It was caught by her son in a butterfly net. It lived with the family and would coo to greet them on entering the house. One of its favourite perches was on Mrs. Griffin's head, and it would remain there while its owner was engaged in sewing or reading the papers.

SHALFLEET - FARMER LOSES TOE IN ACCIDENT. — Mr. Donald Priddle, aged 25, of Lower Dodpitts Farm, received severe injuries to his right foot in a gun accident on Tuesday afternoon, the unusual nature of which emphasises the care which should always be exercised in handling firearms. On his way home from mangold pulling in a field near the Newbridge-road, he loaded his gun on the chance of shooting a rabbit en-route. He stopped on the way to talk to his brother John and while doing so unwisely rested the barrel of the gun on his right foot. When he lifted the gun to continue his homeward walk the trigger caught in the buttonhole of his coat, and the gun was discharged into his foot.

— — — — — ◆ — — — — —

1939.

Surprisingly, clay pipe production was still being carried on at Newport until at least the late 1930s according to a recent obituary for one of the last of the clay pipe makers. The inclusion of the obituary generated another interesting scrap of information the following week ...

January 7th, 1939.
AN ISLANDER'S NOTES.
BY VECTENSIS.

Clay pipe making, once a flourishing industry at Newport, has now died out owing to the dwindling demand for clays in these days of briars and cigarettes. The last of the Newport clay pipe makers (Mr. James Edgar) passed away a few days ago at Gloucester, where he was living in retirement with relatives. He was a very clever clay pipe maker, the third generation of his family to follow the calling, and there was still sufficient demand for his productions to keep him employed until he retired about a year ago. In conversation with the writer a few years ago Mr. Edgar said that some 30 years ago, when he came to work at a clay pipe factory in Orchard-street, Newport, there was still a good trade being done with France, but it gradually died away. 'However, I still turn out a few for the R.A.O.B.' remarked Mr. Edgar. Asked why he thought clays had gone out of favour, he replied: 'Because they are too cheap. They are fine pipes, and some people still know it, but they won't be seen smoking one. Still, more people than you would think smoke them indoors, where no one can see them.

Mr. Edgar was not ashamed of his productions; he always smoked one indoors and out. He had some rare moulds for making fancy clay pipes, which were family heirlooms.

The article brought a follow-up letter in the following issue...
January 14th, 1939.
My reference to the dying out of the clay pipe making industry at Newport has brought me a weighty and interesting gift from Mr. W. A. Hurst, of Messrs. Hurst and Son, engineers, of Newport, in the shape of a metal mould used for making clay pipes, with the figure of a lady reclining on the bowl. Mr. Hurst informs me that his firm have had a considerable number of these moulds through their hands in recent years as scrap metal, but all except this one has gone the way of scrap - into the furnace. I propose to offer it to the Island Museum at Carisbrooke Castle for preservation as a relic of a formerly flourishing Island industry.

------------◆------------

TOWN AND COUNTY NOTES
LAYING A CABLE TO THE WIGHT. — A a new submarine cable was laid between Southsea and Nettlestone Point, Seaview, during last summer. The cable was approximately 6 miles long and weighed 160 tons, and it was coiled in the hold of a cargo steamer, from which it was 'paid out' as the vessel was towed across the Spithead... Getting the cable ashore at Seaview presented some difficulty as the tide was out and the vessel could not approach very near... The distance to the shore was carefully measured, the cable cut to the required length, and the end was then floated ashore on barrels.

ONE OF THE MOST PROSPEROUS TOWNS. — Cowes comes seventh in the list of the most prosperous towns in Britain. This is shown in the Ministry of Labour's Unemployed Index. According to official figures, there are 5940 workers in the town, and of these 97.3 per cent. are in employment, mainly, of course, in the shipyards and aircraft factories.

CAPT P. MACDONALD AND BILLETING OF CHILDREN. — In the House of Commons on Thursday week Captain Peter Macdonald asked the Minister of Health whether he would reconsider the decision to make the whole of the Isle of Wight a reception area for purposes of evacuation ...

ARMISTICE DAY. — 11th of November, 11 a.m., is a sequence of elevens that will ever be remembered by those who took part in the Great War and ... as 11 o'clock approached what were the thoughts passing through the minds of those who survived? Doubtless of old comrades, loved ones, and friends whose names are engraved on the many war memorials to be found in every town and village in the land. Surely, too, for the 5800 ex-Service men in the mental homes, for those 2000 warriors who are sightless, and a further 2200 still in-patients at hospitals, of the 61,000 suffering from neurasthenia, epilepsy, or tuberculosis, aftermaths of the war, to say nothing of the 32,600 who have lost limbs or of the 130,000 widows and orphans...

———————————◆———————————

In the 1930's it was still possible to demolish ancient buildings with little or no danger of protest, but things looked different for a while in 1939 when Cowes Council announced that they were proposing to demolish Northwood Lodge Gate, situated at the junction of Granville and Park Road and once the main entrance to Northwood House.* Built in the classical style, complete with doric columns, it had been designed and built for the Ward family by John Nash in the early 1800s but was now pronounced a hazard for buses trying to round the corner.

The fact that it was the work of one of Britain's most famous architects seems to have been of little consequence and for the moment its future looked bleak. To add insult to injury the pretty lodge was to be replaced by the arguably drab and unimaginative bath-house which still stands on the site to this day.

For once there were protests. This letter is typical of the many that appeared over the next few weeks calling for its retention and complaining of 'Council vandalism' ...

January 7th, 1939.
PROPOSED DEMOLITION OF NORTHWOOD LODGE GATE.
Mr. R. H. Matthews has sent the following letter to the clerk of the Cowes Council: 'Sir, — It is with a feeling of very deep regret that I have learned that your Council is contemplating the destruction of the lodge and gate to Northwood Park at the junction of Granville-road. As a civil engineer and a motorist of many years standing, I quite appreciate that some drastic improvement is necessary to enable buses and other large vehicles to negotiate safely the turn from Granville-road to Park-road, but surely the destruction of one of the few worthy pieces of architecture in the town is too high a price to pay for the improvement if some other course is open. The obvious course is the removal of the nondescript buildings on the acute angle opposite to the gate... If the question of finance be raised it surely cannot be sufficiently serious to justify the proposed vandalism, which would inflict a prominent loss on the town of one of its outstanding objects of interest which can ill be spared. The amenities of the town have already been sufficiently outraged by the incongruous block of buildings recently erected on the Parade.

Faithfully yours, Robert Matthews, Southgate, London.

———————————◆———————————

During the 1880s and 90s, the pages of the County Press were regularly filled with accounts of the shortcomings of the Island's railway companies. By the early years of the 20th century the railways had improved beyond measure and for the most part the only references to the Island's railways during the 1920s and 30s were positive ones.

Accidents on the railways were now virtually unheard of so when the most serious one for many years took place it received generous coverage...

* See photograph, page 67.

January 23rd, 1939.
DERAILMENT NEAR CARISBROOKE.
RAILWAY SERVICES STOPPED.

The derailment of the mail train from Newport to Freshwater, near Great Park Farm, Carisbrooke, shortly after five o'clock on Thursday morning was the most serious accident on the Island railways since they were taken over by the Southern Railway in 1923.* The train, consisting of an engine, two brake vans, two passenger coaches, and two wagons loaded with coal, was the usual early morning train carrying mails to Yarmouth and Freshwater. It was just regaining speed after negotiating the rise from Carisbrooke, on the run downhill into Watchingwell-station, when the whole of the train left the metals near the bridge which carries the line over a lane near Great Park Farm. The engine became uncoupled and it ran about 20 yards along the line before coming to rest. The coaches and wagons crashed into each other and were extensively damaged, while the rails were twisted and the sleepers splintered. The guard's van struck the bridge and the others were poised at precarious angles. About 90 yards of the line were damaged. It was fortunate that there were no passengers, otherwise they might have sustained serious injuries ... The mails were salvaged by Post Office vans from Freshwater, the bags having to be taken across fields in relays. In spite of the delay they reached their destination about 9 a.m... A railway official informed the 'County Press' last night that clearing the line was proceeding well... The engine was put back on the rails shortly after midday on Thursday. It was decided to burn the trucks and two carriages which remained ... which means that the work will be considerably expedited.

The following week's edition gave more details of the clearing up exercise ...
January 14th, 1939.

The railway line at Great Park ...was cleared in time for the resumption of traffic at midday on Saturday last ... Interested passengers saw much evidence of the accident along the banks of the line, where fires which had been lighted to destroy the wooden parts of the coaches and wagons involved in the derailment were still burning, while bent rails, discarded chairs, splintered sleepers, and 14 pairs of wheels still awaited removal. Much of the metal debris had already been conveyed to Newport, and further wagon loads were deposited in the siding at Calbourne Station... And thus was the formidable task of clearing nearly 100 tons of rolling stock, precipitously perched on an awkward embankment, accomplished in little more than 48 hours, in addition to replacing on the track the 45 ton locomotive, W.31, 'Chale.'... The cost of the mishap must have run into hundreds of pounds.

———————————————◆———————————————

At the turn of the last century there were still some 25 working mills on the Island. By the end of the 1914-18 war this number had halved as companies like Hovis and McDougall built gigantic mills directly on the quayside of Britain's larger seaports. The

---

* See photograph, page 67.

likes of the Baltic Mill in Liverpool and Solent Mill in Southampton were able to process huge quantities of imported wheat on the quayside and they were devastatingly efficient. Britain's rural mills were no match for them and over the next 20 years most of them were to disappear...

April 22nd, 1939.

OLD-ESTABLISHED ISLAND MILLING BUSINESS CLOSING DOWN.
RETIREMENT OF MR. JOHN ROACH OF EAST MEDINA MILLS.

Consequent on the retirement at the age of 80 of Mr. John Roach, of East Medina House, the business of millers and corn merchants carried on by members of the family for 142 years since 1797, will close down as soon as the present stock at West Mill, Newport, has been disposed of. This decision marks the end of the business concern which has been prominent in the commercial life of the Island for all those years, and it will be a matter of regret to many, as the firm of T. R. and J. Roach had built up an enviable reputation for quality and straight dealing, a reputation which Mr. John Roach has scrupulously maintained during the 64 years that he has been associated with it. Mr. Roach's familiar tall and genial presence will be much missed by customers in all parts of the Island whom he has called for orders week by week for the last 57 years … For 38 years of that long period Mr. Roach cycled on his rounds. He only gave up cycling three years ago. He estimates that he has averaged 50 miles a week, so he has covered about 100,000 miles awheel on business during his life, facing all weathers, yet, happily, he still enjoys good health.

At one time the firm owned three mills in the Newport district - East Medina, West Mill and Lower Shide Mill. Lower Shide Mill was sold some years ago, and East Medina, where the Roach family started their business operations, was disposed of to the Newport Corporation and closed in 1937. West Mill has remained in their hands until now. It was rented for some years by Mr. Roach's father and then purchased in 1878 … Mr. Roach was one of the first local businessmen to make use of the telephone in the Island. As far back as 1886 he had a system of private lines linking his three mills and a store in Newport installed by the National Telephone Co. at an annual rental of £39. That was about 10 years before the company established a public service in the Island. Just after the Great War Mr. Roach was the first miller in England to make use of an American machine for cutting maize and wheat. It was installed at East Medina and when that mill was closed it was still the only machine of its kind working in the Island … One reminiscence, not a particularly happy one, was referred to by Mr. Roach. He was persuaded by a local iron founder to have an an iron water wheel in place of the customary wooden one, but it proved a complete failure, and the experiment cost him about £200. Water wheels remained the power units at both East Medina Mill and West Mill but at Shide Mill one of the earliest types of steam engine, a beam engine, was installed and it could still be seen at the back of the mill near the pathway across the railway leading from Medina-avenue to Pan-lane until recently, when the increased price for scrap iron made its removal worth while.

MEWS

sparkling

GRAPE FRUIT CRUSH

Still the most popular non-alcoholic drink, contains the actual fruit cells of free-ripened grape fruit.
You'll easily recognise the distinctive pebbled bottle.

THE WEEK'S NEWS.

FRESHWATER - AN UNUSUAL CINDER. — Mrs. Windebank, of Stroud-cottages had an unusual find when taking the cinders from her grate on Thursday week. Among the cinders was one of which was an exact representation of a sitting swan. The head, folded wings, and feet could be clearly seen. The find has attracted considerable interest, and one morning this week Mrs. Windebank had eight visitors to see it before breakfast.

FRESHWATER - A LATE ARRIVAL.— Mrs. Nickerson, of Clarendon-terrace, informs us that a letter she posted from Freshwater Post Office on October 2 last year, reached its destination at Beaulieu, a matter of seven miles away as the crow flies, on Monday last, seven months later.

THE MILITARY TRAINING ACT — 361 MEN REGISTER. — The Military Training Act came into force on Saturday, when 361 men between the ages of 20 and 21 years registered at local employment exchanges in the Island. The percentage of conscientious objectors was less than the 1.8 % returned for the country generally. A medical board will sit at the Foresters-hall, Sun-hill, Cowes, commencing on Monday, June 12th. Five doctors and a military representative will be in attendance and men who are passed as physically fit will be allocated to their various units and instructed to report to them on July 15th. (June 10.)

ISLAND CAMPS FOR MILITIA MEN - ERECTIONS COMMENCED NEAR NEWPORT. — Work commenced on Wednesday in erecting a permanent camp to be used for the training of militia men at Staplers Heath, near Newport. The camp will consist of wooden barrack huts with larger store-huts and other accommodation. It is expected that the total number of militia men to be stationed there will be in the neighbourhood of 200... A series of hutments are being erected at various points in the Island to serve as quarters for the men of the Royal Engineers on detachment work with their equipment. A similar hutment camp is being erected on the east side of the Newport-Cowes road, opposite Albany Barracks, where an artillery encampment existed during the Great War. (June 17.)

TRAFFIC WARDENS. — Following their successful introduction last year traffic wardens have again been engaged for the summer for traffic control duties at the Island's busiest road junctions. They first appeared on Wednesday, and 14 wardens will be continuously employed until September, with an additional four during July and August. Their function is to relieve the regular police who have thus more time to devote to other more important duties.

———————————◆———————————

The protests over the demolition of Northwood Lodge had met with partial success and it had eventually been decided that the archway was to be saved. However, just when things were looking promising...

June 24th, 1939.
NORTHWOOD PARK ARCHWAY DEMOLISHED.
The Works Committee of Cowes Council reported that as they were of the opinion that the archway leading into the car park at Northwood Park was unsafe they had directed that it should be taken down. - Mr. Lallow said it was with regret that the committee had directed the surveyor to have the archway removed. Since the demolition of the lodge it had sagged two or three inches and had become a danger to the public. — Sir Godfrey Baring, while not now deploring the removal of the archway as it had become a danger, pointed out that although they had been told that it would remain it had only survived the lodge a few weeks. Now that one of their few remaining architectural beauties had been destroyed they were left with the public baths. He was glad, however, that the archway had been removed, because without the support of the lodge it looked utterly ridiculous, whereas now the whole place just looked ugly.

THE WEEK'S NEWS.
TONIGHT'S BLACKOUT — From midnight to-night (Saturday) until four o'clock to-morrow (Sunday) morning, there will be a black-out of the Isle of Wight. This is part of a large scale Royal Air Force exercise, involving most of south and east England, and the authorities are anxious that no lights should be visible from the air. Street lighting will be restricted and it is desirable that vehicles should, as far as possible, be kept off the roads during the darkened period... In time of war, darkening of large areas exposed to attack is likely to be an essential feature of the defence of this country.

NEW MILITARY CAMP AT NORTHWOOD — Work commenced this week on the erection of a military camp to accommodate 600 men on a 14 acre site adjoining the Newport-Cowes road at Northwood... The accommodation to be provided comprises some 40 wooden huts. It is intended to use local labour entirely if enough men are available and it is anticipated that between 200 and 300 will be needed. We understand that the camp will be occupied by Royal Engineer searchlight units.

BOMB EXPLODES ON CAR FERRY — A bomb explosion on the Southern Railway car ferry in mid-Solent injured two members of the Royal Ulster Rifles stationed at Parkhurst... The ferry was on its way to Fishbourne with members of the regiment and trucks returning from a bombing course in the Portsmouth area. They were taking back with them a bomb which had failed to explode with the idea of destroying it... Part of the lorry was blown out but there was no damage to the ferry.

THE I.W. COUNTY PRESS, CO., LTD. — The operations of the company resulted in a net profit for the year of £5508 2s. 11d.... The directors recommend the payment of a final dividend of 10 per cent. (making 15 per cent. for the year) and a bonus of 5 per cent., both free of tax... The circulation of the paper was now 19,403 copies a week, which was very satisfactory.

An officious and unpopular A.R.P official was putting the stretcher-bearer party through their paces. He lay on the ground and said, "Now, remember, I am completely smashed up. Nearly every bone in my body is broken. Now let's see how you pick me up." The stretcher-bearers picked him up efficiently, laid him on the stretcher, and asked, "Well, was that all right?" "Yes, quite satisfactory," snapped the officious one, "except you didn't have the look of regret in your eyes I expected."

◆

By now war with Germany was almost certain and Hitler was expected to invade Poland at any time. The day before the invasion took place Britain had signed an agreement with Poland to the effect that if Germany were to attack either nation, the other would aid in its defence and so, following the invasion of Poland, the writing was on the wall.

On the Island there was a hurried exodus of tourists...

August 26th, 1939.

THE ISLAND AND THE CRISIS.
GENERAL DEFENCE PRECAUTIONS TAKEN.
VISITORS LEAVING AND BOOKINGS CANCELLED.

On Thursday, when the international situation was very threatening, the Heavy Artillery Territorials were called out to man their war stations, a continuous watch was started by the the Observer Corps, and the general national instructions as to A.R.P. services were immediately acted upon... At the A.R.P. headquarters at the County-hall, Newport, steps were taken to protect with boards and sandbags the portions of the building used by the A.R.P. workers as an administrative centre, and in every town and village special constables went out to watch vulnerable points... The emergency came as another sickening blow to those who cater for visitors, following one of the worst seasons on record owing to bad weather. Many visitors left on Thursday and yesterday (Friday) before the end of their holidays, and hotel and boarding house keepers received many cancellations of bookings. The broadcast warnings urging people immediately to purchase the necessary materials for blacking out lights in buildings and for restricting motor-car lights led to a rush yesterday morning on shops supplying these things... So great are the motor-car conveyance bookings on the ferries and steamers that on one route it was announced yesterday that no more could be booked until Monday afternoon. On Thursday morning there was nearly an hour's delay on telephone calls to London and later in the day the demands became so great that no call was accepted for more than three minutes' conversation... On Wednesday night, for the first time for many years the street lamps which at certain points in the Ryde area have been kept alight all night, were extinguished, and again on Thursday and last night. The Post Office windows in Union-street were on Thursday pasted over with thick brown paper and the staff have since been working with the aid of artificial light.

The previous Sunday, Britain had declared war on Germany and almost immediately a mass evacuation of children had begun throughout Britain.* Within a few days of war being declared Island residents were awaiting the imminent arrival of nearly 5,500 children to be billeted in homes across the Island. In the event, less than 2000 arrived...

September 9th, 1939.

THE ISLAND AND THE WAR.

Like the rest of the country, the Island received the announcement on Sunday that a state of war exists between England and Germany with a certain sense of relief, having now fully realised that if a horrible necessity, it was still the necessity, in order that Hitlerism and all its pagan policies should be banished from the earth, and the blessings of perpetual peace firmly established. With our traditional patriotism, we have now set to work to make the temporary exiled children in our midst feel that they have here a real home away from home, to attend the sick and visiting mothers with loving care, and to discharge every duty laid upon us by the compelling exigencies of the times with scrupulous care in the letter and in the spirit.

RYDE. — Arrangements had been made for the reception of 2900 evacuees in the Borough but only 615 were received... The Haylands area has the largest percentage of mothers and children under school age and the wives and children of London holiday visitors have been billeted in the town.

NEWPORT. — The week has been one of unceasing activity for civil defence workers. Sandbag filling has accounted for much labour... Air raid wardens are continuously on duty and their numbers have been increased at night, when special watch is kept for those contravening the lighting regulations... A "war-time" service of Southern Vectis buses, operating all over the Isle of Wight, came into effect on Thursday. The main effect is fewer buses during the period of running and the earlier last bus on all routes.

SANDOWN-SHANKLIN. — The accommodation of the district has not been overburdened in the billeting of evacuated children for the numbers did not reach those expected. A contributing factor was the reluctance of some parents at last minute to let their children go, the evacuation not being compulsory... On Friday Sandown billeting officers expected to receive 923 unaccompanied children but only 220 arrived. At Shanklin the anticipated number was 1315, whereas the actual number was 752. Sandown expected 374 mothers and children but only 71 arrived.

VENTNOR. — The watermen commenced packing up their gear during the week-end and the beach has presented a deserted appearance during the week... Several provision traders, especially milk dealers and bakers, have suffered loss owing to the arrival of only about a third of the expected number of evacuated children. Arrangements were made at one hotel for the reception of 100 children and not one turned up. Milk had to be wasted and some of the bakers declined to take bread back.

---

* It soon transpired that not only were the evacuations premature but some of the locations chosen were prime targets for enemy action.

Adders, or vipers, caught as a hobby in April by Mr. C. Cassell and Mr. Banting of Shanklin. It is estimated that if these had been allowed to breed they would have produced 330 offspring.

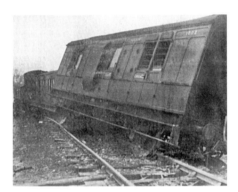

The derailed train near Carisbrooke.
[Photo, Thomas]

A calf with two heads at Blackwater Mill.

The old Gateway and lodge entrance to Northwood Park and the new building which is being erected for public baths behind it. The photographs were accompanied by a letter from Mr. Kirk regretting the Council's decision to demolish this old building, "as the town has little enough of architectural value." It is to be pulled down to widen a dangerous corner.   [Photo, Kirk, Cowes.]

COWES. — The accommodation at the Gurnard Pines Holiday Camp being rather severely taxed, about 100 of the evacuated children were moved to private billets in the village on Monday. A further supply of gas masks was received in Cowes on Saturday and there are now sufficient to meet all demands.

ST HELENS. — Some 600 buns were distributed among the 200 evacuated children at St Helens on Tuesday and Wednesday... A teacher from Portsmouth told our correspondent that the children had settled in wonderfully well... and the children meet each morning at 10 o'clock in the Methodist chapels and Services'-hall for gas drill.

ISLAND GIRL ARRIVES HOME FROM BERLIN.

One of the last English visitors to leave Berlin was 19-year-old Miss Lewis of Alverstone Garden Village. Miss Lewis had been spending her holidays with friends in Berlin. She left there to return home at 7 a.m. on Sunday and did not know that a state of war existed between England and Germany until she arrived at Folkestone. She said that listening in to foreign broadcasts was banned in Germany some days previously. Her German friends were very charming people and did not want war. That was the pity of it.

———————————◆———————————

The year which had seen Europe pitched into a second world war ended on another gloomy note ...

December 30th, 1939.

RATIONING STARTS ON JANUARY 8th.

The Ministry of Food announced on Thursday that sugar, as well as butter, bacon, and ham, will be rationed from Monday week (January 8th). The sugar allowance will be 12oz. a week for each person. Meat rationing will be introduced probably in February ... Farmers have to give 12 days notice of their intention to send cattle to Newport Market on and after January 15th, so they should immediately get the necessary forms from Mr. Edward Way, of Messrs. Henry J. Way and Son, Newport. Consumers must register with their butchers not later than Monday week. This does not apply to pork ... Special allowances of sugar will be made to confectionery manufacturers, brewers, and bee-keepers. As in 1918, meat will be rationed on the basis of value. The weight of the ration will therefore vary with the consumers choice of quality ... Tripe, liver, hearts, kidneys, tongues, rabbits, poultry, game, and fish will not be rationed. Manufactured products like sausages, brawn, pies and pasties will also be unrationed. Mr. W. S. Morrison, Minister of Food, states: "The ration will be well up to the ordinary requirements of the people ... Anyone who wants to make marmalade will buy the oranges required for it and show the invoice at the Food Office, where any extra allowance will be made available on the basis of 3lb. of sugar for every 2lb. of oranges.

———————————◆———————————

1940.

TOWN AND COUNTY NOTES.

THEY KEPT A PACT. — On January 1st ten years ago, the assistants in a local shop discussed the past and speculated as to what the future might bring. Seven of them made a pact that whatever might happen, they would meet on Jan. 1st 1940 to talk over their experiences. As the years went by some left the Island and some were married but on Monday all except one kept the pact and met together at lunch in a local restaurant. Mr. C. M. Dabell, their former employer, visited them and wished them the compliments of the season.

MORE LAND UNDER THE PLOUGH. — The Minister of Agriculture announced on Monday that after less than 130 days of war, well over 1 million acres in England and Wales had been scheduled for ploughing. Much of this had already been ploughed despite the unusually wet weather.

Damage on Shanklin Front. — At this week's Shanklin Council meeting Mr. B.J. Kemp directed attention to damage done on Shanklin seafront. There was not a whole pane of glass in the Council's huts on the north side of Small Hope, and he suggested that the windows should be boarded up or covered with wire. The Clerk said he had been shocked to see the condition of the shelters. Seats had been torn out and were being cut down - sheer wanton damage...

The Corporation's horse "Joe," being no longer fit for work, has been painlessly destroyed.

FIRST ISLAND PRISONER OF WAR. — The good news has been received that Commissioned Engineer Colin Dodsworth, son of Mrs. Dodsworth, of 4 High-street, Newport, missing as the result of the loss of the submarine Starfish, is a prisoner of war "somewhere in Germany." His wife received a postcard signed and addressed in his handwriting on Saturday. The message on the card was merely a formal printed notice in German but the signature is unmistakably his.

———————————◆———————————

As far as the Island was concerned the first casualty of war occurred when an RAF coastal command bomber was forced to crash-land at Whitwell.

For the time being the County Press were able to report such matters in whatever detail they saw fit but that was all to change in a short while...

January 13th, 1940.

AIRCRAFT CRASH AT WHITWELL.
THREE MEN KILLED.

On Saturday morning a bomber belonging to a coastal squadron crashed in a field near The Hermitage, Whitwell. Three of the four occupants were killed. The fourth was conveyed to the I.W. County Hospital, where he is reported to be slowly recovering.

The bomber was observed off Ventnor, and it came very close inshore at Steephill Cove, flying not more than 20 feet above the water. It rose with apparent difficulty to clear the cliffs near Binnel Bay, and soon afterwards crashed. The disaster attracted many people to the spot on Saturday and Sunday, but no one was allowed to get close to the machine, which was guarded by sentries with fixed bayonets... The news of the accident was quickly conveyed to Sergeant Rugman at the Ventnor Police Station and police representatives were soon on the spot. Mr W. Whillier (caretaker of the Hermitage Youth Hostel) and Mr. R. C. Parker, of Hermitage Farm, removed the injured man from the wreckage and telephoned for an ambulance to take him to the hospital.

◆

The war very soon led to the introduction of petrol rationing and many cars were removed from the roads by drivers unable to obtain a fuel allowance. At the same time car manufacturing came to a virtual halt as the factories were switched to war production. This led to a sharp increase in the value of cars; so much so that at the end of the war many owners were able to sell their mothballed cars at a handsome profit...

February 3rd, 1940.

MOTOR CAR TAXATION.

Figures show that Island motorists have laid up a good many cars until more favourable times. The number of licences issued December to January last year was 5263 and for the same period this year the number was 4268, 995 less... The number of cars in use has been further reduced by the surrender of current licences during the last four months of 1939, the number being 453, involving a refund of £1517. What has happened is that people who could not claim the use of a car for business purposes have decided to lay up their cars for the time being, but it is probable that many will take out quarterly licences later in the year, so that they can use their cars for pleasure as far as the petrol rationing admits.

◆

The slaughter of livestock and the subsequent sale of meat products was now strictly controlled by the Government. There were allegations of bureaucratic waste and inefficiencies...

February 24th, 1940.

MEAT CONTROL CRITICISMS.
ALLEGATIONS OF WICKED WASTE

At the meeting of the Newport Food Control Committee on Thursday it was decided to call the attention of the authorities to what were described as wickedly wasteful methods of meat control and supply.

OVER 100 UNBORN PIGS SACRIFICED.

Mr. P. G. Jenkins, the local food control officer in the last war, proposed that the Committee should make a strong protest to the Ministry of Food with regard to what he could only describe as the meat muddle in the Island... They had been told by the Government to stop all waste, to lend money for the prosecution of the war, and to pay big income tax demands with a smile, yet there were evidences around them of the very wasteful methods of Government officials. He was informed on good authority that at Newport a day or two previously 16 sows were killed for public consumption, and that out of those sows over 100 unborn pigs were taken. He could not imagine anything more wickedly wasteful... As regards transport, that week, pigs were sent from Newport to Wroxall to be killed, then taken to Cowes, and back to Newport. In the previous week there were some 200 pigs in Newport Market. A hundred were sent to Southampton, some to Winchester, and some to Portsmouth, and the local butchers were left with very short supplies. 11 beast were allocated in Newport Market on Tuesday, and they were not killed until that (Thursday) morning, with the result that much of the meat would be unfit for use during the weekend. The transport methods seem designed to be as costly as possible, yet we were supposed to be short of petrol. Every animal which came to Newport Market was carted two or three times, either dead or alive, before the meat reached the butchers.

Mr. J. R. Hayles, a pork butcher, supported... For several weeks local pork butchers ... saw most of the good home-produced pigs sent to the mainland, while they had to put up with imported pigs from New Zealand, some of which had been so long in store that they were unfit to eat and the butchers refused to have them in their shops... If the carcasses of pigs were handled during the summer as they were now, much of the meat would be unfit for sale... It was unanimously agreed to send the protest to the Ministry...

◆

THE WEEK'S NEWS.

THE ISLAND "MONSTER" A FOX* - The shooting in a copse near Bembridge last week of an old fox in an advanced stage of mange has, it is to be hoped, quashed for ever the stunt about an Island "monster." The animal was shot by Mr. W. Clark, of Bembridge. The little hair left on its body, save round its neck, gave it the appearance of a mane. This may be the foundation of the statement that the monster resembled a lion. The poor beast had larger paws than usual but there was nothing to give it the appearance of a Shetland pony. The ludicrous description of the old fox in certain sections of the weekend Press was certainly somewhat exaggerated.

Addressing a big gathering, the speaker said boldly: "Gentlemen, I have been born an Englishman, I have lived an Englishman, and I hope I may die an Englishman." A Scotsman in the audience retorted: "Mon, hae ye no ambition?"

THE 26 YEARS OLD CONSCRIPTS. — The number of men aged 26, who registered in Cowes and nearly all the Island on Saturday numbered 467, of

---

* There had been numerous sightings over the last few weeeks of a "monkey-like beast" roaming the Island's roads...

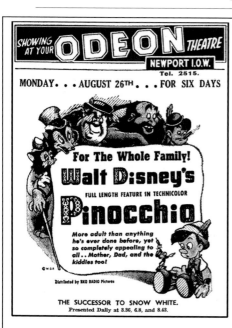
GATCOMBE PARISH COUNCIL.

OFFICIAL SCRAP IRON DUMPS.

HELP FEED THE FURNACES
and
THE RED CROSS AGRICULTURAL FUND
by
bringing your old Iron and Steel to either of the following Dumps :—
The Old Pond, Gatcombe Village.
Rickyard, Sheat Manor Farm.
Broadway Corner, Loverstone, Rill, and Cridmore.
Greenings Lane. Chillerton.

Official and Other Notices.

ISLE OF WIGHT COUNTY COUNCIL.

AIR RAID PRECAUTIONS.

THE County Council has been requested to give publicity to the necessity for maintaining in a fully efficient state measures to meet the use of gas by the enemy.

Members of the public whose respirators have not been inspected recently should ensure that these are gas-tight and serviceable, and should practice wearing them for periods of at least 15 minutes once each week.

It should be borne in mind that the best way to avoid liquid gas spray is to remain under cover. The Government emphasises that it must not be assumed that because the enemy has refrained hitherto from the use of gas he will not make use of it in future.

ON ACTIVE SERVICE.

In the case of Islanders who die in action or from wounds, thus giving their lives for their country, no charge will be made for recording their deaths in this column, so long as space permits in view of the serious restriction in paper supplies.

PRICE.—Oct. 21, whilst on duty, Sapper George Henry Price, R.E., eldest son of Bombardier and Mrs. C. H. Price, of No. 1 Southfield - terrace. Bettesworth - road, Ryde, in his 21st year.

RAE.—On Oct. 17, 1940, killed on duty as the result of enemy air action in London, Frederick Alan Rae, of the London Fire Brigade, youngest son of Mr. and Mrs. R. D. Rae, of St. Eloi, The Avenue, Totland Bay, aged 22 years.—" Greater love hath no man than this, that a man lay down his life for his friends."

SHEPPARD.—On Oct. 18, as a result of an accident whilst engaged on air operations, Sergt.-Pilot Edmund Eric Sheppard, son of the late A. K. and Mrs. Sheppard, of 3 Chapel-road, Binstead, aged 23.

WANTED.

whom three were conscientious objectors. There were 137 objectors in the 14,106 men in the southern region, or 1.40 per cent.; nationally the percentage was 1.23.

A new wireless set. Neighbour: "How many controls are there on your radio set?" Owner: "Well, there's my mother-in-law, my wife, and my daughter."

It has been stated that Lord Haw Haw is an Anglo-Irish man named William Joyce,* a former organiser in the South of England for the British Union of Fascists. This probably explains why Haw Haw somewhat frequently refers to the Isle of Wight in his broadcasts. He has referred to the pylons on St. Boniface Down, and a few days ago gave his impressions of Cowes Week as an example of the "bloated capitalism" under which he says the British people are downtrodden, and from which German people have been freed!

<hr>

It had been suggested that the Island's cinemas should open on a Sunday for the benefit of the thousands of soldiers based on the Island. The public were invited to comment on the proposal and the forthcoming responses were predictably varied. Those against were, it is fair to say, more vocal than the others and in letters to the editor they frequently cited religious reasons or maintained that it was the beginning of a slippery slope. Not everyone was opposed, however...

April 20th, 1940.

SUNDAY CINEMAS.

To the Editor of the I.W. County Press.

Sir, — The attitude of the Rural District Council in refusing a request for Sunday cinema films in Freshwater is inexplicable. Do they seriously suggest that the cinemas are the Devil's temples? If so we had better close them altogether, for surely we cannot rely on the help of heaven merely by forcing the troops to keep out of them only on Sundays. We should remember that we owe our material security to the men who fought our battles for us in the last war, and we are relying on another generation to do it for us this time. We may rest assured that heaven will not forsake this nation because our fighting men go to Sunday cinemas. We should recall also the great and simple teaching of Christ, that we should love one another and understand that evil exists in the mind of him who is apt to imagine it in others. —

I am, Sir, yours faithfully,

A.H. DABELL, Captain, R.A. The Mount. Blackgang.

<hr>

* This was correct. Joyce, a disaffected British resident, left the UK at the outbreak of war and offered himself to Berlin for the purpose of broadcasting German propaganda to Britain. The Radio Luxembourg transmitters were used to beam the broadcasts into Britain, and Joyce, to the annoyance of the British authorities, soon had millions of listeners in the UK. Controversially, he was hanged for treason at the end of the war despite not being a British subject and thus theoretically not capable of committing treason.

In a bitter irony, just as the war started in 1939 the British economy had begun its recovery from the depression and was enjoying a boom, so much so that the County Press was now regularly appearing as a 16 page edition. With the outbreak of war, despite generous stocks of newsprint, (see page 3) the decision was taken to immediately reduce the paper's size. It was halved to eight pages and apart from the occasional 12 page issue it was to remain that size until April 1940 when the decision was made to further reduce the size to just six pages...

April 20th, 1940.

THE "COUNTY PRESS" AND THE WAR
IMPORTANT NOTICE.

In common with all other newspapers, the "County Press" has to be reduced in size, owing to the hostilities in Scandinavia and the consequent cessation of supplies of paper pulp. This has caused the amount of paper allowed to be drastically reduced to less than a third of our normal supplies in time of peace. Although the paper is thus reduced in size, the cost of production is greater than ever. Added to this, our staff has been vitally depleted; two more members joining the Forces this week. The kind indulgence of readers and the loyal help of correspondents is therefore asked for during a time of very great difficulty.

Correspondents are requested carefully to eliminate all trivial and irrelevant matters from their reports, and to forward them to the Head-office with the least possible delay... We cannot find space for long letters on any subject, especially on such general questions as vaccination; and we can only promise occasionally to publish brief letters on local topics.

◆

THE WEEK' S NEWS.

INTERNMENT OF MALE ENEMY ALIENS - ARREST OF 16 IN THE ISLAND. — The Home Office issued instructions to the police on Saturday to arrest and send to internment camps all male enemy aliens between the ages of 16 and 60 *... The arrests were made in the Island early on Sunday morning. They numbered 16, and 15 were arrested, conveyed to Cowes and left by the 4 p.m. steamer under a military guard. The other man was away on the mainland for the weekend but he was arrested on his return on Monday.

THE GERMANS IN PARIS. — The American Ambassador to France gave the first news of the fall of Paris. The Germans entered the city at 7 o'clock last night. The last evacuees left the capital at midnight, when the orders were given for the gates to be closed... Enemy machine-gun posts were established inside the gates. Paris is a city of the dead. Every house and every shop is closed, and no one is to be seen but police and civil guards, who have handed in their weapons...

---

* This proved highly unpopular on the Island. Some of the 'enemy aliens' were respected and long standing members of the community, having lived here for over thirty years.

OFFICIAL NOTICE - INSTRUCTION IN THATCHING. — Classes in Stack Building, Thatching, and Spar-making will be held at the following centres from 6.30 p.m. to 8.30 p.m. - 27th May, Idlecombe (Mr. H. H. Morris). 28th May, Wacklands, (Mr. C. Allen). 29th May, Dean Farm, (Mr. T. W. Attrill). 1st June, Westover, (Mr. F. W. Long). A competition will be held at the end of the instruction. All interested are invited to attend. Basil Jenkins, Agricultural Education Officer.

SOLDIERS PAY FOR OBJECTORS. — Northampton Town Council have decided that any conscientious objector in its employ should have his service terminated, but, if he wished, should be re-engaged for the duration of the war at the pay of a serving soldier, plus a billeting allowance of not more than £1 a week.

———————————————◆———————————————

During July and August three soldiers and one civilian were accidentally shot by military personnel....

June 29th, 1940.
SOLDIER ACCIDENTALLY KILLED BY SENTRY'S SHOT.
An inquest was held at the High-street Methodist School, Ryde, on Private Alfred Henry Peters, aged 23, who met with his death from a sentry's shot, which passed through four seats of a bus before wounding him. He died in the County Hospital on Saturday... The sentry deposed that the trigger was caught by his finger as he was releasing the safety catch of his rifle. He was accustomed to a different type of rifle, with the safety catch on the opposite side. The Coroner accepted his explanation and returned a verdict of accidental death.

———————————————◆———————————————

Because from at least the early days of 1938 there had been a grim acceptance that war was on its way, many preparations had already been put in hand. Unaccountably, air raid shelters for Newport schoolchildren had not been one of them...

July 6th, 1940.
THE SAFETY OF OUR CHILDREN.
To the Editor of the I.W. County Press.
Sir, — The sight of children running out of school after an air raid warning, some having to run a considerable distance either to their own homes or to strangers' houses, has caused a lot of anxiety to mothers. The children of the village schools have been given their rightful protection; why have ours been neglected? - I am, Sir, yours faithfully,
E. KELLY. 51 Melbourne-street, Newport.

To the Editor of the I.W. County Press.

Sir, — May the parents of Barton school-children voice their indignation at the lack of air raid shelters. The distress of the children who had to run home was appalling. The Nodehill girls who have to go to various houses are no safer.... Surely our children are worth a few pounds spent on them. Money can be found for the upkeep of flowers on the Monument and Town-hall; these are very nice, but not a necessity in wartime. Maybe the same authorities are not responsible but it is public money just the same. Other Island towns and villages have provided adequate protection, why not Barton?

I am, Sir, yours faithfully, (MRS) F. SAMPSON. 35 Ash-road, Newport.

(*At a meeting the following Wednesday, Newport Council were roundly blamed for time wasting over the matter and subsequently announced that tenders amounting to over £3500 had been accepted for the construction of school shelters. Mr. Gould, the managing director of Moreys, offered to allow 75 children from the school in West-street to use their company shelter, declaring, "it was nothing short of a scandal that Newport Council had allowed this to happen."*)

Barely a fortnight had passed since the recent shooting when another two occurred. The inquests were fairly matter-of-fact, the Coroner describing the actions of a soldier who had shot his comrade as, "a little careless"...

July 13th, 1940.

TWO SOLDIERS ACCIDENTALLY SHOT.
TRAGIC MISUNDERSTANDINGS.

The Acting Deputy-Coroner conducted inquests on Tuesday on two soldiers stationed at different Island Military establishments, both of whom were accidentally shot by comrades on July 4th. They were Lce.- Corpl William Miller, a married man with two children and Fusilier Joshua Dyer, who was married only about a month ago.

In the case of Miller, two Sappers of his company described how several men, including deceased, were in a hut at a searchlight post, when there was a shot and Miller fell, fatally wounded. - Sapper Douglas Harvey said that on the afternoon of July 4th he was sitting on his bed cleaning a rifle which had been issued to him that day. Not knowing that there was a round in the chamber, he pressed the trigger, there was a report, and Miller fell... Harvey explained that he was not used to the type of rifle issued to him. Prior to that day he did not have a rifle of his own, but used to borrow one when he went on guard duty. This rifle was fitted with a cut-off, which prevented a round entering the chamber from the magazine unless released, as well as a safety-catch. The rifle issued to him that day was not fitted with a cut-off... The Coroner observed that the difference in the rifles seemed a material point. In returning a verdict of accidental death, the Coroner said... he was not disposed to blame anyone, for at the present time it was difficult to blame people in the position in which the country was placed. He attached no blame to Harvey.

In the giving evidence in the inquiry as to Dyer, Fusilier George Turner said that at about 1 p.m. on July 4th he was walking down the drive of the headquarters of his battalion and the deceased, who was on guard, challenged him in fun and presented his bayonet. Witness unslung his own rifle, also in fun, and half aimed at Dyer. There was a report, and Dyer fell. Witness said he eased the bolt of his rifle backwards and forwards, but he did not remember pulling the trigger. He was unable to explain how his rifle came to be loaded... The Coroner commented that it was very easy to make a mistake with automatic action and all who had to handle firearms should be additionally careful. Turner had been a little careless, but he did not consider it criminal carelessness.

Verdicts of accidental death were recorded in each case.

In Britain the first six months of the war saw very little fighting and no bombing at all but once France had been taken German planes were able to operate from French airfields and soon bombs began to fall on England leading to what became known as the Battle of Britain.

The very first bomb that fell on the Isle of Wight exploded harmlessly on Blackgang golf course on June 16th and the only other hostilities were the occasional reconnaissance flight and then a solitary episode a few weeks later when on a Sunday morning in early July the streets of Cowes were machine-gunned by a lone raider.

The uneasy peace eventually came to an end when Hitler decided to invade England. To prepare the way for the invasion, the initial part of the plan called for the destruction of the coastal ports and defences of southern England and so for the next four months the South coast became the subject of intense bombing raids. The Island could scarcely escape and from August until the end of November the population were subjected to terrifying bombing raids.

The summer of bombing began with a major attack on Ventnor just before midday on Monday, August 12th when 18 bombers each dropped four high explosive (H.E.) bombs on Ventnor in an attempt to destroy the radar installation on St Boniface down...

August 17th, 1940.
AIR BATTLES OVER THE ISLAND.
BOMBS ON SEA COAST TOWN CAUSE FIRST CIVILIAN CASUALTIES.

... A raid on Monday, when a large formation of dive bombers attacked a military objective (*Ventnor*) * near one of our south coast towns, caused the first local civilian casualties, three people being injured when bombs, falling wide of their objective, badly damaged two houses, and caused minor damage to houses over a wide area... Our correspondent at the town raided writes: Eighteen machines made for an objective near the town, and immediately

---

* Because of wartime reporting restrictions the County Press were now only able to refer to events taking place in "a south coast town". With the aid of the book 'Isle of Wight At War' by Adrian Searle, it has been possible to cross-reference the County Press reports and identify some of the otherwise anonymous locations. The names of the locations which have been able to be identified in this way are shown throughout this and subsequent reports in brackets.

released their bombs. The din and noise were indescribable. Huge craters were caused on high ground, and several fires broke out. Houses and shops at the eastern end of the town and near a neighbouring village were badly damaged. Windows were blown out and dozens of ceilings collapsed. The behaviour of the population was wonderful and help to sufferers was quickly provided, in spite, in many instances, of serious personal risk. Miss Williams, an organist, and Mrs. Henderson, wife of a Post-office official, were the more serious casualties. Mrs. Henderson was alone in her house and when the bombing began she took shelter in what was regarded as the safest room. Bombs blew out a part of a wall and Mrs. Henderson was imprisoned by falling debris. Two rescuers found her badly injured and rendered first aid. Miss Williams had a miraculous escape from death... She was in the act of alighting from a car when a bomb fell close by. The concussion threw her to the ground and wrecked the garage, the debris falling on her. She sustained a fractured thigh.... Pavements in the main streets were strewn with glass from broken windows and shopfronts. Tiles were ripped off Holy Trinity Vicarage and the church sustained slight damage. Many other houses in the upper part of the town and glasshouses at a nursery were damaged, but the inhabitants displayed wonderful sang froid... Chalk dust from craters on the downs covered everything over a wide area...

Anti-aircraft gunners brought down a German machine in flames into the sea off the East Wight... During another raid on Tuesday afternoon some 30 or more German machines were over this district (*Ryde*) flying at a great height... One German plane was brought down in Spithead, and the pilot bailed out by parachute... A German machine returning from the direction of Southampton was hit by anti-aircraft fire and smoke was streaming from its tail. Eventually it blew up and fell into the sea... A Heinkel, flying low over the Solent received a good buffeting from anti-aircraft fire. It appeared to be hit severely but came flying in towards the Island and passed at about 200 feet over a pier, which it machine gunned... A little later the plane approached again in obvious distress and seemed about to land but turned and disappeared out to sea. It is extremely doubtful if it ever reached its base.

———————————◆———————————

The bombing raids continued but the attention of the Luftwaffe shifted from dockyards and ports to the airfields across Southern England. The Island was caught up in the action with bombs falling on Nettlestone, Ryde, Newport, Freshwater and Ventnor...

August 24th, 1940.

MORE SOUTH COAST AIR RAIDS.
A TOWN MACHINE-GUNNED.

On Sunday afternoon a south coast town (*Newport*) had its second experience of machine-gunning from enemy planes returning from a raid further inland. A Messerschmitt twin-engined bomber-fighter, flying low, passed over the centre of the town, chased by one of our fighters, and sprayed several streets with machine-gun bullets. They rained down on the roof of a large timber works.

One wounded a man. Deceived by the fact that the anti-aircraft gunfire had

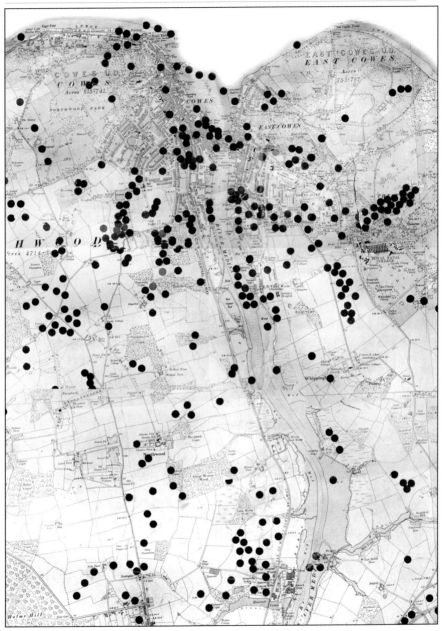

Part of a military map of Island bombing locations compiled during the war. This section shows the bombs that fell on Cowes and East Cowes. The original, a tapestry of large Ordnance Survey maps joined together, measures some 18 feet by 15 feet and is kept in the County Records Office at Newport.

ended, he ventured to look out of his back door. He was immediately struck in the side of the head by a bullet... which inflicted a severe scalp wound which necessitated the insertion of five stitches...A Messerschmitt fighter was shot down and fell in a wheat field (*Tapnell Farm, Freshwater*), where it caught fire and was burnt out. The pilot baled out and landed on a neighbouring down, where he was quickly captured by military officers. Two enemy bombers were shot down into the sea and only one man of the eight in their crews was saved by a motor-boat from the shore.

DELIBERATE BOMBING OF SEASIDE RESORT.

Four bombs were dropped on Monday from an enemy bomber on a south-coast town (*Ventnor*) which has already suffered rather heavily... In the late afternoon the drone of the engine was heard far above the coast. Then came a very sudden whistling noise followed by heavy explosions. Huge clouds of black and white smoke spread over the town... Considerable damage was done to property, the heaviest by far which the town has suffered. One of the bombs made a direct hit on part of an unoccupied hotel which has probably entertained in peacetime more Germans than any other on the south coast. The building was demolished... Another hotel opposite the one mentioned sustained much damage, and private residences in the path of the explosions were twisted into fantastic shapes... Mrs. T.H.F. Pethick displayed admirable composure when a bomb exploded on a hotel a few yards away from her residence. She stopped a bus containing many passengers which was proceeding towards the hotel, forced three little children to lie flat on their faces, and then took the same position, protecting her little dog... A German pilot brought down on Sunday off the same town was rescued by local watermen. He was educated at Bournemouth and knew the area where he was rescued very well. He was about 22 years of age...

———————◆———————

A fourth person was accidentally shot by a soldier; this time, a civilian...

August 24th, 1940.

HAVENSTREET COWMAN ACCIDENTALLY SHOT

The tragic circumstances of a Havenstreet resident's death were related to the Coroner at Ryde yesterday (Friday). The deceased was Frank Sparshot, aged 42, of No. 2 Council Houses, Church-Lane, who died in the County Hospital on Tuesday after having been shot by the accidental discharge of a rifle... Mrs. Evelyn Sparshot said her husband... was deaf owing to the last war, in which he served with the Royal Engineers.

Lce. Corpl Patrick Donolan deposed that at 10 p.m. on Tuesday he saw a man mounting a cycle, and called on him to stop. He did not do so, and witness again called twice in a louder voice without result. He ran after the man, whom he found stopped by a sentry. Asked why he did not stop deceased made no reply. Pte. Douglas stood by deceased in the on-guard position, with bayonet fixed. Witness heard a rifle discharged and found that deceased had been shot in the back of the head... After the occurrence Pte. Douglas was placed under close arrest.

Pte. James Douglas said he heard somebody shout "Stop that man." and loaded his rifle. He shouted to the cyclist to halt, but he came on, and when he was stopped, witness stood in the on-guard position with his rifle loaded, but he could not remember whether the safety catch was over. While deceased's identity card was being examined witness's rifle went off and the man fell to the ground. Witness could give no explanation of the rifle going off. His finger must have been unconsciously on the trigger. He did not think there was any danger from the man after he produced his identity card. By Mr. Palmer, representing the family: There were four men standing round. You were in the on-guard position with your rifle pointing towards his head, and another man with a bayonet. Do you think it a reasonable and proper thing to do? — Witness: I am supposed to keep in that position until we know he is all right. — Mr. Palmer: But he couldn't go far with four men standing round him. Do you think it was necessary to point the rifle at his head? – Yes...

The jury returned a verdict of death by misadventure, adding the following rider: "We are rather alarmed at these unfortunate incidents, which keep recurring, and we think a little more latitude should be given to civilians by the military authorities."

———————————————◆———————————————

The County Press coverage of the First World War was extraordinary in every sense of the word. The military authorities appear to have exercised little or no control over Britain's newspapers, especially the provincial ones, and many intimate and detailed accounts of life at the front appeared, complete with locations in many cases.

The government decided this was not to happen a second time and the reporting of the two wars, at least as far as the County Press was concerned, could not have been more different. In a marked departure from the previous war, hardly a letter home from a soldier ever appeared in the County Press and the progress of the war was reported for the most part not by spacious campaign reports as in the past but instead, in small paragraphs accompanying other national news items.

Conscientious objector tribunals took place just as they had during World War I but the hearings which had occupied so much space twenty years before were hardly referred to this time. News reports of Islanders dying in battle, previously reported in great detail, now became vague unvarnished accounts of those either "lost in aerial action", "lost defending London" or "died in battle," and locally the reporting of the war was confined to accounts of bombing raids on anonymous Island locations.

At the end of August the first two civilian deaths were reported...

August 31st, 1940.

SOUTH COAST AIR RAIDS.
SHOWERS OF INCENDIARY BOMBS.

The first fatal air raid casualties in a south-east coast area occurred on Friday week... Scarcely had the take-cover warnings sounded when heavy anti-aircraft fire was heard on the outskirts of a coastal town (*Ryde*) and a large German bomber, flying very low, came careering across the housetops with two British

Spitfires on its tail pouring machine-gun bullets into it as hard as they could. Away over a valley they went till the German released his bombs in a desperate effort to get away. The nearest buildings were a row of recently built bungalows and several Council houses (*Nettlestone*) occupied by people with families of little children. Bombs fell at the back of these houses but none were severely damaged. The bungalows were not so lucky. Windows were shattered and furniture was strewn about... A gardener, who was the fatal casualty, was working in the garden at the rear of his home. He shouted to neighbours to take cover and then ran into a wooden shed. When a bomb fell near, the shed partly collapsed, and the gardener was found wounded in the throat, side, and leg, and the washing mangle had been blown on top of him. He was removed to hospital but died before arrival...

FATALITY AT SEASIDE RESORT.

A woman was fatally injured when five bombs were dropped at a popular south coast resort (*Sandown*) on Friday week. The woman had been taking tea at a hut facing the seafront, close to a public recreation ground. One bomb fell and wrecked about a dozen huts... another fell in a canoe lake, a third on the sea wall, a fourth damaged a breakwater, and a fifth fell in the open sea. The woman victim was a widow who lost her husband in the last war, and had left her home in North London in the early months of the war in order to avoid the air raids which she anticipated would be made on London.

PLANE FALLS DOWN A WELL.

... One of our fighters made a forced landing in fields near a village. The pilot, a Polish airman, safely descended with his parachute. He had just previously shot down a Messerschmitt 109 fighter, which fell into a well*. (*in Greatwood Copse, Shanklin*) The wings and tail of the machine were torn off as it plunged through some trees and the fuselage went down into the well, from the mouth of which flames and smoke poured, while muffled explosions could be heard as the petrol tanks exploded... The pilot baled out at a great height and was at least a quarter of an hour coming down. He was carried well out to sea and eventually his parachute came to rest on the water about a mile and a half from the coast. When he was rescued he was so badly wounded that he died in a very short time...

1500 INCENDIARY BOMBS - DAMAGE TO ONE SMALL BUILDING.

A large area of the countryside (*Folly, Ningwood, Carisbrooke and Freshwater*) was showered with incendiary bombs during the night of Tuesday-Wednesday. The object of the raiders was obviously to set growing corn on fire, but they were at least a week too late. Well over 100 fell on one field and altogether it is estimated that at least 1500 must have been dropped over a line of country about 3 miles long. When they were blazing it looked as if the conflagration of terrifying proportions had started, but the bombs soon harmlessly burnt themselves out... The corn was not damaged. On Wednesday morning the fields were dotted with little heaps of white ashes from the bombs and with the metal ends of the missiles. A number of aluminium rods, about 4ft. long and about an inch thick were found. They were apparently the "sticks" on which the bombs were carried, so made that the incendiaries would scatter.

---

*In the 1980s some parts of the Messerschmitt were recovered from the well.

Bombs continued to fall on the Island throughout the summer. The Island had not been specifically targeted by the Luftwaffe since the recent Ventnor air raid, the bombs that had fallen being largely the result of raiders on Southampton and Portsmouth dropping their remaining bombs as they flew over the Island on their way home.

Luckily they had done little damage, most of them falling harmlessly in rural areas and open countryside, but towards the end of September the Island, Cowes in particular, became a specific target once again...

September 28th, 1940.

SOUTH COAST AIR RAIDS.

A district on the South Coast (*Cowes*) which had been free from air attacks for some weeks was again the target for large-scale raids on Tuesday and considerable damage was done at a port. The raiders were driven away from another coastal town by the heaviest barrage of anti-aircraft fire yet seen in the district, the sky being black with the smoke of the bursting shells, and as they turned back the enemy formation was attacked by a flight of our fighters... Many watchers saw this thrilling dogfight... and they saw three of the raiders brought down. Two crashed into the sea with flames and smoke pouring from them and another came spinning down out of control. Boats which put off to the spot where the third machine fell could find no trace of it...

AIR BATTLES OVER THE ISLAND. BOMBS ON FRUIT FARM –
TWO GERMAN BOMBERS DOWN.

Between 4 and 5 o'clock on Thursday afternoon there were exciting battles in the air over the western half of the Island... Two H.E. bombs were dropped on a fruit farm (*Freshwater)* and watchers saw six enemy machines and two of our fighters crash, two on land and the remainder in the sea. The crew of one of the German bombers which crashed were blown to atoms with their plane when the bombs it was carrying exploded as it hit the ground near a large haystack. The other enemy machine to fall on land, a Messerschmitt 110, landed almost intact in the valley below a down. The pilot had a bullet wound in the shoulder but the air gunner was uninjured. They were both quickly taken in charge by the military... Both pilots of our fighters baled out and descended safely. One could be seen very high up on his parachute, and as there were several enemy fighters above who might otherwise have machine gunned the escaping pilot, four of our fighters circled round him until he was low enough to be out of danger of attack...

NEWPORT COUPLE'S EXCITING EXPERIENCE.

Mr. and Mrs G. Strand, of the Medina Cafe, Newport, had the exciting experience of seeing five planes crash, one within 100 yards of their car... They heard a plane so close that Mr. Strand stopped the car. It was a German bomber and just as it passed overhead, flames burst from it and it crashed into a field 100 yards away. At once there was a deafening roar and flames shot up to a height of 100ft., while pieces of the plane were hurled in all directions... Of the plane and its crew all that was left was the engine and small fragments scattered over a wide area. Mr. Strand estimated that not one fragment, apart from the engines, exceeded six pounds in weight. While they were standing there they saw three other aircraft crash in the distance.

PREVENTION OF ENEMY LANDINGS

VOLUNTEERS are required immediately from men between the ages of 16 and 50, or from very active men accustomed to outdoor work up to the age of 60, to take part in work for the Protection of Possible Landing Grounds, or in connection with Defence Works during the next three weeks.

Volunteers must be sufficiently able-bodied to be able to dig; no further qualification is required.

Men who are engaged in the following occupations should not volunteer :—
  (a) Agriculture ;
  (b) Work with Builders and Contractors ;
  (c) Industrial work connected with supplies for the Navy, Army, or Air Force ;
  (d) Transport Services.

Notification by post of the time and place of work will be sent to those registered.

When called, Volunteers who possess pickaxes or spades will be asked to bring them along. Others should prepare themselves by borrowing from neighbours or friends. The rest, as far as possible, will be equipped with supplies lent to the Local Authorities. Will those who have pickaxes and spades, but cannot volunteer for work, kindly inform the undersigned?

Will all employers of labour kindly release for whole days if possible, but half-days in any event, those in their employ volunteering for this work?

Applicants should register at the nearest Post Office, where facilities for registration will be available until further notice.

P. E. WHITE,
County Hall, Newport, I.W.   Clerk of the County Council,
12th July, 1940.

MODEL 7322.
Well shaped Front Lacing Twilfit Corset of outstanding value made in Courtauld's Tested Quality Rayon broche. Suitable for medium to full figures. Six suspenders are attached. In Tea-rose. Sizes 24-36 ins. **16/11**

MODEL O3242.
A satin corselet with lace brassiere, semi-low back for informal wear and suitable for a short figure. Tea-rose. Sizes 32-44 ins. **9/11**

MODEL 7093.
Girdle side fastened all the way down. Made in strong "Tested Quality" Rayon broche. Well boned at front. In Tea-rose. Sizes 24-36ins **8/11**
Twilfit Corsetry is fitted with "Twil-grip" Suspenders.
"The Wise Woman Knows they won't Ladder Hose."

MODEL 1316.
Wrap-round in broche. Elastic in waist and over hips. Six suspenders. Suit-able for average to full figures. Tea-rose. sizes 24-36 ins. **16/11**

Look for Courtaulds "Tested-Quality" mark on all TWILFIT models incorporating Rayon.

Made in England
Fully guaranteed

Twilfit
Regd.
GIVES YOU FIGURE.. .. CONFIDENCE

DABELLS
NEWPORT

GERMAN RAIDERS MACHINE-GUN CHILDREN AT PLAY.

German airmen added another to their sickening list of inhuman crimes this week when they machine-gunned some 30 or more children who were playing on a recreation ground in a South Coast Borough (*Ryde*). This latest atrocity was committed on Tuesday evening. Three German planes swooped down and flew not higher than 150ft. over the town. Many houses and business premises were hit by machine-gun bullets... The Nazis' first target was the gasworks but finding they could do little damage they swooped down on a recreation ground where a number of boys were playing football and several younger children were enjoying themselves on the swings. Some of the youngsters, with commendable presence of mind, ran to a hut for shelter. Others threw themselves on the ground and by good fortune none was hurt. A 13-year-old boy evacuee had his school cap torn off by a bullet and later retrieved it with a hole through the peak... As the machines passed out over the sea, still flying very low, they sprayed the Esplanade with machine-gun bullets, and pedestrians ran for shelter or either threw themselves down in the streets... In view of the danger of such attacks in cloudy weather the foolishness of people who persist in unnecessarily walking about the streets after the alert has sounded is again emphasised.

◆

THE WEEK'S NEWS.

OFFICIAL SECRETS CHARGE. – George Mace Wall, 27, a radio engineer from Ryde pleaded "Not guilty" to an indictment charging him with recording information calculated to be directly or indirectly communicated to an enemy... The information was alleged to have been recorded by Wall and was extremely secret and concerned experimental work in the South of England... Accused was found guilty and sentenced to six years penal servitude. Passing sentence, Mr. Justice Hallett said, "You should be glad you are not being tried by a German court, because if you were, you would not have long to live. In this country, rightly or wrongly, we take a much more lenient view."

A man who had a slight motoring accident, which necessitated the application of sticking plaster to his nose, was called upon to be interviewed by the local Inspector of taxes. "Had an accident to your nose?" The latter asked sympathetically. "No," said the taxpayer shortly, "I've been paying through it for so long that it has given way under the strain."

YOUTH ASTONISHES RYDE MAGISTRATES — A 14-year-old labourer astonished the Juvenile Court at Ryde on Thursday by stating that he was earning £3 a week on war work."Are you sure?" asked the Chairman and for answer the boy produced a pay packet showing £2 7s. 11d. for a short week. He was accused, with five schoolboys whose ages ranged from 11 to 13, with being concerned in stealing and receiving National War Savings books and stamps to the value of £7 19s. 6d... Fined £1.

*19-year-old Harold Blow of Gunville was driving a lorry into Newport one morning
when a German airman, complete with flying jacket, stepped out into the road in front
of him and waved him down.*

Showing remarkable coolness for a 19 year old, Harold took it all in his stride ...

October 19th, 1940.

GERMAN AIRMAN GIVES HIMSELF UP TO LORRY DRIVER.

During air fights over a South Coast district on Wednesday a German single-
seat fighter was shot down. It crashed on Bowcombe Down, and the pilot, who
was only slightly injured, walked over a mile to the nearest road, where he
stopped a cattle dealer's lorry, driven by a youth of 19 named Harold Blow, and
asked to be driven to the police. Blow first drove him to a village policeman's
house but as the constable was not there, he took him to his home at Gunville,
where he remained in the charge of Blow's mother while his captor telephoned
to the police. About half an hour later police and soldiers arrived, and he was
taken into custody. Blow said that when the man came out of the hedge and
held up his hand he at first thought it was one of our own airmen, but on seeing
his uniform and hearing his broken English he realised he was a German. "I said
to him," continued Blow "'Are you armed?' He shook his head and said 'No, I
no fight,' but I wasn't trusting any German, so I ran my hands over him before
I told him to get into my lorry. On the way he told me that he knew the district
very well and that he intended to walk into Newport. He explained that he
knew the locality because in peace time he was employed on liners which called
at a port in the area where he descended." His captor's mother, a strong
countrywoman, said "I wasn't frightened of him. He was frightened, not me. He
trembled like a leaf, and described in broken English and by signs how one of
our fighters had swooped down on him several times and brought down his
machine by machine-gun fire. He showed me a photo of his wife and little
daughter and said he did not want to fight England. I said 'Then why do your
people come over here dropping their horrible bombs on women and children?'
He shook his head sadly and replied 'I know. It is terrible. It is very bad for our
women and children too.' I gave him a cup of tea and a plate of meat more to
keep him occupied than anything else, and he took some chocolate and some
toffees out of his pocket and gave them to my little girl. I put them away out of
her reach, and he said 'It is quite all right,' and he ate a piece of chocolate
himself, apparently to emphasise that it would be quite safe for my little girl to
eat it. When the police and soldiers came he looked very frightened and
whispered 'Shall I be all right?' I told him he would be treated well, as we didn't
kill or torture prisoners in England. He said it was his first flight over England.
As he left he shook hands with me and my son, and thanked us for our
kindness."

When a Press representative told Mrs. Blow that there were six "victim"
stripes painted on his machine on the down she said "If I had known that I
should have felt more like putting my carving knife through him than giving
him something to eat. I fancy he was a little frightened of me, as he kept on
saying that he was not a bomber."

THE WEEK'S NEWS.

SERIOUS CHARGE AGAINST A GODSHILL WOMAN. — At Ventnor on Monday Mabel Victoria Attrill (25), was charged "that she did feloniously kill and slay Frank Cave by shooting him in the back with a shot gun at about 7.30 a.m. on Sunday October 20th."... Jealousy of another woman was suggested as the motive. Miss Attrill was committed for trial at Winchester Assizes.

NEWPORT WOMAN'S JOYFUL EXPERIENCE. — A Newport woman who had mourned as a widow for two months had the great joy on Friday week of receiving a postcard from her "late" husband, First-class Stoker Ernest Hiscock, aged 39, saying that he was alive and well in Germany... Mrs. Hiscock said: "I could hardly believe my eyes when I saw the familiar signature 'Ern'... All I am worrying about now is that I have drawn the insurance money and have spent most of it on clothes for the children. What they will do about that I don't know."

THE ISLAND MURDER CASE. — Mabel A—, 25, housekeeper, pleaded not guilty at the Assizes to the wilful murder of Frank C— at Godshill on October 20th... Addressing the jury, the judge said it seemed that relations between the prisoner and the dead man were anything but harmonious... prisoner had resented the dead man's association with another woman... The jury, after a few minutes absence, returned a verdict of not guilty, and the accused was discharged.

◆

The recently downed Messerschmitt was the subject of a court case a few weeks later. Enterprising and well-equipped souvenir hunters had made their way up on to Bowcombe down where the plane, perhaps unwisely, had been left unguarded. In the space of three days the determined souvenir hunters reduced the aircraft to a "heap of scrap"...

November 16th, 1940.

GERMAN PLANE "MUTILATED" - SOUVENIR HUNTERS FINED.

Portions of a Messerschmitt 109*, ranging from an electrical generator to an engine cover plate about 3ft. long, were exhibited in Court during the hearing of summonses against seven souvenir hunters charged with removing parts of a German aeroplane contrary to Defence Regulations. They were William Adsett, 36, electrician, Robert Church, 17, apprentice, Charles Hunnybun, 17, and Kenneth Harbour, 17, labourers, Cyril Stotesbury, 15, apprentice, Clive Burt, 16, and John Upward, 15, driver's mate, all of Newport.

.Edward Crinage, sub-contractor to the R.A.F, told the court that on October

---

*The pilot was identified after the war as Horst Hellriegel. As it happened, he was not responsible for the "victim" stripes. The Messerschmitt was not, in fact, his but belonged to a colleague. Hellriegel was simply borrowing it that day as his regular aircraft was not serviceable.

19th he inspected a Messerschmitt 109 aircraft which had landed on the downs. Three days later he found that the plane had been reduced to "a heap of scrap." Everything removable had been taken, the fuselage and parts of the engine cut out by hacksaws, and the wings and fuselage mutilated... In a statement to Constable Wheeler, Adsett said he went to see the plane on October 20th and found 50 or 60 people round it. The plane was not guarded and several people were using hammers and chisels to take parts away... Asked by the Bench why the plane was left unguarded an Intelligence Officer explained that the practice was to guard fallen German planes until they had been inspected by R.A.F officers, and subsequently the military removed the armament, wireless equipment, and flying instruments. The military finished their job on the Saturday evening and the guard was removed. "As it happened," said the officer, "in this case it was very unfortunate, as a message was received that the plane was wanted for exhibition in Canada."

Adsett was fined £2, Church and Hunnybun 10s., and the other defendants 5s. each.

--------------◆--------------

As unlikely as it sounds, a Sandown housewife was sentenced to death for spying for Germany. After all these years, whether she actually did or not is still a matter for conjecture.* According to some she was simply a harmless eccentric while others still regard her as a dangerous spy...

December 28th, 1940.
DEATH SENTENCE ON SANDOWN WOMAN.
CONVICTED OF TREASON.

After a two-day hearing from which the public were excluded Mrs. Dorothy O'Grady, 42, described as a housewife, of Osborne Villa, The Broadway, Sandown, was convicted at Hampshire Assizes on Tuesday of offences under the Treachery Act, 1940, and sentenced to death. The trial took place before Mr. Justice Macnaghten, Mr. J.G. Trapnell and Mr. Fox-Andrews appeared for the prosecution, and Mr. J. Scott Henderson for the defence.

The case was committed from Ryde Petty Sessions on October 15th. Mrs. O'Grady was charged with nine offences, to all of which she pleaded not guilty. The first, under the Treachery Act, alleged that between August 1st and September 10th she conspired, with intent to help the enemy, to commit an act designed or likely to impede the naval, military, or air operations of H.M. Forces; the second, under the Treachery Act, was that between August 21st and September 10th she committed an act likely to bring assistance to the military operations of the enemy; the third, also under the Treachery Act, alleged that she committed an act likely to impede the military operations of His Majesty's Forces; the fourth charge related to the forcing of a safeguard on August 9th; the fifth, under the Official Secrets Act, alleged that for purposes prejudicial to the interests of the State she feloniously approached a prohibited place, namely, the foreshore; the sixth and seventh charges dealt with the making of a plan, which might have been practically useful to the enemy, and which was likely to be prejudicial to the defences of the realm; the eighth was one of sabotage, alleging that the accused cut a military telephone line; and the ninth and last charge alleged that she had in her possession a document containing information which purported to be information in respect of measures for the defence of a place on behalf of His Majesty.

After an absence of a little over an hour the jury returned a verdict of guilty on all the charges, except those relating to conspiracy and forcing a safeguard.

Prisoner had nothing to say, and the Judge, amidst an impressive silence, assumed the black cap. "On evidence that admitted of no doubt," he said, "the jury have found you guilty of treachery. For that crime the law prescribes but one sentence, and it is my duty to pass that sentence upon you." He then pronounced the solemn words of the sentence of hanging.

The prisoner listened in silence and was led from the Court.

It will be remembered that Mrs. O'Grady was summoned to appear before the County Bench at Ryde in August to answer charges under the Defence Regulations, but failed to appear and a warrant was issued. She was found staying under an assumed name in the West Wight, and when arrested and taken to Yarmouth Police Station she said "I was too scared to attend." The subsequent proceedings at the Ryde Court, where she was committed for trial, were also held in camera. Mrs. O'Grady and her husband first came to the Island about five years ago on Mr. O'Grady's retirement from the London Fire Brigade. He was also a naval pensioner and is about 20 years older than his wife. They lived for a time at Lake, then left the Island for a while and returned to reside at Osborne Villa, The Broadway, Sandown, about 18 months ago. When the air attacks on London started Mr. O'Grady responded to the appeal for ex-firemen to return to the service and he has been engaged in this heroic work ever since. He was totally ignorant of his wife's actions, which led to the charges being preferred, and it is stated that she has consistently refused to see him since her arrest. Mrs. O'Grady was a very reserved woman; even her next-door neighbour at Sandown did not know her name until the police called in the course of their enquiries. She was in the habit of going for long walks accompanied by her black retriever, and it was her persistence in going to places, access to which had been prohibited by the military authorities that led to her being suspected of treasonable intentions.

A number of women were sentenced to death for similar offences in England during the last war, but none was executed.

---

* For the most part, Mrs O'Grady's wartime activities still remain a mystery. In 1995 the then MP for the Island, Barry Field, was asked to take part in a campaign for a posthumous pardon for Mrs O'Grady. He agreed until he was given sight of the still secret case papers when he declared "I am staggered by the treachery this woman sank to. Far from being a simple seaside landlady, she was a highly skilled agent who produced masterpieces of defence systems for the Third Reich. She could have altered the course of the war."

1941.

THE WEEK'S NEWS.

That a young soldier was fatally injured on Monday by the accidental discharge of a sub-machine gun better known as a Tommy gun, was related to the Island's Assistant Deputy Coroner.... Corporal Jack Morris deposed that he found the Tommy gun left at a post and put it into store not knowing whether it was loaded. Later he took the gun into the room which he shared with deceased, holding it by the pistol grip with the muzzle pointing to the ground. It was held in his right arm and as he closed the door with his left it went off...shooting deceased in the head...The jury returned a verdict of accidental death.

ASHEY RACECOURSE UNDER THE PLOUGH. — Those who have enjoyed the race meetings in the verdant valley of Ashey will be interested to learn that the course is being ploughed up by the farmer, Mr. W. H. Brown. Even the grandstand, which has been a landmark for many years, is being pulled down and its site ploughed up.*

A New York paper has published a list of individuals whom it considers worthy of mention for what they achieved in 1940. One Englishman receives mention. He is the soldier in London "who dislocated his jaw while yawning during an air raid."

The following are extracts from letters from mothers received by the Milk Board: (1) Please send me a form for supply of milk for having children at reduced prices. (2) I posted the form by mistake before my child was filled in properly. (3) I have a baby 18 months old - thank you for the same. (4) Will you please send me a form for cheap milk. I have a baby two months old and did not know anything about it till a friend told me. (5) I have a baby two years old, fed entirely on cows.

FIRE WATCHING - NEWPORT A PROSCRIBED AREA. — ...All proprietors of businesses in the borough ... must submit schemes for the efficient fire watching of their premises... The order empowers them to compel all male workers between the ages of 18 and 60 to undertake 48 hours fire watching duty a month.

———————————◆———————————

Just six months after her original trial, Mrs O'Grady's appeal came to court...
February 15th, 1941.
SANDOWN WOMAN'S DEATH SENTENCE QUASHED.
14 YEARS' PENAL SERVITUDE.

Sentenced to death at Winchester Assizes under the Treachery Act, Mrs. Dorothy Pamela O'Grady, 42-year-old Sandown housewife, successfully

---

* The racecourse had been closed since a destructive fire in 1931. See Vol 3 page 174.

appealed to the Court of Criminal Appeal on Monday.*

Mrs O'Grady's husband was allowed to sit in Court and listen to the arguments, at the conclusion of which Lord Caldecote gave his judgement in camera. Afterwards, in open Court, he announced, "The conviction on the two capital charges under the Treachery Act has been quashed, and sentence has been passed by the Court on charges on which the appellant was convicted, but on which the judge passed no sentence. This Court has passed a sentence of 14 years' penal servitude on the counts other than those under the Treachery Act."

Mrs. O'Grady was present in the dock to hear the decision. She answered her name in a quiet, steady voice, standing between two wardresses. She wore a coat of blue serge with a high fur collar. The offences for which she was tried took place in the Isle of Wight.

Mr. J.G. Trapnell, for the Crown, applied for the case to be heard in camera, stating that it had been so heard at the Assizes."Appellant's counsel, Mr. J. Scott Henderson has informed me," said Mr. Trapnell, "that he intends only to raise points of law, but I am instructed to ask that the appeal should be heard in camera in case it should be necessary to go into the facts. It is a matter of precaution." Mr. Trapnell added that there was no objection to the technical law reporters remaining in Court so long as they dealt only with matters of law and submitted their reports to the Court and the Crown before publication.

Lord Caldecote said the appeal would be heard in camera and, when the time came, they would consider whether the judgement should be delivered in open Court.*

───────────────◆───────────────

Throughout World War II news was strictly controlled, but Islanders were fully acquainted with events on the frontline since they had now become a direct part of it.

The port of Southampton, the dockyards of Portsmouth and the shipyards of Cowes became strategic targets and inevitably the whole Island suffered as a result, either from directly targeted bombing raids or from bombers returning home who appear to have jettisoned their remaining bombs.

It is hard to imagine what it must have been like night after night and the following catalogue of bombing raids can only give the merest hint. It is a compilation of County Press reports of air raids during just the first six months of 1941. Again, place names in brackets have been drawn from Adrian Searle's book. Bear in mind that the raids of 1941 were by no means the worst the Island suffered...

*For over 60 years the contents of the Home Office file on Mrs O'Grady remained an official secret. The file was eventually declassified in 2006 only to be removed from public view a few weeks later "in the conduct of official business." Six months later, when National Archives requested the return of the file, the Home Office said it could no longer be traced. Since then inquiries to the Public Records Office as to its whereabouts have gone unanswered. Mrs O'Grady died at Lake in 1985, aged 87, still protesting her innocence.

Bombs dropped in the first six months of 1941

January 5th   Miscellaneous bombs
January 9th   H.E. (High Explosive) bombs. Showers of
              incendiaries,(*Newport*)
January 16th 20 H.E. bombs
January 19th Incendiaries. Bombs (*Somerton*).
February 19th 1 lone bomber. Dropped bombs in sea.
March 1st   8 H.E. bombs. Fell in open country.
March 3rd   3 H.E. bombs.
March 4th   H.E. bombs
March 5th   H.E. bombs
March 7th   1 lone raider. Cottage damaged.
March 9th   Bombs. (*Staplers. Blackwater*).
March 11th   Bombs (*Newport, Ryde, Shorwell, Yafford*)
March 13th   13 H.E. bombs (*Billingham*)
March 14th   16 H.E. bombs and incendiaries (*Arreton*)
March 15th   H.E. bombs. (*Shanklin and Cowes*). 6 killed.
March 23rd   H.E. bombs (*Shanklin*) 1 killed
April 5th   H.E. bombs. (*Yafford, Brighstone*) 1 killed
April 7th   H.E. bombs.
April 8th   H.E. bombs.
April 9th   H.E. bombs.2 killed.
April 10th   Incendiary Bombs. (*Niton*).
April 11th   17 H.E. Bombs (*Ryde, Needles*) 2 killed.
April 18th   5 H.E. bombs.
April 24th   H.E. Bombs (*Swainston. East Cowes, Newport*) "Thousands of
              Incendiary bombs." 4 killed.
April 26th   600 Incendiary bombs. 60 bombs in churchyard.
April 27th   H.E. Bombs (*Ryde*) 1 killed.
May 3rd   4 H.E. bombs on village.
May 10th   14 H.E. bombs.
May 24th   (*Newport Cement Mills*). 20 H.E. bombs.
May 27th   4 H.E. bombs (*Cowes*). 2 in cemetery.
May 28th   3 H.E. bombs.(*Cowes*).
June 1st   16 H.E. Bombs (*Cowes*)
June 9th   6 H.E. bombs and incendiaries.(*Cowes*)
June 12th   1 H.E. bomb and incendiaries.
June 22nd   H.E. bombs. (*Newport. Ryde.*) 11 killed. 50 injured. 130 left
              homeless.
June 26th   2 H.E. bombs. Landmine raid.

The air raids became a part of everyday life, day and night. The next three reports are typical...

March 15th, 1941.

SOUTH COAST AIR RAIDS.

Enemy aircraft were very active over a South Coast area (*Ryde*) on Sunday night. The incoming machines were subjected to an exceptionally heavy barrage of gunfire and some of them evidently jettisoned their bombs before they gained their objective... On Monday night there was another heavy raid on the Portsmouth area but the watchers had the satisfaction of seeing two of the raiders brought down in flames by intense anti-aircraft fire which was almost continuous during the six-hour attack. One machine was blown to fragments in the air as its bombs exploded, and parts fell into shallow water off the Island coast.... There were two baskets of incendiaries near a mental hospital, but they did no harm... On Tuesday night the immunity from casualties unfortunately ended when a stone built residence near a South Coast village (*Yafford*) received a direct hit from a heavy calibre bomb and was completely demolished... In the house were six people, the owner (Mr. D. L. Wadlow), his wife and 10-year-old daughter Pamela, two officers billeted with them, and an officer's batman. Mrs. Wadlow and her little daughter and one of the officers were killed but Mr. Wadlow had a miraculous escape. After he recovered from the shock of the explosion he found himself actually under the floorboards but scrambled out of the ruins of his home with nothing worse than a few scratches... The tragedy has cast a gloom over the village where Mrs. Wadlow's charming generosity has been deeply appreciated... Bombs which fell into the sea during the raid on Portsmouth killed many fish, and people living on the shores reaped a welcome harvest of cod, mullet, and whiting which drifted in on the following day... At about 11 p.m. on Thursday night and enemy bomber making its way home was seen to burst into flames, break in two, and crash into the sea south of the Needles. Mr. J. Cotton, fisherman, of Freshwater Bay, put out in a boat and searched but could find no trace either of the machine or its occupants.

April 26th, 1941.

SOUTH COAST AIR RAIDS.

... A well-known South Coast pleasure resort experienced a sharp attack by several waves of enemy raiders on Thursday night. Thousands of incendiary bombs were showered over a wide area, causing three serious fires. A number of high explosive bombs were afterwards dropped in and near to towns, causing some casualties, four being fatal. A fire caused by incendiaries almost completely destroyed one of the oldest country mansions in the district, the residence of a baronet justice of the peace, and the seat of his family for about 200 years (*Swainston Manor*). Three major fire units fought the flames with water from a large pond in the grounds but the old house burnt fiercely, and it was only possible to save the chapel and servants' quarters.... Nothing but the bare walls of the residence remained. Many valuable pictures and family heirlooms were destroyed, but some pictures, a safe containing jewellery and valuable documents, and furniture from the ground-floor rooms were saved... Bombs

did damage to the windows of a hospital, and caused a huge fire in a forest, which was tackled by soldiers and eventually subdued, although for some hours its glare lit up the sky, and the streets of a town were almost as light as day. Other incendiaries did damage to two farms and haystacks were destroyed. At least 1000 incendiaries fell on downland and burnt out harmlessly.

The loss of life occurred when a villa in a seaside resort, the residence of Mr. and Mrs. F. A. Oatley, (*Cambridge Road, East Cowes*) received a direct hit from a high explosive bomb... the bomb completely demolished the rear portion of it. Those at home were Mrs. Oatley, Mrs. Kings (her mother, aged 86), Mr. Everett Oatley (18), and Mr. Edward Riddell (19, an adopted son). Mrs. Kings and Mrs. Oatley were quickly found and taken to hospital suffering from slight injuries... At the time the bomb fell, two ARP wardens, Messrs. M. Brinton and Cowburn dashed to the back of the house, and as nothing has been seen or heard of them since, it is feared that they probably fell into the bomb crater and were buried by the collapsing walls... A first aid party and wardens worked throughout the night in an endeavour to find the two buried youths and the two missing wardens. After about three hours they succeeded in finding Everett Oatley, but he was dead. Yesterday (Friday) they were still excavating in and around the bomb crater in search of Edward Riddell and the two wardens...

May 3rd, 1941.

SOUTH COAST AIR RAIDS.

During Saturday night an enemy raider dropped between five and six hundred incendiary bombs in the vicinity of a village church (*Nettlestone*). Many fell in fields and burnt out harmlessly. Two bombs penetrated the roof of a cottage... Over 60 bombs fell in the churchyard, where many graves and tombstones were scarred, but the church, where recently several windows were blown out by a high explosive bomb, escaped damage. During the raid on Portsmouth on Sunday night a shell exploded at the entrance to a church (*St. John's Church*) in a seaside town (*Ryde*) and killed Mr. William Kelly, aged 42, who was standing on the opposite side of the road. He was waiting for his wife, who was working in another town and arrived by bus a few minutes after the tragedy... He was removed to hospital, but was dead before arrival, having received a fractured skull....

The bodies of Messrs Montague Brinton and William M. Cowburn, ARP wardens, who lost their lives in going to the rescue of the occupants of a house which received a direct hit on Thursday week, were recovered on Tuesday. After going through the rear of the house the bomb penetrated the ground to a considerable depth before exploding, and it is presumed that the explosion caused a large cavity and that the wardens, who were endeavouring to find one of the occupants trapped by debris who was calling for help, were buried when the ground beneath them suddenly caved in, causing the house to collapse. Relays of rescue parties had been excavating since the tragic happening, but it was not until they had got down between 20 and 30 feet that they succeeded in finding the bodies.

The body of Edward Riddell was recovered on Wednesday. That of Everett Oatley was found about three hours after the bomb exploded.

THE WEEK'S NEWS.

MILITARY SHOOTING FATALITY.— A Coroner's inquest at Newport heard how Corporal Thomas Phillips, aged 20, died after having been wounded by a rifle bullet fired by a comrade. Fusilier Richard Barnett said he was one of seven men on guard in charge of the deceased on Wednesday. Some joking remarks were passed and Fusilier Robert Williams picked up a rifle, aimed it, and pressed the trigger. Phillips fell to the ground. Witness said to Williams "You have shot him," and he replied "I did not know the rifle was loaded."... The jury knew these accidents were continually happening and as patriotic men they wanted to put a stop to them. It was not right that these boys should be allowed to play about with loaded rifles.

ALLEGED DISORDERS AT PARKHURST PRISON.— Wednesday's "Daily Mail" contained the following story of alleged recent trouble at Parkhurst prison :- Rowdy demonstrations against food rationing in Parkhurst gaol have become very frequent in the past few weeks. People walking in the road outside the prison have heard convicts shouting abuse at the warders.... Although the prisoners complain about the rationing they are still better off than many people outside who have to earn a living... Breakfast - bread and butter, porridge, pint of tea; dinner - corned beef, patties, mashed potatoes, beetroot, bread, rice pudding, rhubarb; tea - bread and butter and cheese, pint of cocoa.

Mr. Curtis Goad, of Fishbourne, wrote recently rejoicing in the fact that nightingales had returned to that district, but wondered if they would be able to put up with the intensive gunfire which sometimes takes place at night... He will be glad to hear that an air raid warden who was on duty in the Shide district a few nights ago, when the gunfire was particularly shattering, states that the nightingales carried on with their singing unperturbed by the repeated crashes of shells bursting overhead...

————————————◆————————————

As always in time of war, those of a religious persuasion sometimes found their faith and beliefs tested to the limit. Members of the clergy were no exception...

May 31st, 1941.

CHRISTIANITY AND THE WAR
VICAR OF CARISBROOKE ON SLOPPY SENTIMENT.

In the June issue of his Parish Magazine the Vicar of Carisbrooke (the Rev. Harold Ewbank) writes: We must beware of our usual English sentimentalism - that instinctive softheartedness of ours which quickly regrets the evil that men have done and thinks only of the "poor, pathetic creature" who should be saved at all costs from receiving the due reward of his wickedness. We have seen it often before in those curious petitions for leniency on behalf of a convicted murderer, appeals which ignore entirely the misery and pain the assassin has caused to his victims and their friends. It also occurred after the last war, when we were told that the "poor dear Germans" never meant to do us any harm and were merely driven on by the Kaiser. And after this war we will, no doubt, be told that all this beastliness was not really the wish of the German nation, that the atrocities are all terribly exaggerated or invented, and that we ought to shake hands and be nice and friendly to them all, and then, further, we will be told that that is the Christian way... I fail to see ... why we should be expected to forgive when it implies endorsement of their wickedness... You may think that this is rather strange reading for a church magazine, but I feel very strongly that sloppy sentiment has for too long been allowed to masquerade as Christianity...

Several readers wrote the following week to agree with the vicar, including one who suggested that extermination was the only answer, writing "Modern science has found many ingenious ways to kill strong men. For the worst criminals, the Nazis and Fascists and the Gestapo, there is the lethal chamber; for the rest, the choice between voluntary birth control or compulsory sterilisation. These methods would solve the post-war problem in a generation and make the world "safe for democracy" for our time. I am not acquainted with any other means that give the slightest hope of doing so..."

―――――――――◆―――――――――

As if things weren't bad enough already...

June 7th, 1941.

NEWPORT SCHOOLBOY'S DANGEROUS PLAYTHINGS.

At a Children's Court at Newport Guildhall a 13-year-old boy was charged with having found two incendiary bombs and not handing them over to the police or military authorities. He was similarly charged in respect of a trench mortar bomb. Acting-Sergt Davis stated that at 8.20 p.m. on May 18th, when in Newport High-street, he heard a loud explosion. Later he received an urgent request to proceed to a house where the explosion had occurred. He found that all the windows on the ground floor had been blown out and other damage done. On a table in the house he found a spanner and file and two incendiary bombs which had been taken to pieces. The boy, who was somewhat shocked but uninjured, had found the bombs in a field... As to the second charge the boy admitted having found the mortar bomb on the downs. As he could not unscrew it he threw it out of the window, when it exploded. It was a 2in. trench mortar shell and an Army officer said it would cause casualties up to 150 yards distance... The boy was bound over for a year...

―――――――――◆―――――――――

One by one, the old trades and their practitioners were dying out, and one by one the County Press faithfully marked their passing...

July 5th, 1941.

HARNESS-MAKER TO QUEEN VICTORIA.

The death occurred at the residence of his son, Poleclose Farm, Carisbrooke, on Sunday, after only a week's serious illness, of Mr. William Henry Cheverton, proprietor of the harness-making business in Lugley-street, who had the distinction of having made harness for Queen Victoria. Mr. Cheverton, who was in his 67th year, was the second son of the late Ald. R. B. Cheverton, J.P., who built many carriages for the Royal Family at Osborne, and the business which he conducted for many years was at that time part of the carriage-building establishment. Mr. Cheverton was very proud of the fact that he made a set of harness for the pony which used to draw the little chaise in which the Queen used to ride about the grounds of Osborne. It was a very handsome set, made of red and blue Morocco leather stitched with yellow silk and with gold mountings. It is now in the South Kensington Museum with several of the carriages his father built for the Queen. In his early days Mr. Cheverton established a reputation as a skilful marksman while serving with the I.W. Yeomanry. He several times competed with success at Bisley and continued his interest in shooting as a founder-member of the Carisbrooke Miniature Rifle Club and as a keen shot with a sporting gun. He was also a great lover of gardening and beekeeping, and often judged honey at Island shows. He was actively associated with the harness-making business in Lugley-street for some half a century and retired about four years ago. Almost throughout that long period, for 47 years to be exact, he had as his assistant Mr. G. H. Morgan, who is still carrying on the work. His wife, formerly Miss Julia Rice, of Poleclose, died 14 years ago...

TOWN AND COUNTY NOTES.

BIGAMY. — Mrs. Violet Corbin (31), was bound over for two years at the Hampshire Assizes when she pleaded guilty to a charge of bigamy. Mr. Scott Henderson said Corbin and her husband separated, each taking two children... In March 1940 she met a soldier and they were married by special licence eight days later at Newport... His Lordship said neither of the parties seemed to have any morals; both went their own ways. She would be bound over in the sum of £5 for two years.

SOLDIER ACCIDENTALLY KILLED. — Lce. Cpl. Edward Duke, aged 21, and a survivor of the evacuation from Dunkirk was shot through the head while serving in an Island fort on Sunday by a comrade who had unknowingly taken another man's rifle which he did not know was loaded, and which should not have been loaded.... (July 12)

NEWCHURCH MAN BELIEVED LOST RETURNS HOME. — On Monday there was a very happily family reunion at Newchurch when a young sailor, Stoker Arthur Sibbick, who was believed to have lost his life when HMS Jersey was sunk, unexpectedly returned to his home at 6 Council Houses... His mother was preparing dinner on Monday when an army lorry drew up outside the house, from which her son jumped... The pleasant surprise and relief from anxiety was quickly made known to his fiancee, Miss Lily Woodmore...

SHOOTING FATALITY AT SANDOWN - ACCIDENT THAT SHOULD HAVE BEEN AVOIDED. — A tragic accident in which a soldier lost his life through the discharge of a rifle presumed to be unloaded occurred at the Sandown Hotel, Sandown, on Tuesday. The unfortunate man was Fusilier Samuel Dester aged 30 who was billeted at the Hotel. Fusilier Stanley Cox stated that … he was instructed to borrow the rifle of Lce Cpl Askin, but did not examine the rifle. He went on guard with Fusilier Dester… Dester gave four or five shots with his unloaded rifle. Witness pressed the trigger of his rifle, expecting nothing untoward to happen. The rifle was cocked and a bullet went through Dester's head… The jury found that "Death was due to a regrettable accident that should have been avoided." (September 20)

WANTON DAMAGE TO RYDE BAPTIST CHURCH.— On Saturday the Baptist Church, George-street, was broken into for the second time within a few months. The electric earphone for the deaf, costing over £55, was rendered useless. The pulpit microphone was smashed and thrown into the large baptistry, which is kept filled with water; the first aid equipment was unpacked and its contents scattered in the baptistry, and bottles containing chemicals were found broken in the pews. The new brass Communion table vases were filled with match boxes, and the organist's music, including a leather music case, was also thrown into the baptistry.

--------------◆--------------

Food and clothes rationing had long since become part of everyday life but with an air of quiet resignation the uncomplaining public had taken it all in their stride but a cigarette shortage was an entirely different matter...

August 9th, 1941.

A CIGARETTE, TOBACCO, AND MATCH FAMINE.

There has been an acute shortage of cigarettes, tobacco, and matches in the Island for a fortnight and inquiries made yesterday (Friday) show that no one seems to know when stocks will be more plentiful. Tired of telling customers that they had no cigarettes or tobacco to sell, and of being obviously disbelieved by some, several tobacconists in Newport temporarily closed their shops until they could get a small consignment from the wholesalers, while those who had other goods to sell exhibited large notices in their windows that their stocks of cigarettes and tobacco, and in some cases matches, were exhausted. Both wholesalers and retailers have been having a very harassing time and many lovers of the weed have had to go without, yet if more self-control were exercised it is probable that all would have a reasonable supply. A "County Press" representative discussed the situation with one of the largest wholesalers this week, and this is what he said : "The main cause of the shortage is not the lack of tobacco in the country, but the difficulties with which manufacturers have to contend through losing so many of their workers to the Forces. They simply cannot cope with the demand, which has largely increased since the war. The anxieties of the times have undoubtedly caused more people to smoke, and those who are not new smokers smoke more. I don't think rationing is a practical possibility, so, as the Minister of Supply has already warned the public, unless they ration themselves by making say 10 cigarettes go as far as 15

BUGLE HOTEL
NEWPORT
TELEPHONE 2180.
The Island's Business
and Service Rendezvous.

A.A.   R.A.C.

Isle of Wight THE County Press
AND SOUTH OF ENGLAND REPORTER.
WITH WHICH IS INCORPORATED "THE ISLE OF WIGHT EXPRESS."

RYDE

V. O. S. FOWLER & Co.
Estate House, RYDE

No. 2969. Vol. LVII.   SATURDAY OCTOBER 18, 1941.   6 PAGES—PRICE 2d. (Postage 1½d.)

Births, Marriages, and Deaths.

picture yourself

In something different . . . . you
will like our new hats . . . . it's a
joy to choose from this season's
selections.

This non-coupon fashion will
give spice to your ward-
robe. The new colourings
are : Blackberry, Rosmary
Red, Vineyard, Fairway Green,
New Flannel, Crampian Blue,
and Michaelmas Rose.

Dabells

ACCUMULATOR CHARGING.
You can be certain of getting a really good Charge if you leave your
Accumulator with us. Westinghouse Chargers are used throughout,
and every accumulator is given a full charge at the correct rate. As our
chargers are in use day and night, we require approximately 24 hours
only to complete the charge. You pay no more for Young's Westinghouse Charge. Be certain, leave your accumulator with us.

YOUNG'S The Radio Specialist,
HIGH ST., RYDE, NEWPORT (Opposite Woolworth's), & COWES
For Tax Results Phone Ryde 2469.

TWO-PURPOSE FUEL
IN OPEN GRATE OR CLOSED STOVE
YOU GET A WARM HOT FIRE FROM
OVOIDS
Island Stockists :   JOLLIFFE BROS., LTD.

THE ROYAL SPITHEAD HOTEL
Fully   BEMBRIDGE, ISLE OF WIGHT   Phone 89.
Licensed
THE HOTEL IS OPEN ALL THE YEAR.
LUNCHEONS, TEAS, & DINNERS served EVERY DAY,
INCLUDING SUNDAYS.
Golf, Squash Racquets, Billiards, Table Tennis.
DANCING EVERY NIGHT
Special Tariff to Officers and Families of H.M. Forces.
Bed-rooms with Private Bath-rooms now available.

HILL HOUSE HOTEL
TOTLAND BAY.
A.A. and R.A.C. Recommended.
BEAUTIFULLY situated in Three Acres of Private
Grounds.   Own Fruit, Vegetables and
Poultry.   Telephone : Freshwater 108.

GODWINS
FOR
MEN'S WEAR
IN ALL BRANCHES

WADHAMS'
for
Furniture
Make your choice from one of the
largest stocks in the South of
England.

WADHAM & SONS, LTD.
Shop NEWPORT FREEWATER

Educational.

ROYAL ACADEMY OF MUSIC,
MARYLEBONE ROAD, LONDON,
N.W.1.
L.R.A.M. EXAMINATIONS.

ROYAL DRAWING SCHOOL
OF MUSIC & DRAMA.

THE GUILDHALL SCHOOL
OF MUSIC & DRAMA.
LONDON.
LOCAL EXAMINATIONS

WESTMINSTER HOUSE SCHOOL,
BRAUNSTONE HOUSE SCHOOL,
NEWPORT

THE GRAMMAR SCHOOL
NEWPORT, I.W.

WESTMONT SCHOOL,

SCHOOL FOR BOYS.
VENTNOR COLLEGE

RYDE SCHOOL.

THE MILITARY SCHOOL,
NEWPORT, I.W.

AN APPEAL

Bottle Shortage!

There is an acute shortage of bottles and we would
very much appreciate prompt return. If you have
any, please let us know and we will collect them.

Thank You.

W. B. MEW, LANGTON & Co., Ltd.
ROYAL BREWERY
NEWPORT, I.W.

Established 1861.   THE HOUSE OF QUALITY & SERVICE.   Established 80 Years.

JORDAN & STANLEY,
at NEWPORT & TOTLAND
(Tel. 2319)   (Tel. 87)
for High Class Provisions, Groceries, and Empire Produce,
Wines, Spirits, Ales, Stout, Superior Table Waters.

Big News about FISH
FRESH-SALTED COD
Plentiful-Appetising-Cheap!
9d

HERE ARE TWO SUGGESTIONS :—
FISH PIE
CURRIED COD

FOOD FACTS
No. 54
THE MINISTRY OF FOOD, LONDON, W.1.

BATTERY EFFICIENCY

Strike the Iron while it's Hot!

For the sole purpose of affording you the opportunity of ensuring your battery set being fed with
highly efficient and expertly charged accumulators,
our special accumulator vans are planned to be in
your district every week.

Thousands are taking advantage of this unique
service. If you are desirous of getting the best
out of your set—do make a note of them:

Monday	
Tuesday	
Wednesday	
Thursday	
Friday	
Saturday	

Autumn Woollens
FOR
COATS, COSTUMES, FROCKS, etc.

They're NEW—They're SMART—They're DIFFERENT

Visit the Famous Fabric Department at
Fowler's and see their wonderful new selection
of Woollen Fabrics . . . . Warm Weight
Coating in plain Colours and Checks . . . .
A wonderful choice of Scotch Tweeds and
Suitings . . . . Velours for Children's Wear
. . . . and glorious ranges of Dress Weight
Woollens in the newest Autumn Shades.
Patterns gladly sent.
Price, per yard 6/11 to 19/11

S. FOWLER & CO., RYDE

The LONGER your FABRICS LAST, the LONGER will your
COUPONS ! Buy them for reliability from
BULPITT'S 53 OSBORNE ROAD,
SOUTHSEA.

TEXTOR CLEANING
ADDS life to the CLOTH
SAVES you MONEY and Coupons.
REDUCED price cleaning saves you NOTHING
TEXTOR guarantees—

Official Agents for the Isle of Wight :
MARDERS   NEWPORT
RYDE
SANDOWN
SHANKLIN

TILLEYS
Tel. 2715

THE HOUSE FOR FABRICS
129 HIGH STREET
NEWPORT

ENGAGEMENT
AND DRESS
RINGS

BENZIE **COWES**

EXCEPTIONAL VALUE

*Prompt Delivery to all
parts of the
Island*

COAL
FOR WOOD
HEAT

HEAD OFFICE
STATION APPROACH, NEWPORT
Phone Newport 2628

THOS. H. SEED
AND COMPANY LIMITED
BRANCH OFFICES
COWES
SANDOWN
SHANKLIN
VENTNOR
FRESHWATER

COKE

LOG WOOD   "The Island"
SAME DAY DENTAL
REPAIR SERVICE
HAYWARD'S

CURTISS & SONS,
REMOVALS & STORAGE

Removals & Storage.

T2 UNION STREET, RYDE

ALES
BENNETT
WANTED FOR CASH
MODERN MOTOR CYCLES
AND AUTO CYCLES

STIBY & ELDERFIELD
TAILORS
CLOTHIERS
AND
OUTFITTERS

PARNELL,
UNDERTAKER,

SHERRATT'S
82 HIGH STREET, NEWPORT
PHONE 2166
YOUR LOCAL MARCONI MEN

in happier times these periods of shortage are bound to occur. As a matter of fact, the Island has been extremely fortunate in this matter. The local wholesalers had pretty full stocks early in the war and they have called on them as sparingly as possible, but what with the increased demand and the cutting down of supplies by the manufacturers, the reserve became exhausted about a fortnight ago and unless the public reduce their demands they will have to be satisfied with the supplies as they are received, which is somewhat irregularly, owing to the reasons stated and war-time transport difficulties. The shortage has no doubt been aggravated by the selfishness of some people who, finding supplies were getting short, have been shop crawling and hoarding up cigarettes and tobacco, a very unpatriotic and inconsiderate thing to do, but a very difficult thing to detect and stop. The purchases of Servicemen, who are not taken into account in our quota, also aggravates the situation. If they would only purchase at their own canteens there would be more for the civilians."

-------------------◆-------------------

THE WEEK'S NEWS.

THREE SHANKLIN WOMEN INJURED BY STRAY SHELL. — Yesterday (Friday) morning a shell fired in practice by a battery near Wroxall pitched and exploded in the roadway at the junction of Arthur's-hill and Hope-road, Shanklin damaging eight houses and injuring three women. Mrs. Piper of the Homelands Boarding-house was taken to the Home of Rest Hospital.*

ORANGES IN THE ISLAND! — The first consignment of oranges to reach the Island in nine months was delivered at the stores of Messrs. F. Trim, Newport, on Thursday. It consists of 880 cases of South African Valencias. The supply is being evenly allocated to retailers throughout the Island. Some were on sale in Newport yesterday (Friday) morning and were eagerly snapped up by early shoppers.

As the Mayor and Corporation were solemnly passing down the aisle of Newport Parish Church recently, a little boy, sitting with his mother in one of the pews, gazed wide-eyed at his Worship's red robe, and exclaimed, loud enough for some of the passing civic dignitaries to hear, "Is that Father Christmas?"

SOUTH COAST AIR RAIDS. — A South Coast district which has been free from night raids for about three months had another sharp visitation on Saturday night, when a number of enemy machines, flying very high, came in from over the Channel. When fiercely attacked by anti-aircraft fire they scattered, and they appeared to drop their bombs hastily... Two which fell near a farm on the outskirts of the town fortunately landed into fields among some poultry houses but the only casualty was an injury to a cock-bird which had to be destroyed.

---

* Mrs. Piper later died from her injuries.

WHAT OF THE CIGARETTE. — "Like the snowflake on the river, a moment white, then gone for ever." The demand for them is universal and increasing by leaps and bounds. We should ration ourselves... Rolling one's own is conducive to economy, and gives a better and more hygienic result. No one who makes his own will suffer from throat trouble or smoker's cough.

As part of the war effort thousands of Britain's park railings were removed in order, so it was said, to be melted down to be recycled into munitions. London's railings had been the first to disappear in June of the previous year and now it was the Island's turn....

October 18th, 1941.
IRON RAILINGS WANTED FOR MUNITIONS.
The Minister of Munitions has instructed local authorities to prepare inventories of iron railings on public and private property, which can be utilised for munitions making. He says the need is urgent. Newport has a wealth of scrap of this kind and doubtless the Town Council have set their eyes upon it. There is one particularly valuable stock in the railings which border the old Cemetery in Church-litten, and, although no one would like to see this fine range of railings go, they must if the nation requires them to build tanks. These railings are interesting because they bear the date of their erection (1849) on each of the spear-head tops of the main uprights, and these are so faced that they repeat the number in succession along the whole length of the line. Then there are the railings which front almost every Victorian villa residence in all parts of the town. They, too, will probably have to go. The only legitimate grounds of appeal against their removal are public safety, historic or artistic merit, or utility in confining cattle. If the old Cemetery railings have to be sacrificed it may prove the first step in carrying out a suggestion which has often been made, that the memorial stones should be removed and placed around the walls and the site laid out as a pleasure garden. It would make an admirable haven of peace almost in the centre of the town, and it is already beautified by many fine trees.

1942.

Removal of the railings began early in the New Year. The work was not carried out to everyone's satisfaction...

February 21st, 1942.
THE COLLECTION OF IRON RAILINGS.
The Chairman said a protest had been sent to the Ministry of Works and Buildings as to the manner in which railings were being taken down in the district, but no reply had been received... In some places walls had been left in a very shaky condition. Some children loved to pull things down and householders could see their walls gradually disappearing. The collectors had even started taking away railings from around graves, and the curbings had

been broken by being hit with sledge-hammers. It was sheer vandalism. If this sort of thing occurred in peace time people would lynch those responsible... Ninety-nine per cent of the people did not object to the railings being taken, but they did to their property being knocked about... If the collection of railings was necessary why were not everyone's taken? In certain streets the collectors had gone so far and then stopped. It seemed to him that it was nothing but a rush job to make it pay. Everyone should be treated in a like manner. Railings should not be left because of artistic value. — Mr. Mason spoke of the danger at East Cowes by the removal of railings from around the umbrella tree in York-avenue. The disgraceful state in which the Town-hall had been left was no credit to the Council...

February 28th, 1942.

WASTE IRON.

To the Editor of the I.W. County Press.

Sir, - I entirely endorse your last week's critic as to the removal of iron railings from cottage property, etc. This order is from the Ministry of Works and Buildings. What this ministry exists for is still a matter of conjecture. Builders concerned get approximately 28s. a ton for the removal, delivery, and loading on a barge, slightly more than the cost of carriage. In the Island marine store dealers' yards there are about 3000 tons of scrap. Hundreds of tons are lying about in shipyards, at cement mills, on almost every farm and old machines, etc., having no value, probably 1000 tons. Some has been offered but no replies have ever been seen. To rob house property of its front fences and gates is not only dangerous in the black-out, but gives the appearance of a bombed area. Costing at the rate of £5 a ton to collect, exclusive of delivery, makes me wonder are railings the only thing of interest we can find?

I am, Sir, yours faithfully, G. H. WILLIAMS. Rushdale. Wootton.

————————————◆————————————

THE WEEK'S NEWS.

ARMY EXERCISE FATALITY - SOLDIER SHOT BY BREN GUN. — Pte. Leonard Theobald died on Monday from wounds inflicted by a Bren gun in an incident in the Brading district...The spring seer of the gun was found missing, rendering the gun highly dangerous even though the change lever was at the "safe" position... Sergeant Alfred Gregory said he checked the gun, finding the change lever at "safe" and inserted a magazine when the weapon discharged, wounding Theobald... The jury returned a verdict of "Accidental death." (Feb 28.)

An appeal has been made against the removal of the railings surrounding Newport Cemetery.

SOLDIER SHOT BY HOME GUARD - "LACK OF SUPERVISION" AT RIFLE PRACTICE. — Gunner Joseph Clark, R.A., aged 35, died as a result of a bullet wound received while a platoon of the Island Home Guard were at rifle practice at a military battery on Sunday... Clark was engaged in marking the targets, laying down in a pit during the actual shooting... Lce. Cpl. Allen... opened fire prematurely, believing he had received orders to do so. (March 7)

COLWELL COMMON PLOUGHED UP. — The stretch of Colwell Common to the west of the main Yarmouth-road at Totland Bay has been cleared of gorse and other undergrowth and ploughed. The Rural District Council are offering the land, which extends to about six acres, for allotments, but if it is not taken for this purpose it may be used for agricultural crops.

RABBITS FOR FOOD. *To the Editor of the I.W. County Press.*
Sir, — I saw in the "County Press" of February 28th that the Minister of Agriculture is encouraging the gassing of rabbits. What a waste of valuable food, costing almost nothing to catch. I have been trying with no success to buy one in the shops for weeks, and many other people say the same.
Yours truly, N. KENNEDY. 70 Pellhurst-road. Ryde.

◆

Nearly half the bombs dropped on the Isle of Wight during the war fell on Cowes and most of those bombs fell on the night of the 4th/5th of May, 1942 when the town suffered its worst air raid of the war.
That night, over 200 tons of high explosive bombs fell on Cowes and East Cowes, killing over 70 and destroying large areas of J. S.White's shipyard on both sides of the river...

May 9th, 1942.
SOUTH COAST AIR RAIDS.
DAMAGE AND CASUALTIES AT A PORT.
A South Coast port (*Cowes*), which was subjected to an early-morning low-flying raid by German fighter-bombers a few days previously, was twice attacked by bombers during the night of Monday-Tuesday, resulting in further serious damage to property and a considerable number of casualties.
The first raid started with the dropping of a group of powerful parachute flares, which brilliantly illuminated the target area, and then the bombers came at regular intervals for about an hour, first with incendiaries and then with high explosive bombs, most of them heavy ones. The incendiaries started several big fires in the waterside premises which blazed furiously and further lit up the district making it a clear target, and in spite of a very fierce barrage from the ground defences, which was continuous as long as there was a plane in the vicinity, the raiders dive-bombed the place, and also scattered high explosive bombs over a wide area, including another town. A second attack came about four hours later and, although this did not last as long as the first raid, it was severe and further damage and casualties resulted... Many buildings in the business and residential parts of the town suffered either complete destruction or extensive damage.
It was by far the worst raid the district has experienced and it is satisfactory to be able to give wholehearted praise to every branch of the civil defence service. They were faced with an exceedingly heavy task necessitating untiring

efforts amid great danger, but they never faltered and those who had suffered terribly were the first to pay tribute to their skill and bravery.

A noble example of devotion to duty was set by the A.R.P officer in the town which suffered most. This officer (Mr. S. F. Birchell), who lost a limb in the last war, suffered a crushing blow early in the attack. His wife and her parents were killed and his three-year-old son injured when a bomb hit the private shelter in which they were taking cover, yet he refused to leave his post of duty and carried on throughout the night and following day. Rescue and first-aid parties and ambulance drivers laboured almost without a pause for refreshment; the firemen, in spite of casualties in their ranks, continued to fight the flames with bombs falling around them and those responsible for the care of the homeless and the transport of wounded to hospital worked magnificently...

A gratifying circumstance, amid much to sadden, was the way in which the brick shelters in the streets stood up to the bombing. They saved hundreds of lives. Near misses shattered houses farther away, but in almost every case the shelters remained intact and their occupants were uninjured, although in some instances the shelters were bodily moved by the blast. There was one case where a shelter actually fell into a crater made by a bomb which exploded only a yard or two from it, but some of those inside were got out unharmed, although several lost their lives. Practically the only criticism heard was that some of the shelters were not unlocked earlier when they were badly needed....

The public generally bore the ordeal with admirable fortitude and pluck, although the state of some of them next morning was pitiable as they tried to rescue precious possessions from their ruined homes, or searched for missing relatives... The homeless were evacuated to other towns and villages. They were received with every sympathy and some of those who helped in securing billets for them were constantly at work throughout the afternoon and evening of Tuesday until past midnight. Many others left the town fearing another raid the following night and they could be seen on foot, on bicycles, or in cars, making their way to safety with their portmanteaux and parcels of bare necessities. It was a pathetic spectacle, but everything possible was done to succour them... There were numerous amazing escapes from injury. One family whose house collapsed into a crater were extricated unscathed and a 5-weeks-old baby was rescued alive from a wrecked house in which the mother and 14-year-old sister were killed.

The following experience of a mother and her 11-year-old son is typical of what many had to endure. Almost the first bomb which fell shattered their home. They were sheltering under the stairs and escaped injury, but fearing that the house would totally collapse they left it and sought shelter in a street refuge. On the way they had to fling themselves on the ground three or four times as other bombs whistled down uncomfortably close. They spent nearly an hour in the shelter and several times it seemed as if their last-minute had come, as the shelter rocked with concussion as bombs fell near... When the raid was over a fellow shelterer, a man who was a stranger to her, asked the mother what she was going to do as she could not go back to her ruined home. She said she would like to get to relatives at a place 5 miles away, so he immediately got out his car and took her and the boy there. On the way they collided with a cow and

DEATHS.

ABROOK.—In May, by enemy action, Evelyn Francis Abrook, dearly-beloved wife of Sapper W. Abrook, of 2 Ryde-road Cottage, Whippingham, aged 26.—The family wish to thank all who sent flowers and letters of sympathy.

BARNES.—In ever-loving memory of our darling Floss, aged 32, and Arthur, aged 38, killed by enemy action in May.—From their broken-hearted Mum, Dad, Eve, and Alf.

BURCHELL.—In May, 1942, by enemy action, Isabella Elizabeth, wife of Sydney Frank Burchell, of Comrie, Ward-avenue, Cowes.

BURTON.—May 5, at Laburnum, Worsley-road, Gurnard, Sarah Ann, widow of Frederick Burton, aged 82.—The daughter and relatives of the above wish to thank the many friends for kind expressions of sympathy, also letters and lovely floral tributes. Will they please accept this as the only intimation.

CHIVERTON.—In May, by enemy action, Mary, Vera, John, Pat, Paul, and Jean.— The relatives thank the Council and all persons who so kindly helped in any way. Please accept this, the only intimation.

COLE.—In May, 1942, by enemy action, George Henry Cole, C.C., and his wife, Elizabeth, of Crathie, Baring-road, Cowes.

COOK.—In May, by enemy action, Capt. H. J. Cook, aged 76; also Mary Hannah Cook, aged 72, of East Cowes.

COSH.—In loving memory of dear mother, sister, and nephew, taken from us in May by enemy action.—Mr. and Mrs. Cosh wish to thank all kind friends for their sympathy, help, and floral tributes. Please accept this as the only intimation.

COSTER.—In loving memory of my darling wife and children, killed by enemy action in May.—Her broken-hearted husband Will.

COSTER.—In loving memory of Sallie, Marjan, and Peter, killed by enemy action in May.—From Ken, Grace, and Joyce.

DOWNER.—In loving memory of our dear ones, Mum, brother Sid, and Grannie, taken so suddenly from us by enemy action.—Mrs. and Mr. H. Page wish to thank all kind friends for their sympathy, help, and floral tributes. Please accept this as the only intimation.

EGGLETON.—In loving memory of dear Gordon, killed by enemy action in May.— From his loving brothers and sisters, Roy, Kath, Pam, and Jack, Alice, Reg. and Daphne.

EGGLETON.—With treasured memories of my dear brother, killed by enemy action in May.—Never forgotten by his loving sister Vera, also Eric and Pat.

EGGLETON.—In ever-loving memory of my dear son Gordon, who was killed by enemy action in May.—From his ever-sorrowing mother.

GALTON.—In May, by enemy action, Robert Frank Galton, aged 41; Florence Elizabeth Galton, aged 40; Maureen Jean Galton, aged 10, of East Cowes.

GUSTAR.—In ever-loving memory of my brother, Frank Gustar, his wife May, and his two little children, Sally and Allen, who were killed through enemy action in May. Safe in the Arms of our Lord.— Fred, Anne, Ernie.

HANN (Alice Frances).—In May, while on duty during enemy action.—Her sons and daughters send their most sincere thanks to all concerned and gratefully acknowledge the many expressions of sympathy and beautiful flowers.

HARVEY.—In loving memory of my darling husband Frank, taken so suddenly from me by enemy action in May. So kind, loving, and devoted always.—From his broken-hearted wife Ray.

HUGHES.—In memory of our darling daughter Gwen, killed by enemy action in May. Safe in the Arms of Jesus.—From her broken-hearted Mummie and Daddie.

HUGHES.—In May, by enemy action, Gwen Hughes, of Cowes, aged 4.

INCE.—In May, by enemy action, George Henry, beloved husband of Doll and father of Mary, aged 43.

INCE.—In May, by enemy action, George Henry, beloved son of Mrs. Ince and the late Mr. J. Ince.—From his loving mother, brothers, and sisters.

INCE—MARSHALL.—In memory of our brothers George and Char, taken from us through enemy action.—From Alice, Arch, and children.
Two of the best in every way
We will keep in our memories for ever and a day.

JEANS.—In May, by enemy action, Marjorie Winifred (née Maker) and Anne Elizabeth Jeans, of East Cowes.

JOHNSON.—May 9, at 49 West-street, Ryde, Sarah Ann Johnson, aged 82.

JOLLIFFE.—On May 8, at Cowes, I.W., Sarah Annie, the beloved wife of Henry Samuel Jolliffe and mother of Ethel, in her 71st year.—In heavenly love abiding.

KERSEY—BARTON.—In loving memory of our dear daughter, son-in-law, and grandson, killed by enemy action during May.— From mother, Dad, brother and sister.

LAIDLER.—In May, by enemy action, Mrs. Laidler, of 4 Netherton-road, Brockhurst, Gosport.

LOUGHTON.—May 6, at St. Mary's Hospital, Parkhurst, Alexandrina May, only daughter of the late R. B. and Mrs. Loughton, formerly of the Globe Hotel, Cowes.

MAKER.—In May, by enemy action, Dora Mabel and Edward Henry Maker, of East Cowes.

MORRIS.—My dearest Uncle Reg, who was killed in May.—Always his loving Betty.

TUTTON—HUGHES.—In ever-loving memory of Mr. Tutton and his little grand-daughter Gwennie, killed by enemy action in May.—Always to be remembered by their friends opposite, Maisie and Fred and little Maureen, Brian, and Michael.

VARNEY.—In loving memory of Uncle Bill, Auntie Lou, and Betty, of Arctic-road, killed by enemy action in May.—From Les and Doll.

The deaths column in the issue of May 9th, following the bombing of Cowes on the night of May 4/5th. (Edited to show only those who died as a result of the bombing.)

at another place the car became enmeshed in fallen telephone wires, but in spite of all difficulties the journey was safely completed. Then the motorist Good Samaritan discovered that his petrol had run out, but he was enabled to make the return journey as a motorist living near siphoned out of his own car sufficient petrol for the journey, which was completed safely. The motorist's action was just one example of the fine spirit of comradeship which prevailed among those who had to withstand the terrifying experience...

During the first raid bombs which fell wide of the mark did damage and caused casualties in the outskirts of another town (*Shide*). One of the heavy calibre fell in the back gardens of the villa residences on the main road, completely demolishing three residences, seriously damaging half a dozen more, and doing minor damage to many others. Thanks to what would appear to be providential protection several residents had wonderful escapes and there was only one fatal casualty, the victim being Mr. George Kirkup... He happened to be in the kitchen of his house where he lived alone, and he was apparently instantly killed when the building collapsed... The rescue squad worked splendidly, regardless of an ever present danger they knew to be at hand and soon extricated Mr. Kirkup but he was beyond human aid.

A most tragic result of the raid occurred when two cottages about a mile from the town, at the junction of main roads, (*Lushington Hill, Wootton*) received a direct hit. The occupants of one of the cottages, Mr. and Mrs. W. Chiverton, and two children were rescued, but their other six children, whose ages ranged from five weeks to seven years, including twins two years of age, were killed. Mrs. Abrook was rescued from the other cottage after being buried under the ruins for six hours. Here a party of soldiers gave much appreciated help in the rescues.

Mr. and Mrs. F. Adams and their child emerged from their garden shelter after the raid to find hardly a trace left of their home, which had received a direct hit.

An enemy aircraft dropped incendiary and high explosive bombs at another coast town on Monday night (*Ventnor*). One bomb fell on the cliff face between a disused gasworks and the pier, causing widespread destruction of glass over a residential area. A newspaper and printing office had its front windows blown out and there was minor damage to other business properties in the same street... Apparently the raider was being chased from the coast and jettisoned its bombs. A few miles out it crashed into the sea. There were no casualties except a few minor injuries from flying glass, but Mrs. Cass, wife of a postman and a special constable (who was on duty at the time), collapsed and died from shock.

---◆---

ISLAND NOTES.

To the Editor of the I.W. County Press.

Dear Sir, — The burials of the unfortunate victims of a recent air raid were the first in the district, and seem to prove that our organisation is at fault in more than one respect. May I ask who was responsible for the burial of these victims?

Although there was an official ban in place prohibiting the photographing of bomb damage this picture of Arctic Road, Cowes somehow appeared in a Toronto newspaper in June 1942. It shows the damage inflicted six weeks earlier, on the night of May 4th/5th, when the town suffered its heaviest ever bombing raid during which over 70 people were killed. Captioned "A Nazi Raid did this to a south coast town in England," its appearance in a British newspaper would have been unthinkable.

Above all, why paupers' graves? Are these people, old as they were, not worthy of something better? Why did a certain friendly society fail to interest itself sufficiently to make inquiries. Does the friendliness cease when a person is of the same order but of a different lodge? DISGUSTED RATEPAYER.
[We understand that the sum officially allowed for such interments is alleged to be insufficient for the provision of some of the usual funeral arrangements. Editor, I.W.C.P.]

A RARE TREE. — The General Purposes Committee have instructed the Borough surveyor not to re-fence the Church-litten burial ground now that the iron railings have been removed, but that he should erect a fence around the weeping beech tree. The Mayor explained that the tree was a rare one; there were reputed to be only two in this country and for that reason it was thought wise to protect it from damage by children. Mr. King thought fencing unnecessary as, if the children were told that it was a valuable tree, they could be trusted not to interfere with it, or for that matter, with any of the trees there.

"SOME" CHICKEN — Mr. J. P. Read, of 27, Green-street, Ryde, recently had a pure Light Sussex chicken hatched with four legs. This little freak was quite able to run about on its own, and would sit on its second pair of legs, smaller in size, which had grown from the rear of the body. Although it appeared in good health, after 10 days' existence Mr Read decided to destroy it in the belief that it might eventually develop some disease which would cause it suffering.

———————————◆———————————

There seemed to be no end to it. The air raid sirens sounded even as the dead were being buried...

May 16th, 1942.

SOUTH COAST AIR RAIDS.
FUNERAL OF VICTIMS.

The funerals of the victims of the two heavy air attacks on a South Coast town* (*Cowes*) last week took place on Tuesday and Wednesday, when a large number of sympathisers gathered at the respective cemeteries. On the former day, while the long procession was proceeding to the burial ground, an air raid alert was sounded and gun-fire was plainly heard. Despite the danger that looked close at hand above the low clouds very few people were driven from paying their last respects to their unfortunate fellow townspeople. The coffins were borne in motor wagons which were draped with Union Jacks... The A.R.P. Services provided the bearers except in one instance - that of a Wolf Club, whose coffin, on which were his cap and neckerchief, was carried by senior members of his Scout Group. As the procession wended its way from the Cemetery entrance to the communal grave several large bomb craters, which bore testimony to the savagery of the raid, had to be passed... When the remainder of the victims were interred on Wednesday there was again a large

*The "South Coast town" was identified when the following week's death column contained repeated references to Cowes inhabitants "killed by enemy action".

number of sympathisers present... There was no procession to the Cemetery as on the previous day, as the coffins had been placed in the communal grave, the sides of which had been draped with Union Jacks, in readiness for the graveside service...

Six children of one family under seven years of age, who were killed in another town, were buried together on Friday week. One of the parents who were rescued has since died.

———————————◆———————————

TOWN AND COUNTY NOTES.

FATAL SHARK-SHOOTING ACCIDENT AT GATCOMBE - SOLDIER KILLED DURING PRACTICE. - The Coroner held an inquest at Parkhurst on Wednesday on the body of Sergt. Hubert Tost, of an infantry regiment, aged 32, who died from a bullet wound in the head. He was engaged in hip-firing practice in a coppice near Garstons Farm... Cpl Edward Bowles deposed that he had fired at three tins, and then, thinking he saw another to his left, he swung round and fired... He immediately heard a shout "Stop firing."... Sergt Tost had been hit in the head... The Coroner said he had no hesitation in recording a verdict of accidental death...

More than 700,000 Polish Jews have been slaughtered by the Germans in the greatest massacre in the world's history.

THREE SANDOWN BOYS INJURED IN AN EXPLOSION. — The danger of boys picking up objects where military operations have taken place was again emphasised by an unfortunate occurrence on Thursday morning. Three boys about eight years of age, Billy Bradley, David Williams and Maurice Dove, were playing near Jaels-lane (sic) when Bradley picked up a metal object. The other boys advised him to throw it away and when he did so it exploded. As a result he is in hospital with wounds in the chest, legs and groin, and the other boys received less serious wounds.

ACCIDENTALLY SHOT WITH TOMMY-GUN. — The Island's Deputy Coroner held an inquest on the body of Gunner Horace Shambrook, aged 20, who lost his life by the accidental discharge of a Tommy-gun by a comrade on the previous Friday evening... Lce-Bombardier Frank Staines stated he examined a Tommy-gun before handing it over to Gunner Garrett and saw that the safety catch was applied. At about 6.15 p.m. when in the guard-room, he heard a shot, and a few moments later Shambrook staggered in holding his stomach with his hands and, saying "He has shot me," he collapsed... A verdict of accidental death was returned, the Coroner pointing out that it was clear that Gunner Garrett had no idea how to operate a machine gun.

The phrase "Careless Talk Costs Lives" entered the English language. It not only cost lives; sometimes it cost money....

September 19th, 1942.

FIRST ISLAND CARELESS TALK PROSECUTION.

Miss Doris Bessie Hannaford, 30, of Camp-road, Freshwater, employed as a cafe manageress at Cowes was charged "that she did on July 25th in Yarmouth communicate to another person information in respect of HM vessels which would, or might be, directly or indirectly of use to the enemy contrary to the Defence of the Realm Regulations." The defendant pleaded not guilty saying "I did mention the words, I admit, but I did not think it was of any importance." The evidence was heard in camera, and after the Bench had retired, the Chairman said they had decided to convict accused on what was a very serious offence in war-time. Talking about the movement of ships in public places like buses was a most serious offence and very heavy penalties had been inflicted. They were being lenient with accused in fining her £10.* — Asked if she wanted time to pay, defendant said she had to support her mother and would need time to get in touch with somebody who would lend her the money. Two months were allowed for payment.

————————————◆————————————

In 1942 Germany's U-boats were at the height of their success (after the war Churchill confessed it was the one time he thought Britain might actually lose the war) and merchant ships bringing food and materials to Britain were sunk in their hundreds. To make matters worse the Channel Isles were now under German occupation and the export of tomatoes and potatoes to the British mainland had ceased.

To help make up the shortfall, councils in the southern parts of the country were set the task of ploughing up suitable plots of land for tomato and potato growing on an industrial scale. On the Island, Ryde, Newport and Ventnor councils achieved some impressive results...

September 26th, 1942.

THE ISLAND'S GROWING TOMATO INDUSTRY.

VISITS BY MINISTRY OF AGRICULTURE OFFICERS.

The Ryde Corporation's tomato farm at Knighton was visited on Monday afternoon by Capt Beaumont, MP, Mr. Tom Williams (Parliamentary Secretary), of the Ministry of Agriculture, and Mr. Roy Hay, the well-known broadcasting horticulturalist. With them was Mr. F. G. Short, an expert on seeds from the firm of Messrs. Harrisons, seed merchants of Leicester... On this, their second visit they saw instead of 15,000 plants as last year, 52,000 plants on the slopes of the sun trap valley and heard that already 15 tons had been disposed of, with a further crop of approximately 60 to 70 tons to be gathered, given reasonable weather conditions... After inspecting the growing fruit the visitors saw young girls at work in the packing shed preparing baskets of fruit for transport to the Midlands and the North Capt Beaumont said ... Ryde Council had set an

---

* For a cafe manageress at that time, £10 would represent the best part of a month's wages.

Official and Other Notices.

What I Don't Do

I don't burn Paper

I don't smash Bottles

I don't throw Bones away

I don't throw Tins and Odd Bits of Metal on the Garden

I don't mix up valuable Rags with Household Rubbish

I don't keep Rubber Articles till they perish

What I Do Do

Sort my Salvage

Put it in clean Dry Heaps or Bundles.

Ask my Neighbour to do the same.

ISLE OF WIGHT COUNTY SALVAGE DRIVE
JULY 18th–AUGUST 1st.

It has been brought to my notice that there is much distress among cats and dogs, due to the recent raid. Many animals running away in fear have since returned to find their homes gone and their owners evacuated. Owing to lack of petrol, the R.S.P.C.A. Inspector cannot frequently be in the district, but any animals that are found vagrant and homeless were better painlessly destroyed, and taken to MR. WHITE, Shoe Repairer, Pelham-road, Cowes, where there is a lethalising-box, and who will certainly attend to any lost stray animals brought to him, and put them to sleep.
L. G. WILSON-HEATHCOTE,
Hon. Sec., I.W. Branch R.S.P.C.A.

COUNTY OF THE ISLE OF WIGHT

NOTICE TO THE CIVIL POPULATION ON THE SUBJECT OF INVASION

The issue of posters relating to invasion does not mean that invasion is necessarily imminent or likely at the present time, but is intended to give publicity to the arrangements which are being made to meet such an emergency. The Germans never cease preparing for invasion, and while at some periods the immediate threat diminishes, at other periods it increases and preparations to meet it demand long-term planning and practice. The following points need to be emphasised.

STAND FIRM

The first essential is that all persons should stand firm and, except under definite orders, or in discharge of their duties, keep off the roads. The general public are on no account to leave their homes for some supposedly safer area, and so start the refugee movements which can only cause disaster. THEY WILL IN ANY CASE BE IN LESS DANGER AND SUFFER LESS HARDSHIP BY REMAINING IN THEIR OWN NEIGHBOURHOOD.

In areas not immediately threatened with enemy attack the public will be expected to carry on essential activities so far as possible.

CAN THE CIVILIAN FIGHT?

The Stand Firm policy does not mean that the civil population are expected to adopt a purely passive role. On the contrary, the Government has always expected that the people of these islands will offer a united opposition to an invader and that every citizen will regard it as his duty to hinder and frustrate the enemy and help our own Forces by every means that ingenuity can devise and common sense suggest.

Of course, the civilian is not expected to attack large military formations, but if stray enemy marauders or small parties of enemy soldiers are moving about in an area not in the effective occupation of the enemy, the Government expects that every stout-hearted citizen will use all his powers to overcome them.

If his help is asked by the military, as it may well be, it is his duty to answer whole-heartedly any call, however exacting, that may be made upon him.

WHAT IS YOUR JOB IN INVASION?

If you have not got one, apply to your Invasion Committee, who will find one for you which will be of real use in time of invasion and which will enable you to say, when the enemy has been driven back, "I did my part."

Young or old, strong or weak, EVERYONE must lend a hand if your country is invaded.

Issued by the County Invasion Committee.

Children's Dresses—hundreds and hundreds, all different. In fact, we can help you in every item of Kiddies' Clothing

DABELLS

example to the Island which it was pleasing to know was being successfully followed by other authorities. He hoped that the venture started in the tragic times of war would be proceeded with even greater effectiveness in the days of peace...

NEWPORT.

The visitors inspected the Newport Town Council's tomato crop at Froglands, Carisbrooke, in the evening... So far about three tons of fruit have been dispatched to the North of England, under the arrangement made with the Cooperative Wholesale Society, the price received being 9d. a lb. Capt Beaumont was informed of the valuable help given by the farmer (Mr. M. Morris), in preparing the ground and the soldier helpers who have worked at intervals attending to the crop... Young women are employed in picking and packing and more help in this direction would be welcomed. There are about 15,500 plants on two acres of ground.

At the tomato site at St. Lawrence, Ventnor, two acres of meadowland have been ploughed up and planted with 20,000 plants of a number of varieties. And the party walked through the ranks of plants of wonderful growth, all carefully staked and tied and it was a revelation to see the marvellous crop on every plant... Ventnor Council are seizing the opportunity by marketing their crop to advertise the town as a seaside and health resort. A slip of paper is inserted in each box of tomatoes sent away bearing the printed message: "Tomatoes From Sunny Ventnor, Isle of Wight. We shall be delighted to welcome you as a visitor when peace returns."

Up to Tuesday about 130 tons of outdoor tomatoes have been exported by the Vectis Shipping Company, Newport. Most of them have gone to big industrial towns in the North of England

◆

ISLAND NOTES.

ALARMING SUBSTANCE AT SEAGROVE BAY. — For two years signs of an unusually rapid subsidence have been evident in the land surrounding Seagrove Bay, Seaview, and during the last few weeks these have increased at an alarming pace. The state of the Esplanade even to the casual observer gives signs of the movement of the land, large slabs of concrete having been pushed out of place and extensive cracks appearing in what has for years been a comparatively good surface. All 14 houses on the Esplanade show obvious signs of a serious position. In some cases houses have been cleared of furniture and appear unsafe for habitation...

THE MOTHERING INSTINCT. *To the Editor of the I.W. County Press.*

Sir, — At a farm in Bouldnor yesterday I saw in the corner of a cow shed, a broody hen sitting on and doing her best to cover a large litter of retriever terrier puppies. The terrier mother was sitting happily nearby, while the broody hen and the puppies, who were themselves fast asleep, appeared thoroughly happy and contented. The hen was sitting on top of the litter but was obviously not able to cover them all completely and a black circle of the puppies' coats appeared as an outer ring. I presume that this is what should be called an aberration of the mothering instinct, but I thought it would be of interest to animal lovers. — I am, Sir, yours faithfully, MARGARET SPICER. Woodend, Yarmouth. 23rd October 1942.

PUT OUT YOUR JUGS! — The Ryde Dairymen's War-time Association advertise that from October 25th milk will no longer be delivered in bottles.

Children have lost much owing to the war; the liberty of the sea-shore, the freedom of the tuck-shop, and cakes that are really cakes. They are often separated from their parents, exiled in strange homes or left in day-nurseries. And now toys and games are put out of reach by scarcity and preposterous prices, which are far beyond the means of many householders. Are toys mere trifles? Not altogether. In the wartime creche where one woman helps many to go out to work, the presence of abundant toys and games is a great help to those in charge.

———————————◆———————————

Another soldier was accidentally shot and killed by his colleagues bringing the total so far to seven. In each of the previous inquests the Coroner had suggested that in times of war such things were bound to happen and following his directions juries had so far returned verdicts of accidental death but when a young soldier was shot by his colleagues outside Brading railway station one November night, the Coroner for once took a different view.

This time he had no hesitation in condemning the actions of the other men involved. "The poor man" said the Coroner, "had been wantonly shot"...

November 28th, 1942.

ESCAPING SOLDIER FATALLY SHOT.
STRONG COMMENTS BY CORONER AND JURY.

A remarkable story of how seven shots were fired at a soldier who had broken arrest was told to to the Deputy Coroner at an inquest in Ryde on Monday. The deceased was Peter McHenry, 23, a regular soldier in the Royal Artillery... who died at the County Hospital on Saturday from gunshot wounds... Battery-Sergt.-major Percy J. Gregory deposed that at 6.30 p.m. on November 19th he heard that McHenry, who was under close arrest for removing a newspaper from the rest-room and for committing a common assault, had escaped. He instructed Sergt. Rogers to detail a search party. This consisted of four gunners and a sergeant and they carried rifles. He ordered them not to open fire... Sergt. Edward Rogers said he was instructed by the previous witness to search Brading Railway station. They were not to use their rifles unless in self-defence, and then to fire low... His attention was directed towards the up platform, where he saw the outline of McHenry standing between the lavatory and a white gate. He heard one of his escort call out, "Halt. Is that you McHenry?" and McHenry replied "Yes" and turned towards the white gate. The next thing he heard was a single round fired in his rear. He did not give any order to fire... He was surprised when he heard the shot fired...

Whilst he was making for the entrance to the station he heard more shots ring out behind him. When the first shot was fired he thought one of the men had got excited and fired accidentally. He thought that altogether seven shots were fired... McHenry was found lying in a prone position in the road outside the station... Dr. William Gross, house surgeon at the County Hospital said deceased was admitted at 10.50 p.m. on November 19th. He was severely shocked and had a gun-shot wound through the left upper thorax, lung, diaphragm, and kidney region. An operation was performed and the kidney removed but deceased died as a result of shock and internal haemorrhage...

In reply to the Coroner, Capt. Barratt said under King's Regulations there was no justification for the use of rifles on that occasion. They should only be used if actual violence was offered to the escort. — The Coroner: If this man was escaping there would be no justification for using the rifles? — Capt. Barratt: No...

In summing up, the Coroner said ... it was a very serious matter and, in his view, the poor man had been wantonly shot; in the excitement of the moment the men completely lost their heads and fired their rifles in a most dangerous manner. It was only by luck that there were no passengers on the station or people coming down the road to join the train. They simply blazed away in a public place like a railway station. He was not satisfied that the battery-sergt.-major had exercised all the care that he might have done... The Coroner said the jury could consider whether they thought a charge of manslaughter might not be preferred against the sergeant and the men...

After conferring in private the Foreman announced that their verdict was "that death was due to misadventure"... They considered that the orders given by the battery-sergeant-major were inadequate. They expressed sympathy with deceased's relatives.

———————————◆———————————

In the early years of the war it was common practice for some U-boat commanders to assist torpedoed survivors with food and water, simple medical care and directions to the nearest land but the practice was forbidden in September 1942 after what became known as the Laconia incident.

The Laconia, a British troopship, was sunk in error by a U-boat commander who had not realised until it was too late that it was carrying over 1800 Italian prisoners of war (Italy and Germany were allies at that time). Four U-boats mounted a rescue attempt of British and Italians alike but came under attack from an American bomber despite clearly displaying Red Cross flags across their decks, and as they tried to pull the survivors from the water they narrowly avoided being sunk themselves. As a direct result Admiral Döenitz, commander of the German fleet, banned further 'good samaritan' rescues by U-boat commanders. In future, he ordered, survivors were to be left in the sea, declaring "rescue contradicts the most basic demands of the war - the destruction of hostile ships and their crews."

An Island family were lucky enough, if that is the word, to be torpedoed just before the ban came into place. Their subsequent account of the behaviour of the U-boat crew must have taken many by surprise...

December 12th, 1942.
SAVED BY GERMAN SUBMARINE.
ISLAND FAMILY'S AMAZING EXPERIENCE AFTER BEING
TORPEDOED.

Sergt. E. W. Littlecott, RAF, his wife (a Whitwell woman), and their five-year-old son David, arrived safe and well at Whitwell this week after an experience which makes both a pathetic and thrilling tale of adventure... Here is Mrs. Littlecott's story : "I went out to join my husband in Singapore with David four years ago and we had a happy time until the Japanese came into the war. David and I were evacuated to South Africa last December... and my husband joined us in August and we were all looking forward to the trip home... We were unlucky as somewhere off the African coast our ship was struck during the night by two torpedoes fired by a German U-boat. She immediately took a big list, which made it difficult to launch the boats, but the ship did not sink for a time and we were able to get away in a lifeboat... There were 84 of us on board, although the boat was only supposed to take 60, and the water and food had to be strictly rationed. We had two small drinks of water a day and a ship's biscuit.

Just as it was getting dark on the fifth day several German U-boats surfaced near us and the captain of one of them shouted to us in good English to come alongside. We were all taken on board the U-boat. The women and children were taken below and the men remained on deck. I didn't like going down into that maze of pipes and wheels but the commander and first lieutenant reassured us, and I must say they and the crew were real gentlemen. They gave up their bunks to us, gave us hot food, and generally made us as comfortable as they possibly could. I was worried because I had been separated from my husband, but we later found that as there was no room for the men in the U-boat they had been given hot soup on deck and then returned to the lifeboat which the U-boat took in tow for the night. The Germans dressed the wounds of several men who were injured by the torpedoes. The commander was a very nice man. He said he regretted that it had been necessary to torpedo our ship, that it was war, adding that we need not worry as the war was over as far as we were concerned. I thought by that remark that we should be taken to Germany, but evidently during the night they had called up a French cruiser and she appeared next day and took all the boat's complement on board and landed us at Casablanca. Before the U-boat appeared we had been trying to make for the land by sail, but it was a very slow business and what might have happened to us but for the German submarine crew does not bear thinking about. On reaching land we naturally thought our troubles were over, for the time being at any rate, but that was far from being the case.

We were badly treated by the French at the internment camp. The conditions were unhealthy and the food bad. We had mouldy bread, very little of it, and almost all the food they supplied was thin soup... Most of us had bad attacks of dysentery owing to the bad feeding and conditions. When I think of that camp the least said the better, but I shall have great difficulty in ever thinking kindly of the French again... I shall never forget the day when the American officer came and said we were free. The French guards actually had the impudence to ask us to tell the Americans that they had treated us well... I am thankful to say we are little the worse for our experience now...

THE WEEK'S NEWS.

OTTER KILLED. — Mr. Charles Trueman, of 8, Lake-hill, killed an otter in the marshy locality to the north of the golf links on Tuesday. His dog disturbed the animal from a clump of rushes and it sped to a near-by stream, down which it commenced to swim. Harried by its pursuers the otter tried to take refuge in a large iron pipe, but it was dislodged and dispatched.

A LUCKY BLACK CAT. — While the Missions to Seamen's motor-launch Nai Louis was visiting ships and distributing woollies to the crews on Tuesday those on board, as they drew close to a merchant ship lying at anchor, were surprised to see a black cat sitting on the ship's rudder. After rescuing the cat those aboard the launch made inquiries and found that the cat belonged to the vessel. The crew were delighted to get their pet back again. Apparently the cat had fallen overboard and had swam round to the stern of the vessel where it succeeded in climbing onto the rudder to await rescue.

A "MICKEY" POTATO. — A huge freak potato, actually four potatoes grown together and weighing 3½lb., giving a remarkable representation of "Mickey Mouse," has been sent to us by Mrs. Henderson, of West Cliff Lodge, Niton Undercliff. Dressed to make it more realistic, "Mickey" has been on view in our head office window.

RARE RATS AT NEWPORT. — A rat of unusually dark colour was recently caught in business premises in the centre of Newport. It was shown to Mr. Percy Wadham, who has identified it as a black or ship's rat, (which can be bearers of bubonic plague, which they transfer to man by means of their fleas), a breed which is very rare in this country.

1943.

ISLAND NOTES.

THREE BOYS WOUNDED. — The misfortune of three boys who were foolish enough to play about with mortar bombs left on the downs after military exercises, will, it is hoped, prove an effective warning to others not to meddle with any strange object they may find in these dangerous days. Seeing one of these projectiles among furze bushes on Christmas-day two brothers, Edward and Raymond Ridett, of Moons-hill, Totland Bay, aged 13 and 11 respectively, pelted it with stones until there was an explosion and they were both wounded, fortunately not seriously, in the face and legs. On Monday Gordon Spirit, aged 14, of Madeira-road, found another bomb. It was providential that he was not killed as a companion says he tried to unscrew the top before he threw it against a large stone. It then exploded, wounding him in the leg, and he is now in the County Hospital.

The reports about the massacre of the deported Jews in Poland which reached London last week from Polish underground sources, tell the most horrible tale of the war. It appears that these unfortunate people are now being moved further to the east under conditions which amount to slow, cruel, calculated mass-murder. Men, women, and children, already emaciated by starvation in the ghettos, are crammed into unheated cattle-trucks and sent without food on a journey of days or weeks, which few of them survive. More than a million human beings have already perished in this way...

———————————————◆———————————————

For most of the war the Isle of Wight was a prohibited zone and entry to the Island was restricted to those who had a valid reason for their visit. It meant the end of tourism for four years and in some instances prevented relatives from seeing each other. In the New Year of 1943 the ban was lifted for two months...

January 2nd, 1943.
VISITORS TO THE ISLE OF WIGHT.
BAN LIFTED FOR TWO MONTHS.
For a period of two months only - between January 1 and March 1, 1943 - people will again be able to visit the Isle of Wight without having first to obtain special provision but nobody will be allowed to take up permanent residence here. The news is contained in an announcement by the Ministry of Home Security... The removal of the embargo on the admission of visitors to the Island has given great satisfaction at Ventnor, and there have already been several inquiries for accommodation....

"Peterborough," of the "Daily Telegraph," comments "An easier time is in store for the firm but pleasant mannered official who stands on the gangway in Portsmouth Harbour and inspects the identity cards of all boarding the little steamer for Ryde. Some time ago my own reasons for visiting the Island were submitted to a close and patient scrutiny. There was an hotel opened in Ventnor, a little town greatly favoured by German visitors before 1914, where I was given an excellent dinner... The Islanders will welcome the sight of new faces."...

A member of the "County Press" staff was rung up on the telephone by a London daily paper and asked what the reactions of Islanders were to the waiving of the restrictions. The enquirer remarked "I suppose all the hotel proprietors are delighted," which shows how little many people on the mainland appreciate what the effect of the war has been on the Island's chief peace-time industry. Unfortunately the removal of the restrictions will have little or no effect in this direction at this time of the year, but the relaxation is welcomed as an indication that the authorities now consider that the Wight is no longer a gravely threatened outpost of England...

———————————————◆———————————————

If it seems undue space has been given over to accounts of bombing raids, nothing could be further from the truth. What appears in this book is but a fraction of the reports that appeared. For the best part of four years Islanders lived under a constant shadow, carrying on with everyday life in the knowledge that a bomb might kill them or their children at any moment. This report of the aftermath of a bombing raid on Ventnor is, like all the others, a sensitive, unsensational account of what had now become a part of life ...

January 23rd, 1943.

ISLAND COAST TOWN RAIDED.

An Island coast town (*Ventnor*) had its fifth and most serious air attack on Sunday. There were seven fatal casualties. Coming in from sea level, in one place severing telephone wires, two German fighter-bombers dropped two bombs in the main street... The attack was on the upper part of the High-street, where repairs to several properties had recently been carried out. The town was also attacked with cannons and machine-gun fire. One bomb fell on the lawn of a private house, wrecking it and killing two of the occupants, Mr. W. A. Phillips and his daughter-in-law. Mrs. Phillips, Sen., and other relatives were injured. A brewery was badly damaged. In transit this bomb cut through the gable of St Boniface Villa (Mr. O. Channing), doing much damage and ricocheted onto the back premises of Crawford's wireless shop, and finally exploded on the lawn. The other bomb demolished four or five residential and business premises. In flats above four people were killed, viz., Mrs. and Miss Norman and Mr. and Mrs. T. Gull. Their bodies were extricated with much difficulty. Mr. and Mrs. W. H. Harris, who lived opposite, had their premises totally destroyed... Mrs. Adams, wife of Mr. H. J. Adams a musical society's conductor, was killed on alighting from a bus, and a soldier in the street was badly injured... Two hotels were partly wrecked, and a Wesleyan church was further damaged, and a Spiritualist church had its windows torn away. A Co-operative store premises were badly damaged and a public library had its windows shattered. Mr. Gull was a driver for ARP services, and a great favourite with his colleagues. His body was not extricated until the following day. There was wholesale damage to shop fronts and windows, some caused by blast and cannon fire. The rescue and first-aid parties worked magnificently...

On Wednesday two German bombers, after causing damage in a neighbouring town (*Shanklin*), machine-gunned the district on passing the coast. Men working in a cemetery had narrow escapes from the bullets, which pierced the roof of a chapel and ripped off branches of trees...

—————————◆—————————

TOWN AND COUNTY NOTES.

HEAVY FINE FOR WASTING FOOD. — Phoebe Carpenter, of the Vectis Tavern, Cowes, was summoned for promoting food to be wasted... As a result of information received, the Food Executive Officer made an inspection of defendant's premises and found 7lb. of lard, 11½lb. of margarine and 13lb. of bread, in a refrigerator in a dirty condition and unfit to be eaten... Giving evidence defendant said for two or three months she had been saving the lard and margarine and friends had given her some for a 21st birthday party. She intended to make cakes, pastry, etc., with it. She was hoping to keep it until April, and put it in the refrigerator although she knew it was not working...

Fined £5, the Chairman saying it was a serious matter to waste all this good food in wartime.

Mr. John Roach, the well-known Island miller died at East Medina House, Newport, on Saturday... Mr. Roach was one of the first Island millers to adopt steam power in place of the water wheel. He installed one of the earliest steam power units, a beam engine, at Shide Mill, and until a few years ago, when the price of scrap made its disposal worthwhile, this old engine was an object of interest to all mechanically-minded passers-by on the footpath from Medina-avenue to Pan-lane, as it stood silent and rusty among the tottering walls of the mill. (March 6)

Central heating of offices, blocks of flats, hotels, theatres, and cinemas may be banned after March 31st. This step is now under consideration by the Ministry of Fuel.

Gandhi's three-week fast ended at 9.30 on Wednesday morning (5 a.m. BST), when his wife handed him a tumbler containing slightly diluted orange juice.

LONDON SHELTER DISASTER. — On Wednesday evening a serious accident took place near the entrance to a London Tube shelter, causing the death by suffocation of 178 people... There were nearly 2000 in the shelter when a middle-aged woman carrying a baby, tripped on a flight of steps leading down from the street. Her fall tripped an elderly man behind her, and he fell similarly and within a few seconds a large number of people were lying on the lower steps, completely blocking the stairway. Those coming in from the street could not see what had taken place and continued to press down the steps so that within a minute there were hundreds of people crushed together and lying on top of one another... By the time it was possible to extricate the bodies it was found that 178 had died and that a further 60 were in need of hospital treatment. (March 6)

———————————◆———————————

Hurdles, fence panels woven from hazel branches, were once a common sight in the countryside. Today, cheap and abundant fence wire has replaced them and they are rarely seen except as party pieces at craft-fairs or agricultural shows.

Mr Wells of Ryde had been a hurdle maker all his life. The world was a smaller place in those days and he had been known to many people in the district, and when he died his passing was marked in the County Press.

From their very first days the County Press were never superior or condescending and they were certainly never snobbish. They were as likely to publish the obituary of a road sweeper as they were that of a wealthy landowner. Always speaking well of working-class people, the short essays were never patronising but were generous, even affectionate, vignettes...

March 6th, 1943.
HURDLE MAKER'S DEATH
One of the small and swiftly declining band of Island hurdle and spar makers, Mr. Joseph Eli Wells, of 17 St. John's-road, died on Saturday after three weeks illness, aged 69. A native of Ryde he spent over 45 years following his rural occupation and worked chiefly in St. Urian's Copse, Bembridge. He was apprenticed to his father, the late Mr. John Wells, and in early days used to start from Ryde shortly after 4 a.m. and walk to Bembridge to commence work at daybreak. They would remain busy in the woods until dusk, with Sundays as their only rest day. It was only a few years since, that, owing to rheumatism, Mr. Wells made the daily journey to Brading by train and then tramped across the marshes. In winter he conscientiously remained in the copse engaged in his craft often not seeing another soul until he returned in the evening. He was, however, known to many people in the district who in the spring and summer went to the woods to gather wild flowers. He was more or less a self-educated man and a great reader. Visitors were often surprised at meeting one who from outward appearance and dialect was a typical rustic, yet could converse convincingly on a wide variety of subjects, politics by no means the least; he was a convinced Liberal. Mr. Wells was keenly interested in football and his one annual outing was travelling to London to see the final of the English Cup. Affectionately known as "Old Joe" he was a God-fearing man whose simplicity of life and contented disposition won him the greatest respect. The funeral took place on Tuesday… On the coffin rested a cross of wild daffodils, the first to bloom this spring in his beloved St. Urian's Copse…

———————————◆———————————

There are literally thousands of paintings and drawings of the Isle of Wight going back several hundreds of years and ordinarily, anyone looking for images of the Island in the past is usually spoilt for choice. However, there is one period that stands alone in being virtually undocumented. It is easier to find images of Newport High Street in the 1700s than it is to find them for the years 1939 to 1945.

A search for photographs of air raid damage will only ever turn up just a handful. There are two reasons; firstly, the taking of any photographs of war damage was prohibited and secondly, and perhaps the more effective reason, film for domestic cameras was virtually unobtainable. For that reason it is only the imagination that can provide a picture of Newport High Street after an early morning air raid in April 1943. The raid left the streets around the Guildhall covered in brick rubble, slates and piles of broken glass, which was all that was left of the shops which had been standing a few moments before, while up above, all four clock faces on the Guildhall tower had been blown out...

April 10th, 1943.
SOUTH COAST AIR RAIDS.
DAMAGE AND CASUALTIES IN MARKET TOWN.
An old borough and market town near the South Coast (*Newport*), which had fortunately hitherto escaped serious attention from enemy raiders, suffered badly in a low-level attack by a formation of eight fighter-bombers – M.E.109's - soon after daybreak on Wednesday. The enemy planes opened up with their

Issued in support of the National Food Economy Campaign by

ISLE OF WIGHT ELECTRICITY

Isle of Wight Electric Light & Power Co. Ltd.   Central Office : 14 Union Street, Ryde
Telephone No. 2231/2

SAVE THE MERCHANT SHIPS by avoiding waste and serving more home-grown foods. Patriotic meals can be made interesting—come to the next Kitchen Front Club meeting and learn how to get the best from home produce.

Help the National Effort by turning out your Old & Disused Gramophone Records.

Collecting Depots :

Messrs. Murdochs, Timothy Whites, or other Record and Gramophone Shops, or notify any of the above and they will be collected.

Proceeds are to be divided between the British Legion and the Great Ormond Street Hospital for Sick Children.

This space is kindly given by Messrs. Jolliffe Bros., Ltd.

TO THE WOMEN OF THE ISLAND

Your Services are urgently required for local work of National Importance.

Full and part-time employment is available near your homes.

Good wages.   Excellent working conditions.

Help the offensive by offering your services

NOW.

For details apply to your nearest Employment Exchange.

G. CANNING
The Model Bakery, WOOTTON.

Owing to two of my Staff being called up for National Service, and the inability to secure further suitable labour, I have been obliged to

CURTAIL MY DELIVERY

until more normal times.

On and after **MONDAY JULY 19th** I shall cease to call on my customers at **Kite Hill, Fishbourne, Binstead, Havenstreet, and Briddlesford,** but I have arranged with the Westminster Bakery to do so.

I wish to thank everyone for their past patronage, and trust the time will not be long before we can recontinue business.—Yours truly, G. CANNING.

cannon as they approached the town, still flying very low. Swinging round in a half circle each dropped a bomb and then raced away for the coast... The bombs were well scattered over the town, hence the damage both to business and private property was extensive and unfortunately there were casualties, including a number killed. The attack did not last more than a minute.

A bomb, which fell in a timber yard and killed three men, bounced at least 300 yards after first hitting the ground. It passed through the roof of the residence of Mrs. J. H. Flux, while she was in bed in the room immediately below, bringing down debris on her bed but she escaped injury. It then struck the ground in the next-door garden, ploughed up the soil for about three yards, passed through a concrete wall between the gardens and ricocheted over two roads and several houses before exploding in the timber yard... Another bomb hit a garage, passed out through the open doors, and travelled another 150 yards before it completely demolished and set fire to a large grocer's and provision merchant's shop and store. Most of the casualties occurred when terraces of houses in Clarence-road and Chapel-street were hit. In Clarence-road four houses were demolished and five occupants killed, including Mrs. Dudley and her six-year-old daughter Valerie...

A bomb passed through the roof of a cinema in the High-street, badly damaging the building, and then exploded in a big draper's shop next door, completely demolishing it and an electric light company's offices, and badly damaging the Guildhall and the offices of a county newspaper. There were no casualties here...

The most complete example of devastation was at a doctor's residence which received a direct hit. Hardly one brick of the large house remained on another, and unfortunately the doctor and a maid were killed. The doctor had been in practice in the town for some 25 years. His devotion to his noble calling, his outstanding skill, and unfailing kindliness and sympathy had won the affectionate esteem of a very large number of residents in the district... His death is an irreparable loss to the community.

The damage to the Guildhall was extensive. Practically every window was broken and the flying glass scarred the furniture and walls in the Court-room. Coping stones on the roof were dislodged, ceilings and plaster brought down, and the four faces of the clock in the tower smashed. Fortunately the valuable pictures in the Council-chamber escaped serious damage.

No words of praise can do adequate justice in commending the magnificent work of the Civil Defence Services and their military helpers who came so readily to their assistance, and of those responsible for the treatment of the injured and the comfort and feeding of the homeless and distressed. A special word of appreciation must be given to the W.V.S. and the Church Army, whose vans and other means of providing tea and refreshments for workers and sufferers alike, were a bright gleam in a very sad picture. Once more these women voluntary workers showed a wonderful spirit of unselfishness, pluck, and unremitting concern for the unfortunate, and these qualities were also exhibited by the public generally, who were courageous and cheerful in a very trying ordeal.

Mr. Humphries, the driver of a train approaching the town, showed admirable good sense and presence of mind. Seeing the enemy machines heading towards the town, he pulled up his train in a tunnel until the danger had passed.

On their way back, near a village on the coast, the raiders fired cannon shells at a herd of cows. Five were hit and two were so badly injured that they had to be destroyed.

————————————◆————————————

The Daily Mail had sent one of its reporters to investigate rationing on the Island. He interviewed the Mayor of Ryde who later confessed that he may have been a little loose with some of his answers, and then he scuttled back to Fleet Street to write his article.

When it appeared its contents were roundly dismissed by the County Press. The Daily Mail article was, it declared, nothing more than "frothy fiction" and "a mischievous tissue of falsehoods"....

April 17th, 1943.

A "DAILY MAIL" SCREED.

Saturday's "Daily Mail" contained two-thirds of a column of frothy fiction written by a gentleman with a hyphenated name, who pretends to have found the Island "flowing with plenty." None will be more surprised than residents of the Island both at what this visitor found and what he failed to find here. Island users of razor blades will read with incredulity that a local hairdresser at once on request handed him three, and they will certainly judge that the visiting scribe has a Nazi-like habit of reckless lying when he states that he "found razor blades in almost every shop." Equally surprising is the statement that he saw no queues for fish or anything. He could have seen them gathering daily both for fish and cakes in Newport and other Island towns had he looked for them. Mainland readers of the "Daily Mail" will have gained the idea from this mischievous tissue of falsehoods that prime Isle of Wight lamb is easily obtained on production of food coupons, although it has been absent from our shops for at least two years. Of course, having found such a plethora of good things, the writer of the article must seek a reason for it and so he has had to invent one. It is that when everyone in the summer of 1939 fully expected the speedy advent of war, the caterers of the Island laid in in such stocks of supplies that they have lasted for nearly four years.

————————————◆————————————

ISLAND NOTES.

VISITORS TO LEAVE ISLAND BY SATURDAY NEXT. — A police notice in an official advertisement warns all visitors in the Island who do not come within the permitted categories of the regulations to leave by Saturday next, April 10th. Failure to do so will render them liable to prosecution.

Dance. — A banana and a lemon were prizes at a dance held in East Cowes Town-hall on Saturday... These rare fruits were given by Mrs. Milmore, of 3 Cross-street, on condition that the proceeds of the competition should be divided between the Red Cross and the East Wight Air Training Corps.

£4 FOR A BOTTLE OF BRANDY. — The Chairman said that during the recent emergency the stock of brandy in the Forest House hospital ran out, and they had to pay £4 for a bottle of Martell's Three Star. That was an awful price to have to pay, and he hoped if any residents in the Island had any brandy they would remember the hospitals... The present price of the best brandy was £5 a bottle. The county clerk kindly obtained one for the hospital at £4. When it was required for a patient fighting for life they could not use cheaper brands.

ORANGES FOR CHILDREN. — During the next few days a consignment of oranges from South Africa is expected to arrive in the Island. Two pounds may be purchased on the production of a child's ration book. After they have been on sale five days any that remain may be purchased by adults.

------◆------

The Post Office had recently announced that in future their official abbreviation for the county of Hampshire would be "Hants." Critics denounced the decision saying that the abbreviation should surely be "Hamps" but the Post Office appear to have done their homework...

June 26th, 1943.
HANTS FOR HAMPSHIRE.
To the Editor of the I.W. County Press.
Sir, - It would be preferable if the critics of the use of the designation "County of Hants" made sure of their grounds before embarking on a terminological crusade. The word "Hants" is not a modern Post Office abbreviation, nor can it reasonably be regarded as being horrible or vulgar; it is simply a shortening of one of the ancient names of the area which, in some very old maps, is designated "Hantshire." In the legal documents we shall continue correctly to use the customary terms "County of Hants," or, alternatively, "County of Southampton."...

------◆------

The sacrifice of the nation's railings was seen at the time as a patriotic necessity but figures released after the war revealed that it had been little more than an empty gesture* and it was further revealed that much of the nation's railings were not re-cycled at all but had simply been dumped at sea, in the mouth of the Thames Estuary.
It was becoming clear from events on the Island that a deeply flawed scheme had already started badly...

July 3rd, 1943.
ALLEGED UNFAIRNESS IN TAKING IRON RAILINGS.
Mr. Fowler said he was acting as spokesman for the many people who had approached him on the matter of the way the removal of iron railings had been carried out. He desired to make it clear that no one who had complained objected to giving up anything if it was absolutely necessary for the war effort;

------

* The removal of London's railings, for example, amounted to only 1500 of the 10 million tons of scrap metal recycled during the war.

what they complained of was the unsatisfactory manner in which the railings had been removed and a lack of impartiality. People were told that the railings were badly needed by the nation, and that the only railings which would be exempted were those of the distinctly artistic or protective nature. That seemed quite reasonable, but those conditions had not been observed at Ryde. People on one side of a street had had theirs taken, yet exactly similar railings on the other side still remained. Those who had lost railings were naturally asking why the others had not been taken. It was disquieting to hear that many of the railings taken were still lying about on dumps in the Island... Many had wondered at seeing an advertisement in a daily paper recently, offering surplus iron railings for sale from Government stocks, if they were their railings... There had also been much lack of consideration of people's property in removing the railings... He knew of one case where a gateway had been removed causing considerable inconvenience to the owner because of the undesirable use of the passage at night where the irritation had been increased by the fact that the gateway was placed in the owner's garden after removal, and it had remained there 18 months; in fact, it was still there... Mr. Cooper said the way salvage in the Island had been generally dealt with was most unsatisfactory. Several truckloads of scrap remained on the railway for months, and it was only after repeated representations had been made by Mr. Gardener (local superintendent of the Southern Railway) that the material was eventually shipped. Mr. Gardener said that was so. He knew of scrap lying in dumps for over a year. The whole position with regard to its disposal from the Island was appalling. If the government wanted it so badly as they indicated when the appeal for metal was made, surely they should have made arrangements to collect it... Mr. Fowler said there were at least 400 tons of scrap metal rusting away on a dump at Ryde, yet they took people's railings. - It was agreed that a representative of the Ministry of Works should be invited to meet a sub-committee of the Chamber to discuss the matter.

ISLAND NOTES.

To the Editor of the I.W. County Press.

Sir, — "Heard in camera." Surely this is becoming a habit with our Council, or is it that some of the senile old gentlemen, whose period of usefulness has long since passed, are trying to emulate the importance of the highest authorities? It would appear to be a poor Council which cannot disclose its actions publicly and trust its "*County Press.*"... It would be well for the taxpayer to back up the Press in demanding an end to these secret sessions... Let us hope that when the lads return and see what has been built up in their absence and what they have been fighting for, they will steadily take it to pieces and see what makes it 'tick.' Much of the ticking will be due to 'back-patting.' I am, Sir, yours faithfully, "FIAT LUX."

BAN AREA LETTERS CENSORED. — Every letter written inside the newly banned South Coast belt is to be censored by security officers at bureaux set up

Order NO. 1464961908

phone 01675 481006

John Knibb International
AirGunSpares.Com

BSA 675 MS 2700
750 HS 3000
~~£300~~ Diff

St 650 - 800 3000
3200
840 - 1250 3900
~~5000~~

BELGRAVE ROAD • VENTNOR • ISLE OF WIGHT • PO38 1JJ
TELEPHONE: 01983 852186 • EMAIL: ENQUIRIES@ROYALHOTELIOW.CO.UK
WWW.ROYALHOTELIOW.CO.UK

2.2

2.2

1.1

100

5.5

120

130

~~2100~~

2 1/2 hrs

2.

2.00

100000

3

97

5

THE ROYAL

on the fringes. Writers of "careless letters" may not get a warning before action is taken against them. It is permissible for people living inside the area to write to friends outside telling them of the extent of the ban but no mention must be made of any military movements. A certain proportion of telephone calls will also be censored.

POINTS FROM CORRESPONDENCE. — Mr. M. Gray, of Holmbush, Alexandra-road, Ryde, writes suggesting that it would be a good thing if half the number of dogs in Ryde were exterminated.

AN EXPENSIVE VISIT. — John Nixon, engineer, of Loughborough, pleaded guilty to unlawfully entering the Island. – P.W.R. Hillier deposed that when defendant came off the Lymington ferry at Yarmouth he presented an identity card bearing a mainland address and when witness asked him for what reason he was visiting the Island he replied "I am on holidays at Bournemouth, and I came over to visit my son who is at a private school in Freshwater." Asked for the address and telephone number of the school, he replied that he did not know. After further questioning he admitted that he had told an untruth. He then said "I am sorry, officer. I thought it would be a good excuse to get to the Isle of Wight on a visit." He told defendant he would have to leave by the next ferry, which he did. — The Chairman said they considered it a grave case for a man of defendant's position and education to get into the Island in that fraudulent manner. He would be fined £5.

––––––––––––––––◆––––––––––––––––

On a quiet summer's evening during harvest time, Kern Farm at Alverstone suddenly became part of the war...

August 21st, 1943.
SOUTH COAST AIR RAIDS.
TWO ENEMY PLANES DESTROYED.
On Monday evening there were probably more spontaneous cheers raised in the Island at one moment than ever before. Thousands of people were watching the anti-aircraft fire directed at a flight of several enemy planes returning from a reconnaissance raid over the mainland. They were flying at a great height, appearing as small dots in the sky to the naked eye, but the A. A. gunners soon got the range and one burst into flames and, blazing fiercely, fell into the sea off the east of the Island. Another spiralled down badly damaged, pieces breaking away as it fell. The wreckage of this machine, a Messerschmitt 109 fighter, was scattered over a wide area at the east end of the Island... The fuselage descended at Kern Farm, Alverstone, where the farmer, Mr. R. H. Barton, and his father were engaged in harvesting work... They heard gunfire and saw parts of the plane drifting down to earth. Their attention was focused on what appeared to be a wing descending to the north of the farm and they failed to see the fuselage until a sudden swish and crash announced its arrival close to where they were working. A pedigree Friesian bull was tethered in the field on a six yards rope and as the fuselage approached it sprang out of the way in the nick

This must be a NO TRAVEL EASTER!

THE Prime Minister has left us in no doubt as to the magnitude of the effort being made this year.

Every truck and carriage, every mile of railway track, every engine is needed to carry troops, war workers and war materials.

There is no room for holiday travel. You should stay at home this Easter and leave the Railways free for the war.

ONLY GOODS LOADS ARE GOOD LOADS

BRITISH **RAILWAYS**

RAILWAY　EXECUTIVE　COMMITTEE

Any dawn now this man may face his supreme test—the liberation of the enslaved peoples of Europe. Then, the ships and trains and trucks which normally distribute our coal will be used to rush supplies to the fighting men. That's why we must cut our use of coal, gas and electricity *now*, for existing stocks of coal are precious —*they may have to last a long time*. Fit fire bricks wherever possible, lag hot water tanks and pipes, go easy with hot water — small things compared with the job of our fighting men but essential if we are to give them all the backing they must have.

We must SAVE FUEL for Battle!

Issued by the Ministry of Fuel and Power

There'll always be MAZAWATTEE

Issued by THE MAZAWATTEE TEA Cº LTD

RATS on your farm MUST BE DESTROYED

At any time, rats are pests. To-day they menace the nation's vital food supplies. Destroying them is no longer just a sport; it's serious, urgent war work that must be done, and done thoroughly.

The rats must be killed before next harvest. Write to your War Committee now

ISSUED BY THE MINISTRY OF AGRICULTURE AND FISHERIES

of time, the wreckage actually falling over the plug to which the animal's rope was attached. Meanwhile, a blazing petrol tank came to rest between two ricks in another field about 100 yards away.... The engine of the plane came down at Hill Farm, Brading, and other parts at Nunwell and Ashey. Mr. Barton said his wife saw the body of the pilot dropping through the air to the west of the farm, and it was subsequently recovered near the Kern plantation. The airman, who must have been killed instantaneously when the plane was hit, was a young man of about 21, wearing an Iron Cross, and was still strapped into his seat...

———————————◆———————————

TOWN AND COUNTY NOTES.

Mr. G. R. Brigstoke has very kindly sent us two old I.W. Race cards for races on "the new course at Whippingham" on dates in August 1842 and July 1843. This explains the naming of the straight piece of road where the East Cowes road branches from the Newport-Ryde road as "the Race-course."... The owners of horses bore well-known Island names, like Mew, Carter, Allen, Hearn, Harvey, Buckell and Wavell...

ISLE OF WIGHT LACE. — A wedding dress of Isle of Wight Lace, about a hundred years old, is to be exhibited in drapery establishments in each Island town. A charge of 1s. will be made to view and the entire proceeds will be given to the Prisoners of War Fund... The manufacture of Isle of Wight lace was once a flourishing industry at Newport. It was carried on at what was known as "Nunn's Lace Factory" at Broadlands from about 1826 until 1870. The lace was noted all over Europe for the beauty of its design and the fineness of its texture.

THE COUNTY COUNCIL STILL HUSH-HUSHING. — We feel very strongly that the County Council are pursuing a very unwise, not to say dangerous, hush-hush policy. On August 4th a special meeting of the Council was held, and reporters were excluded. After two hours' discussion the Press were informed that the business had reference to an officer of the Council and that it was not then possible to make any statement, but that one would be made later. The "County Press" cannot be accused of impatience, but we certainly expected after a lapse of two months that the promised statement would be made ... yet not a word is forthcoming. We were told that the Council had nothing to hide, but at the end of September they are still hiding what, on the face of it, must be an extremely important matter... (October 2)

———————————◆———————————

Newport cattle dealer,"Fred" Biles, was well-known across the Island, the name Biles still being well-known in farming circles today. In an age when self reliance and resourcefulness were possibly more in evidence than today, he had left school at the age of eight and living on his wits had successfully made his way in the world despite not being able to read and write.

A man of the times in every sense of the word, and seemingly a popular one at that, when he died the list of mourners at his funeral was one of the longest for some time...

September 18th, 1943.
DEATH OF MR. "FRED" BILES, OF NEWPORT.

Members of the Island agricultural community, and many other friends made during nearly half a century as a cattle dealer, will regret the death at his residence, Trafalgar Cottage, Newport, on Tuesday, of Mr. Charles Henry Biles, known to all his acquaintances as "Fred."

For over 40 years, until serious illness caused his retirement in 1937, Mr. Biles was a very prominent and popular figure at the Newport and mainland cattle markets, and his business was extensive. Although handicapped by very meagre schooling - he commenced work at the age of eight and could neither read nor write, except to sign his name - Mr. Biles had remarkable business aptitude. He carried in his memory all the details of his deals on the busiest days so that they could be recorded by his wife in the evening. He was a sound judge of horses and cattle, revelled in striking a bargain, and his dry wit in banter with the auctioneer or vendor provided entertainment for others attending sales... A member of a Gunville family, Mr. Biles had a hard boyhood, but showed a flair for buying and selling from his earliest days. When he left school at the age of eight he started selling watercress, flowers, and chalk for whitening doorsteps, and was always proud of the fact that by the time he was 10 he had saved £32, which he lost by lending it to someone who never paid him back! This incident indicated that trait in his character which won him the warmest esteem of those who knew of his generosity. Beneath his rather brusque manner lay a very kindly heart. No appeal for a case of need ever failed to meet with a generous response from him, and most of his charitable acts had the added merit of being unostentatiously done. Examples of this are that he regularly sent gifts in kind to add to the comfort of the old people at Forest House, he was always to the fore in raising money for worthy causes, such as the Red Cross in the last war and the County Hospital, and when a live pig was required for a competition at local fetes, etc., or a subscription list was opened for anything to promote the enjoyment of children, he was always ready to respond. The experiences of his early days left him with an intense desire to improve the lot of others, especially children, and his discriminating generosity is gratefully remembered. He had borne a long illness with characteristic fortitude.

———————————◆———————————

THE WEEK'S NEWS.

QUARR MONK EXECUTED BY NAZIS. — Many friends, especially in Roman Catholic circles in the Island, will be deeply distressed to learn of the untimely and tragic death of the Rev. Dom Jacques Kerssemakers, one of the monks of Quarr Abbey, which occurred in Holland at the hands of the Gestapo... About six months previously he was having breakfast when the Gestapo arrived at St Paul's Benedictine Abbey, Oosterhout and took him to a concentration camp. No reason was given for this, but it is thought that he must innocently have said something which displeased the Germans. Nothing more is known beyond the fact that he has been executed, it being generally thought that he was shot. Dom Kerssemakers was in his early fifties...

VENEREAL DISEASES. — At the beginning of the year 48 patients were under treatment for venereal diseases and during the year the number attending the centre for the first time was 85. In addition, 117 patients, of whom 107 were Service patients, continued treatment after a previous treatment at other centres... It cannot be too strongly emphasised that treatment is confidential, is free to all, and no sensible person should lose time in having adequate treatment.

MATERNITY AND CHILD WELFARE. – Fifty three midwives were in regular practice on the Island, of whom two were employed at Parkhurst Institution... There were 1074 expectant mothers seen by the district nurse midwives and the midwives paid 1903 visits to 436 expectant mothers...

35 YEARS IN THE POST. — On Monday a post-card, which was dispatched from Southampton on June 20, 1908, was delivered to Miss Brading, High Park, Ryde... It has been over 35 years in the post. The recipient's friend wrote "Just a line in case your sister forgot to tell you, I shall arrive about 3.30." As the card does not say when, it may still not be too late!

1944.

ISLAND NOTES.

ALVERSTONE MILL. — In view of the decision of the vendor, Mr. H. A. Guy, to withdraw from negotiations, the Council have instructed their solicitors to return the contract for the purchase of the Alverstone Mill property to the vendor's solicitors. The Council were offered the property and water rights some months ago and decided to purchase with a view to the development of the Sandown water undertaking... The purchase was to be subject to the lease of the mill to Messrs. Leigh Thomas, the Island millers... The discontinuance of boating on the picturesque mill stream, which would have been a consequence of the Council's utilisation scheme, aroused considerable public resentment...

A BADGER COMES TO TOWN. — The badger is one of the most elusive of our wild animals... yet one was discovered well inside the boundaries of Newport on Monday. Mr. S. Smith, who carries on a second-hand motor and spare parts business in the yard of the Plough Inn at Nodehill, Newport, noticed that several rabbit skins hanging near a shed in the garden had been torn and partly eaten. He attributed this to dogs until Monday when, on going into a shed, he saw a strange animal peering out at him from among some straw in the corner. It proved to be a full size female badger. It was destroyed.

A few weeks ago Islanders showed practical sympathy by readily responding to an appeal for bananas for a sick Newport boy. Last week a Ryde advertiser asked for another rare fruit – lemons - for a girl seriously ill... and by

Wednesday 10 small brown paper parcels had arrived at our Ryde office. Altogether 20 lemons were received from donors across the Island. Some donors preferred to remain anonymous, and the majority sent touching little notes.

ITALIAN PRISONERS HELP TO SAVE BLAZING THATCHED COTTAGES. — Italian prisoners engaged on farms in the district, who happened to be passing in a lorry on their way back to their quarters, lent valued assistance to the occupiers, neighbours, and firemen in saving the contents of Laburnum-cottages, two old semi-detached thatched cottages at Wellow, when they were badly damaged by fire on Wednesday evening. The prisoners volunteered to help and, in the words of a witness of their action, "worked like Trojans."

———————————◆———————————

Until now, income tax collection in Britain had been carried out on a twice-yearly or annual basis but the demands of war required a more frequent and efficient way of collecting taxes. In 1944 the phrase "Pay As You Earn" entered the English language when overnight the P.A.Y.E. system was introduced, and at the same time the tax net was broadened to include anyone earning over £100 a year.

In 1939 there were 10 million taxpayers; by 1945 the number had grown to 14 million...

January 29, 1944.

"PAY AS YOU EARN"

The Income Tax Act, 1943, brings the "Pay As You Earn" system into operation as from April 6th and employers will have the responsibility of deducting the appropriate amount of income tax from each payment of wages or salaries. The Act applies to all weekly wage earners and to salaried workers with earnings up to £600... The employee's income tax will be calculated by the employer each pay day on the cumulative total of wages, and the amount to be deducted will be ascertained by the employer from official tax tables supplied by the Inspector of Taxes... Every employee known to be liable to income tax will receive this month a coding notice, which will show the allowances to which he is entitled and the appropriate code number representing those allowances...

———————————◆———————————

Women stepped into the shoes of the men who had left to join the services just as they had done in the First World War. They worked in factories and offices and they carried out invaluable work on the land. To this end, the government set up the Women's Land Army, provided the recruits with a uniform and a small wage, and for the duration of the war thousands of women worked in the fields. For some of them it was a life changing experience...

March 25th, 1944.

SKILFUL ISLAND W.L.A. DAIRYMAIDS.

On Wednesday, at Old Park Farm, St Lawrence, 14 members of the Women's Land Army*, most of them young women who had had no experience of such work before the war, underwent the Women's Land Army dairymaids' efficiency test and they all passed with flying colours. Members who pass the test are entitled to wear a special badge and to a higher rate of pay. They have to reach a high standard of efficiency in milking on the most modern cleanliness lines and are orally examined in general knowledge of dairy practice and the management of cows... It is wonderful how many of these girls have adapted themselves to dairy work. Some were shorthand typists, shop assistants, or domestic servants before joining the W.L.A., but from both health and interest points of view they far prefer their present important national work, hard as it is, with early rising, long hours, and very few holidays. They looked the picture of health, and lipstick and other forms of feminine make-up were pleasingly absent. As to adaptability there was no better example among them than Miss D. Pedrick, of Tapnell Farm, Freshwater, who obtained over 90 per cent of marks and who had the distinction of being adjudged the best milker. Two years ago she was a shop assistant at Freshwater Bay and was too nervous to enter a field where there were cows!...

TOWN AND COUNTY NOTES.

With a wink at the other passengers, the smart young man said to a yokel in the corner seat: "Let's have a game of riddles to pass the time. If I ask one you can't guess, you give me half-a-crown, and I do the same to you." "All right," said the yokel, "but as you're better educated, do you mind if I only pay a shilling?" The young man agreed, and the yokel, invited to begin, asked: "What animal has three legs walking and two flying?" "I don't know," replied the young man. "Here's half-a-crown. What's the answer?" "I don't know either," said the yokel. "Here's your shilling."

THREW A MILLS BOMB. — A 15-year-old office boy pleaded guilty to tampering with an article of military value. P.C. Meadows said that in consequence of an explosion off the Western Gardens. Ryde, on February 27, he saw the accused... who said a Marine Commando left a Mills bomb and a box of detonators at his house. He pulled out the pin and threw the bomb as far as he could towards the sea and ran behind a water tank and the grenade went off, a fragment of the bomb striking a person in the back, but fortunately causing no injury. — The boy's mother said he was very good at home... The magistrates dismissed the case under the Probation of Offenders Act.

---

* So successful was the W.L.A. scheme that the National Farmers' Union who were originally opposed to it, actually campaigned for its retention when it was eventually disbanded in 1950.

D-Day was just nine weeks away. By now there was a confidence in the air that the war was beginning to turn in Britain's favour and the phrase 'post-war' began to appear more and more in County Press articles.

Part of that confidence stemmed from the fact that Islanders were privy to the classified information that a huge military operation was about to take place because the preparations for what became known as D-Day were being carried out right on their doorstep. Since the beginning of the year troops had been arriving on the Island in large numbers and now the Solent was full of warships of every description. As part of the preparations orders were issued restricting movements along virtually the entire east and south coast of England.

For anyone left in any doubt as to what was going on, the last line of this next report suggests that the War Office were confident of the outcome...

March 25th, 1944.

EXTENSION AND VARIATION OF COASTAL BAN REGULATIONS.

Special orders issued by the War Office this week for operational reasons impose, with certain exemptions, a complete ban on visits to a coastal belt 10 miles deep extending from the Wash along the east and south coasts to the Scilly Isles. The orders come into operation on April 1st. In certain respects the new orders vary the conditions under which people are now allowed to enter the Island; for instance, individual permits to enter will not be given by the Police; all residents over 16 in the prohibited areas are required to carry their identity cards; and the former ban on the use of binoculars and telescopes is reimposed... The order prohibits Islanders visiting the adjacent mainland without special permission, and no indication is given as to the conditions under which permits will be granted. Those who will be permitted to enter the banned areas include persons on necessary business; those visiting parents, visiting children; visiting near relatives who are seriously ill; attending college, or school; or entering to live with relatives... Anyone entering the banned areas may be made to justify the visit at any moment. Unauthorised people will be turned back, and will be liable to a fine of £100, or three months' imprisonment, or both. Police and Service authorities cannot undertake to answer inquiries from people wanting to know if they are allowed to enter the banned areas... The War Office states that it is essential that the ban should be strictly enforced for the time being, but it will be removed at the earliest possible moment, and it is hoped that it will be the last to be imposed.

ISLAND NOTES.

THE NEW COASTAL BAN REGULATIONS. — One of the numerous problems which have arisen this week from the new regulations is whether Islanders are allowed to travel to Portsmouth, Southampton, and other places within the banned area on the adjacent mainland, irrespective of the new regulations. The answer is "No."

SOUTH COAST AIR RAIDS. — Early on Tuesday morning an enemy machine, flying very low in and out of cloud, machine-gunning at times, was

eventually shot down. It was a Junkers 188... Its five occupants were killed when the machine crashed. (April 20)

BUNCH OF BANANAS. — A bunch of eight good-sized bananas, given by the officer son of one of the members, was the prize in a competition at the Conservative Club on Saturday in aid of the British Red Cross.

SOUTH COAST AIR RAIDS. — During another enemy air attack on Monday night the raiders met with the most intense barrage yet experienced in a seaside resort.... Though no human casualties were reported, two farmers on whose land bombs were dropped suffered considerable loss of stock. Four cows and two horses were killed, and six cows injured. At a farmhouse occupied by Mr. and Mrs. A. E. Blow and their two children windows were broken and the ceiling came down. Mr. Blow lost the only two horses belonging to the small farm and one cow was killed and six injured. (May 27)

———————————◆———————————

Serial numbers on recovered fragments of German bomb cases had recently provided vital clues as to where they had been manufactured, allowing the Allies to target the factories. Efforts to make the most of this unexpected source of information were being hampered by members of the public who were gathering up fragments to keep as souvenirs...
APPEAL TO SOUVENIR HUNTERS.
DON'T TAKE AWAY BOMB FRAGMENTS.
In an advertisement in this issue the authorities warn the public that it is an offence to pick up and retain fragments of enemy bombs or other missiles, and we have been asked to appeal to the public not to keep such articles as souvenirs. By so doing they may very likely be withholding from experts knowledge of the utmost value in defeating the enemy. For security reasons it is not possible to disclose exactly how such pieces of bomb fragments, etc, may supply our experts with information of vital importance, but it is so, and the ordinary person can have little conception of how valuable such information may be... People who find parts of bomb casings in places where they are not likely to be seen by the official searchers are asked to hand them to the police. Should they be of no value to the intelligence service, and the finders express a wish to have them as souvenirs, they will be returned to them...

———————————◆———————————

By now the impending invasion of Europe was an open secret and the news had even reached Berlin. Only the landing place remained a secret...
May 6th, 1944.
WAITING.
That we must be near the very critical point in the world war is very evident from the signs of the times. The Germans themselves have been telling us that many vessels are assembling off the Island coast ... and whether a matter of

days or weeks, we all realise to some extent that gigantic effort, organisation, and skill are now needed... With the characteristic bravery of the British spirit, we, living in the Island, which has never looked more beautiful than to-day, can courageously go forward each day, singing "The lark's on the wing; The snail's on the thorn; God's in His heaven - All's right with the world."

May 13th, 1944.

THE HUSH BEFORE THE STORM.

At a time when the whole world is waiting with bated breath for the curtain to go up upon the greatest adventure of all time-the invasion by the Allies of the Continent of Europe-the Conference of the Commonwealth Premiers has shown to a watchful enemy a calm unified front... We are assured that all the Premiers are confident that the plans of the Allies will free Europe and the world from the manacles of Hitler's robbers, although the Germans will oppose with military might and with all the political and economic treachery of experts... In the uneasy hush before the storm we are comforted and confident in the unextinguishable certainty that our Forces will do their duty.

------------------------◆------------------------

History was made in the early hours of May 30th, 1944 although no one knew it at the time. A lone Focke-Wulf fighter-bomber flew over Godshill and dropped a bomb which demolished part of the disused Bridgecourt Mill and that bomb would later go down in history as the last bomb from a manned plane ever to fall on the Island* and the Focke-Wulf itself became the last enemy plane ever to fly over the Isle of Wight.

Also unknown to Islanders at the time, another historic milestone had just been passed. Two weeks before, the Isle of Wight had experienced what was to be its last ever air raid...

May 20th, 1944.

SOUTH COAST AIR RAIDS.

The enemy renewed his activity in night raids over the south and west coasts during the weekend.

On Sunday night in scattered raids, during which 15 machines were shot down, a bomb was dropped on a clifftop near a farm occupied by Mr. J. Phillips, the concussion damaging the windows of the farmhouse and one of the buildings.... The German wireless stated that Bristol was the chief target for the night.

A much more severe attack was made on a south-coast holiday district on the following night *(East Cowes)*. Chandelier flares were dropped which brilliantly illuminated several parts of the coast and a sharp attack with high explosives followed during which there was considerable damage to property and a number of casualties, some fatal... Bombs fell in two neighbouring towns that have not been raided since being heavily attacked two years ago. One caused fatal casualties. This fell on a row of houses in the centre of the town, demolishing six. Nine people were killed and about half a dozen injured were

---

* The last enemy activity over the Island actually came seven weeks later when a flying bomb landed harmlessly on Ventnor golf course on the night of July 14/15th.

taken to hospital... Among the killed and missing are Mr. and Mrs. J. Cook and their three children, the youngest a baby of eight months, Mr. and Mrs. W. Adams, Mrs. Moore, and Mr. Polley. Mr. Polley, with other people was in a shelter at the rear of one of the demolished houses when they noticed a small fire in the garden which is believed to have been a flare dropped by one of the raiders. In company with Messrs. E. Moore and T. Skinner he left cover to put out the burning object with a stirrup pump when the bomb fell and the three men were buried by the collapsing houses. When they were extricated by members of the rescue party Mr. Polley, who still had the stirrup pump on his shoulder, was found to be dead... Two people lost their lives when a bomb fell in a residential area of another town *(Shanklin)*. It fell at the junction of two roads, demolishing property in the immediate vicinity, and doing considerable damage to houses nearby. The occupants of the most badly affected premises were buried beneath the debris for some hours, and two of them were dead when the rescue party extricated them.

A resident of one of the towns that suffered was strolling round surveying the damage and stopped in front of the ruins of a demolished house. While he was meditating upon the scene of destruction he noticed a starling with a worm in its mouth fly down and perch itself on the rubble. He kept his eye on the bird, which, after looking round for a moment or two, disappeared into the debris. This roused the sightseer's curiosity, as he could not understand why the starling should want to take a worm into the ruins. On investigating he was amazed to find a starling's nest full of young which must have come down with the house without being injured.

———————————◆———————————

Women were working in factories, offices and on the land, and now they were finding employment on the railways. A County Press representative called at Shide Station to watch their newly appointed signalwoman at work. She could certainly pack a lot into 10 minutes....

June 3, 1944.

FIRST ISLAND RAILWAY SIGNALWOMAN.

Mrs. Ivy Smith, aged 28, of 53 Clarence-road, Newport, has the distinction of being the first fully qualified signalwoman to be employed on Island railways...She and a woman colleague ably controlled Mill-hill station, Cowes, under the supervision of Stationmaster Hill until early in this year, when Mrs. Smith was chosen for training as the first Island Railway signalwoman... On April 11 she was appointed signalwoman in charge of Shide Station. That station is no mere railway halt; its working is complicated by a level-crossing on the main Newport-Sandown Road, and by a considerable branch line traffic from the Pan chalk pit, which supplies the Medina Cement Mills. Working eight-hour shifts alternately with the stationmaster she tackles her important task with the utmost confidence, and an ever ready charming smile for passengers. Changing the levers which control the distant signals is a man-sized job but Mrs. Smith has become so adept at it that she appears to do it as easily as she brushes back the fair hair from her forehead before gripping the lever.

Confidence without hurry marks the performance of her numerous jobs, such as working the intricate electric "tablet" train control system, swinging the heavy crossing gates to and fro, changing the tablet-holders with the drivers as the trains run into the station, issuing and collecting tickets, keeping the accounts, and, last but not least to a good railwayman, keeping the station clean and tidy.

A "County Press" representative admiringly watched her on Whit-Monday afternoon during a busy 10 minutes. In that time she issued tickets to over 50 passengers, opened and closed the level-crossing gates twice, took telephone messages from Newport and Merston, and passed an engine through en route for Merston and a passenger train for Sandown and Ventnor. She had to move "at the double," on the hottest day of the year, but when the hectic 10 minutes were over she was still unruffled, looking smart and very capable in her blue uniform trousers and white shirt. She had discarded her uniform jacket and cap because of the heat. Yes, Ivy Smith is a very fit and happy woman; at least as happy as a young wife can be when her husband is a prisoner of war who has been in the hands of the Japs since October, 1941... As Mrs. Smith remarked: "One of the reasons why I like this job is that it keeps me so busy that I just haven't time to think about it while I'm at work."

———————————————◆———————————————

THE WEEK'S NEWS.

THE FLYING BOMBS. — The "Daily Mail" leader on Friday said the policy of silence on the flying bombs is to be continued, at least for the present. This is the government's decision, and we think it is a wrong one. Details of how many bombs land and how many are shot down would be useful to the enemy, and no one here would wish them to be given. But we can see no objection - rather the reverse - to publishing casualty figures and to giving facts conveying the true state of public morale*. (July 1)

COUNCIL CLERK'S HOME BOMBED. — Mr. Frank W. Hefford began his new duties as clerk to Cowes Council on Monday. On Wednesday, however, he was temporarily called away by the news that his home had been badly damaged by a flying bomb and that his wife and child had been injured and were in hospital. (July 8)

DRIVING A FARM CAR AT NINE. — Master John Morris, the nine-year-old son of Mr. and Mrs. D. L Morris of Kitbridge Farm, Newport has been doing a man's job during the haymaking. His father was astonished when Johnny offered to drive an old Buick car, used for hauling a hay rake. He was more

---

* The V1 flying bombs, pilotless jet engines, were launched from a base at Calais which was destroyed by the invading allies in September 1944. That same month the V2 rocket-powered bomb was introduced, launched from mobile bases. Of the 10,000 V1s fired at England, around a quarter crashed before reaching land, and over half the remainder were shot down.

astonished when Johnny climbed into the driving seat, started up the engine, and drove gaily away. The boy had become so well versed in his father's actions when driving with him as a passenger that he had not the slightest difficulty in managing the car. He has driven the Buick at every opportunity throughout the haymaking.

For the first time for four weeks there was no enemy air activity over this country on Wednesday night. Flying bomb attacks were resumed on Thursday. (July 15)

STARTLING NEWS FROM GERMANY - ATTEMPTED ASSASSINATION OF HITLER. — The startling announcement was made in the B.B.C news broadcasts on Thursday night that an attempt had been made on the life of Hitler, who escaped with bruises and burns. The news stated that the attack was made by a group of rebel army officers and that a bomb had burst six feet from Hitler. It wounded about a dozen of his staff, three being seriously injured, one of whom died...(July 22)

———————————◆———————————

The D-Day invasion had been successful and as a direct result there had been no air raids for over two months. The Island felt able to relax a little...

August 12th, 1944.
HOLIDAYS AT HOME.
RYDE. — Ryde has this week experienced its nearest approach to a pre-war Bank-holiday in the last four years. True, there was still an absence of the usual great influx of visitors from the mainland, but residents normally engaged in peace-time catering for them took full advantage of the opportunity to become happy holidaymakers themselves. Not since August, 1939, has the children's corner on the western Esplanade presented so animated an appearance. It was crowded the whole day long with adults and juveniles, who bathed, paddled, and played games with a much freer abandon, and the turnstiles at the promenading pier most certainly had not clicked so frequently as this year. Trains and buses brought large contingents of people from Newport and other parts of the Island to enjoy a real summer day by the sea, and everywhere an infectiously gladsome spirit was in evidence. Thanks to the holidays-at-home programme of the Corporation there was a number of attractions.

———————————◆———————————

A few weeks later events in Europe only added to the growing sense of optimism when the military authorities announced the ending of the ban on entry to the Island, a possibility they had hinted at some weeks before...

August 26th, 1944.
COASTAL BAN REGULATIONS LIFTED.
THE ISLAND FREED AFTER FOUR YEARS.
The War Office announced yesterday (Friday) that the ban on entry to the

coastal belt of England from the Wash to Lymington, including the Isle of Wight, had been lifted. The announcement was accompanied by the warning that the removal did not mean that there is any less danger from enemy missiles, and the areas involved would still remain regulated areas in which everyone over 16 must carry identity cards, no one is allowed to use binoculars, telescopes, or cameras without police permission, and the military may still retain or impose local restrictions... After patiently enduring restrictions for over four years, with the exception of one short break from January to April, 1943, Islanders will breathe a sigh of relief at this most encouraging sign of the good progress of the war... Long-parted friends will be able to meet again but the picture is not so rosy when the larger and more important question of the revival of the Island as a public pleasure and health resort is considered. Any immediate large-scale influx of visitors is unfortunately out of the question. Islanders know to what a great extent many of the seaside towns have suffered as a result of enemy action, particularly during the sneak day-time raids of a year or so ago. Some hotels and boarding-houses have either been destroyed or badly damaged. Many others have been occupied by the military ever since the dark days following Dunkirk, and they will need a lot of renovation before they can reopen their doors to visitors. The proprietors of many have had to seek a living by working in munitions factories, and not a few have had to realise assets necessary for their business which it will be impossible to replace without Government help, which, apparently, will not be immediately available. In short, an industry which has lain dormant and grown largely derelict through nearly five years of war cannot possibly be restored to full activity for many months. The Island, therefore, cannot hope to reap any great benefit this year by the removal of the ban...

Long-suffering Islanders were at last able to travel to the mainland free of any restrictions and the following week many of them took advantage of their new found freedom...

September 2nd, 1944.
THE BAN ON THE ISLAND LIFTED.
The lifting of the ban on the Isle of Wight did not produce the rush of visitors which was experienced by mainland resorts, but rather gave the inhabitants an opportunity of becoming visitors to the mainland. After four weary years, in the last 12 months of which Islanders have been virtually prisoners in their own area, many residents from all parts of the Island took their first trip to Portsmouth for a long while and once more enjoyed a shopping tour in the Naval port. Ryde Pier Head presented something approaching a pre-war travel scene, and Mr. T. F. Thompson (stationmaster) and his staff had great pleasure in dealing with the increased numbers... One feature giving great satisfaction was the absence of that wearisome ferry check, the product of so much irritation and many pathetic scenes.

The first midday steamer carried a greater number of civilian passengers than usual and it was the same with all the others that followed. The travellers all looked very happy, rejoicing in the knowledge that at last one severe cut had been made in the restrictive cords which had bound them. At Portsmouth the number anxious to make the trip to the Island was very large. The 10.55 steamer left filled to capacity, 150 would-be passengers being left behind to queue for the next boat at about 1 o'clock. As the boats from Portsmouth were full, so those leaving Ryde for Portsmouth were filled to capacity, but after a busy day in the shopping centres the visitors found it something of an ordeal to accomplish the return journey. It was necessary to queue for long periods and then many could only find standing room on the boats.

◆

THE WEEK'S NEWS.

CASUALTIES AT THE FAIR. — There was an alarming incident at the Fair Ground at Seaclose on Thursday evening. Miss Foster, a young woman from Gurnard, apparently lost her nerve while in the chair-planes and must have released the safety chain. She was hurled out of the chair when it was revolving at high speed and might have received fatal injuries but for the fact that her body struck people on the ground below...

TOMATO GROWING IN THE ISLAND 50 YEARS AGO. — *To the Editor of the IW County Press.* Sir, — In view of the development of the tomato growing industry in the Island it might be of interest to your readers to be told of tomato growing 50 years ago. At the age of 10 I planted a row of tomatoes across my father's garden here in the orchard. I trained them to wattle sheep fold hurdles which I was then able to buy at 1s. each, carriage paid from Newport. The plants were given me by an old gardener friend of my father's, only costing me a 7 mile walk after 5 o'clock to get them. I grew a fine crop, but only sold a few as there was a widespread belief at that time that they caused cancer. This belief also applied to bananas in those days. This may interest some of our large growers in the Island to-day and remind them of the struggles of the early pioneers. — I am, Yours Faithfully, ARTHUR WILLIAMS. The Orchard, Gatcombe.

FIRST ISLAND POLICEWOMAN. — The first Island policewoman to do ordinary police duty is Constable Mrs. E. Duncan, of Newport. She has been doing patrol duty in the Newport district for a fortnight. It is probable that other policewomen will soon be appointed. (September 9)

ISLAND AIR RAID CASUALTIES. — From June 1940 until February 29th of this year bombs were dropped from enemy aircraft on the Island on 116 occasions, and the official numbers of casualties are as follow: Killed 199, injured treated in hospital 249, injured treated at first-aid posts 293. The heaviest losses were at Cowes, Shanklin, Ventnor, Newport, and Ryde. (Oct 28)

THE HOME GUARD STOOD DOWN. — A War Office announcement states, "The government have decided that the Home Guard is no longer required to perform active duty. The Force is, therefore, to be stood down with effect from

November 1st, 1944... No decision has yet been taken to disband the Home Guard, and until the Force is disbanded it will remain in reserve and all members of it will remain liable to recall should circumstances render such action necessary..."

Throughout the war, letters home from the front had been subject to strict censorship which meant that by the time a letter appeared in the County Press, a rare enough event in itself, it had been pared to the bone and invariably included little more information than the fact that the writer hoped to be home soon. Suddenly, out of the blue, two letters appeared in the same issue providing detailed accounts of events on the front line; something previously unheard of...

November 11th, 1944.

COWES TROOPER'S EXPERIENCES IN ITALY.

How he was assisted by a German medical orderly in Italy after his tank had been knocked out and he had been wounded is described in a letter from Trooper Robert Reed, Royal Armoured Corps, to his parents, Mr. and Mrs. F. A. Reed, of 1 Hillview, Newport-road, Cowes. Trooper Reed who was wounded on September 22nd is in hospital with serious wounds to his hands and legs...
He writes: We were ordered one night to prepare for an advance on the following day to establish a bridgehead over a river. We moved off at 2 am, got to a ridge before the river and started to shell the enemy's positions on the opposite bank. They returned the fire so that it was practically impossible for us to move. We were ordered to get across at all costs. Our three tanks were the lucky ones that had to do it. One tank broke down before it had moved 200 yards, leaving two of us. Off we went and I shall never forget as long as I live the number of shells which came round us, but we got through and advanced 200 yards and halted. We blasted away at the enemy's positions for between one and two hours and when I turned round to throw some empty shell cases out of the disposal hatch what we had been fearing, came. We received a direct hit from a bazooka, a weapon carried by the German infantrymen. The shell went through the front of our tank into the turret and our ammunition started going off and pieces of shrapnel went into my legs and through my hands. Immediately the ammunition went off, the tank caught fire and I didn't have the power to switch the engine off or turn the petrol off as my hands and legs were numb. I managed to get out just in time and crawled into a ditch. While lying there I had the biggest surprise of my life when a German medical orderly came through the hedge and gave me two shots of morphia, put shell dressings on my wounds and carried me into a house where my mates were and left us. My mates, like myself, had the wind up, for there we were in a house in Jerry's lines with our tanks outside blazing away. This gave him what he wanted as something burning told him there was something unusual there and he started shelling with 210 mm and knocked the house about something wicked and we thought our end was coming any minute. It was a good job we were under a stone horse trough in this house and we lay there from 1.30 until 6.30 that

evening when the remaining tank drew up outside and rescued us. That is all I can remember for I must have lost consciousness from loss of blood. I woke up in a hospital. Two of my mates also suffered as the wireless operator got slight wounds in the face and the sergeant got concussion from falling bricks. The other two, my co-driver and gunner got away without a scratch (lucky fellows)."

———————————◆———————————

TOWN AND COUNTY NOTES.

The new drug penicillin, which has had such marvellous results in the Services, has been made available for the treatment of civilians, but the quantity is limited, and it can only be obtained for a case of saving a life when other treatment has proved ineffective. A case of this nature arose this week at St Mary's Hospital, Newport. Dr. J. Fairley (county medical officer) immediately obtained a supply from Portsmouth and from the time it was first used the patient has shown steady improvement.

PIER DE-REQUISITIONED — It was reported that the War Department relinquished possession of Sandown Pier on November 30th and the Council had resumed letting the Pavilion for entertainments.

The recently issued government facts and figures speak eloquently for themselves. They tell of our efforts in trying times, when nothing but the will of the British people stood between the free world and dire disaster.... By the issue of these breathtaking figures the world can now appreciate that our nation has made unprecedented sacrifices. Scarcely one home in Britain has not been churned up by the war. No fewer than 22,500,000 civilians have been removed from their homes and callings since 1939; 7,100,000 adult women have been mobilised and the Armed Forces this year numbered 4,500,000... Our contribution to the war far exceeds that of any other country. (December 2.)

REPAIR OF COWES BOMB DAMAGED HOUSES. — Mr. A. Holmes said that during November, 12 houses at Cowes had been rendered reasonably habitable, leaving about 290 still to be repaired. The average number of operatives engaged on repairs was 124. (December 23)

———————————◆———————————

Tropical fruits of all varieties were rarely seen on the Island during the war years so when the Island receieved a consignment of oranges in December 1944 an allocation committee was put in place to oversee the fair distribution of the boxes of fruit amongst the Island's traders.

Surprisingly perhaps, the person appointed chairman of the committee was a trader himself and there were vigourous protests when it became known that he had allocated himself a generous 50 cases of oranges ...

December 2nd, 1944.

DISSATISFACTION AT ORANGE DISTRIBUTION.

The Mayor of Newport received a deputation of local fruit retailers on Wednesday to protest against the manner of distribution of the eighth allocation of oranges in the borough. It was stated on the traders' behalf that it had been unfair, and they felt it up to them to have the method stopped. In one case a local trader had received 50 cases of fruit, far above what others had received.

A member of the deputation, in reply to the Mayor, said it was understood that the trader was chairman of the Allocation Committee. It was felt that the position should be occupied by someone not in the trade. Other members with interest in the business should not serve on the committee. The same position might arise over the allocation of nuts at Christmas.

Another trader said he understood from the trader himself that he had 39 cases of oranges allotted at one of his shops and 11 at another...

The trader alleged to have received 50 cases had been asked to attend that meeting, but had replied that he would not do so on any account. It was pointed out to him that it was only fair that he should be there to defend himself, but he would not come.

1945.

In a touching little article a poignant few lines pointed out what the war had meant for the children unfortunate enough to have grown up during the war...

January 6th, 1945.

CHRISTMASTIDE CELEBRATIONS AT NEWPORT.

On Wednesday evening the parents of five families, who wished to give their young people a New Year's treat, decided to pool their resources and give a joint party in the Unity-hall, Newport. With an inspiration which almost amounted to genius, the organiser decided to engage a Punch and Judy exhibition. The result was electrifying.

Owing to five years of war, none of the toddlers had ever seen the renowned pair, with their faithful dog Toby. They sat open-mouthed, drinking in every word of the dialogue, and shrieking with laughter as Punch belaboured all and sundry with his staff. It was a scene to delight the heart of Charles Dickens, the champion of Christmastide celebrations, but it was also a reminder of what the war has cost our children in hours of lost happiness.

◆

ISLAND NOTES.

RYDE. — Mr. Harry Brickwood, J.P., of The Orchard, Bembridge, was a member of a brains trust at the Portsmouth Rotary Club on Tuesday. To a question "Why do people live in the Isle of Wight?" Mr. Brickwood replied, "Once one arrives at Ryde Pier all sense of time goes. I think the Island is the only unspoiled country within handy distance of Portsmouth. I would go there every time for rest and repose. But not for high life - there is none."

Widespread interest has been taken in the sale this week by auction of a large portion of the contents of Mottistone Manor, by direction of Lord Mottistone, who, as we recently announced, is closing the Tudor and Elizabethan wings of the ancient house because of heating and other maintenance difficulties. Nearly 1000 articles were offered for sale including furniture, silver, and books. The disposal attracted buyers from all parts of the south of England and the interest aroused can be gauged by the fact that 900 catalogues were sold prior to the sale. (March 10)

ALVERSTONE SHOOTING TRAGEDY - LODGER COMMITTED ON MURDER CHARGE. William J—, 41, an unemployed carpenter, was charged with the murder of Reginald H—, a farm labourer, aged 52, with whom and his wife J. lodged at Burnt House, an isolated bungalow at Alverstone. J— had been living with deceased and his wife for the last 12 years and had lodged with Mrs H— before her marriage. The deceased was a man of somewhat violent temper... (April 21)

The captain of a steamer took on two hands, one a Kirkaldy man without a written character, the other a man from Dundee possessed of abundant documentary evidence as to his honesty. They had not been long at sea when they encountered rough weather and the Dundee man, when crossing the deck with a bucket in his hand, was swept overboard. The Kirkaldy man saw what had happened and sought out the captain. "D'ye mind yon man from Dundee that ye engaged with a fine character?" "Yes," said the captain, "What of it?" "He's awa' with your bucket."

V2 TRAILS SEEN FROM NEWPORT. — One morning last week, when the atmosphere was extraordinarily clear, several people in the Newport district saw, far away in the eastern sky, the smoke trails of rocket bombs speeding towards some unlucky spot in southern England. The trails stood out distinctly against the background of the flush of dawn. (March 31)

THE WORLD'S GREATEST ODYSSEY.— We are nearing the end of an odyssey without any parallel in history of mankind. Victory will soon be ours... The wonderful war news this week has uplifted all our hearts. At long last the collapse of Hitlerite Germany is imminent. Soon we shall have to apply ourselves to the many problems of making a real peace in Europe. There must be no forgetfulness, no complacency, no passing off of selfish expediency as justice. Above all, let there be no forgetfulness... (March 31)

———————————◆———————————

One of the Island's most familiar landmarks was the huge boulder known as "Chad Rock" which had sat for years alongside the Niton to Blackgang road until it was displaced by the landslide of 1928. The impressive rock had managed to survive the landslide and now, as the war came to an end, a County Press journalist set out to see how it had fared this time ...

April 7th, 1945.
"CHAD ROCK" NO MORE AT BLACKGANG CHINE

Vectensis writes : On Easter Monday it was my delight to re-visit that charming spot, Blackgang Chine. It was a relief to find that it has escaped damage by enemy action. The fell work of the blue slipper clay has gone on, but fortunately cliff falls have not affected any of the chief attractions of the place, and the work of restoring the chine to its former beauty is well in hand. Quite a number of visitors, including some American naval officers, were among those enjoying its pleasures. Walking along to the scene of the great landslide in July, 1928, my impressions were not so pleasing. Nature had healed many of the wounds before the war, but the area has been used by the military as a training ground, and it now lies torn and shattered again, with gaping craters, blasted trees, and splintered rocks. More regrettable still is the fact that the big rock by the roadside, on the western lip of the chasm caused by the landslide, which for centuries had been an impressive landmark, has gone. "Big Rock," or "Chad Rock" as it was known locally, was formerly the outstanding object in views of the Undercliff at this point, and its loss will be regretted by thousands who have visited the district. Apparently it was made the victim of an experiment with explosives, and it has been shattered out of all semblance to its former noble shape - a wanton and almost sacrilegious act when there were so many other rocks about on which to test explosive power.

The County Press reminded "foolish girls" where their duty lay in respect to Italian prisoners of war held on the Island...

April 7th, 1945.
ISLAND GIRLS AND ITALIAN PRISONERS OF WAR.

We regret that it has again become necessary to refer to the relations between a very small and irresponsible class of Island girls and Italian prisoners of war. If they are encouraged the Italians cannot be blamed, but these foolish girls must remember the duty they owe to our national honour and our gallant soldiers overseas. The Italians are here because they are prisoners of war. Amongst them are excellent workers and men of good repute but as a nation they are "working their passage." From a national standpoint, they stabbed France in the back when she was down and they then stabbed Germany in the back when the German star began to set... Some of our men who have been prisoners of war in Italy compare their treatment at the hands of the Italians very unfavourably with the treatment in German camps. On the other hand, many of our men who have escaped in Italy speak highly of the risks taken by Italian families to help them. Let us therefore treat Italian prisoner of war collaborators with dignity, firmness, and respect insofar as individually merited, but immodest familiarity should be sternly rebuked by all who see instances of such conduct.

THE WEEK'S NEWS.

DIM_OUT ENDS ON MONDAY. — Mr. Herbert Morrison, the Home Secretary, announced that on Monday, except in a 5-mile strip round the coast, all black-out and dim-out restrictions are to be lifted. It will not be necessary to draw blinds or curtains in homes, shops, offices or factories. So far as black-out regulations are concerned, every light available may be switched on fully but the regulations regarding waste of fuel are still in force and any excessive use of light may lead to prosecution. Shops will be able to use only the amount of lighting they have had up to now. Advertising signs will still be prohibited. Street lighting need no longer be dimmed... (April 21)

THE SOUTHERN RAILWAY AND THE ISLAND. — Speaking to the Chamber of Commerce, Mr. C. Graseman of the Southern Railway said the railways, as well as the hotels, would suffer from shortages of equipment for some time to come, and would have shabby coaches and shabby hotels. They were still under government control and there were not enough boats to go round. They believed in private enterprise and did not want to be nationalised ... He could not offer them much at present except sympathy and hard work.

PHOTOGRAPHER'S DISTINCTION. — The highest award in the photographic world has been bestowed on Mr. F. W. Beken, who has been made a fellow of the Royal Photographic Society of Great Britain. Mr. Beken has received this honour chiefly on account of his beautiful yachting pictures which have gained him a world-wide reputation. His study of the late King George V's famous racing cutter Britannia was reproduced on the 13 cent stamp of the Silver Jubilee issue of Canada.

A TASK WELL DONE. — Mussolini shot; Hitler dead (according to the Germans); Berlin captured, and the fighting over in Italy and Austria as a result of the surrender of the Germans. With the news of these dramatic events crowding upon us this week, and as the war with Germany draws to its inevitable end with the possibility of the total collapse of Germany before these lines are read, it is not surprising that an item of home news this week has passed comparatively unnoticed, viz., the stand-down of the Civil Defence Services... We believe we are expressing feelings of all inhabitants of the Island when we say to them a very sincere "Thank you!" (May 5)

———————————◆———————————

As the war came to an end, so did censorship. The County Press was now free to relate in some detail the loss and destruction suffered...

May 5th, 1945.

ISLAND WAR CASUALTIES AND DAMAGE.
214 KILLED - NEARLY 11,000 BUILDINGS DAMAGED.

With Germany at last impotent to make further attacks, and in no position to benefit from the information, it is now possible to give details of the effects of local air raids. The enemy subjected Islanders to all forms of aerial attack except

Lost and Found, Inquiries, &c.

LOST, between Newport and Yarmouth, child's blue Sun Suit, Madeira work; reward given.—Hutchinson, Castle View, Carisbrooke. Newport 2819.

LOST, Sunday August 15th, Canoe Lake, silver Wrist Watch, brown leather strap; reward.—Finder please return Police Station, Ryde.

£5 Reward. — Lost, long, thin, green-cloth Aquascutum Raincoat.—The above reward will be paid to anyone returning it to Major R. S. Savile, J.P., Bembridge.

LOST, on August 6th, between Shalfleet House and Newport, small steel Bench Vice.—Finder rewarded on returning same to Newport Police Station.

LOST, on August 16th, approximately 6 p.m., between South-street and the Quay, Yarmouth, gold Ring set with diamouth; reward. — "Wren" Berwitz, Gordon House, Yarmouth.

Personal.

I am well and happy and would like to see you, Hazel.

RECEIVED letter August 16th; freely forgiven; longing to see you soon.—Mother.

After the war is over,
When all our boys come home,
Travelling will be so easy
No need to groan or moan.
Punctual will be the driver,
Unharassed will be his mate,
For we'll have enough staff to serve you
After the "Berlin" date.

THE

SOUTHERN VECTIS

OMNIBUS COMPANY

V2's, but, looking back, we can all be proud of the way Vectensians "took it."

From the night of June 16th, 1940, when the first German bombs fell on the downs behind Blackgang Chine, with no worse results than a few broken windows, to July 14th, 1944, when the last enemy missile, a flying bomb crashed on the Ventnor golf course with no worse results, 1748 high explosive bombs and mines, including six flying bombs, descended on the Island in 125 raids, to say nothing of hundreds of thousands of incendiaries.

They killed 214 people (92 men, 90 women, and 32 children), seriously injured 274, inflicted minor injuries on 320, and destroyed or damaged 10,873 buildings, the vast majority being dwelling houses.

The Island was a dangerous spot. It was one of the nearest points on our side of the Channel to the enemy occupied seaboard of France. It was also a natural bastion defending the great ports of Southampton and Portsmouth. It was obvious that no effort would be spared to defend those important objectives from air attack, and it was only natural to expect that the Island, a vital part of those defences, would have its full share of enemy attention.

Apart from the very heavy raid on Cowes on the night of May 4th/5th, 1942, and the tip-and-run daylight raids which followed later, sadly knocking about the towns of Ventnor, Shanklin, Newport, and Ryde, and further damaging Cowes, most of the bombing was indiscriminate. It was done by planes bound for other objectives whose crews quailed before that terrific Solent barrage, turned tail, and jettisoned their loads anywhere to facilitate their getaway. Happily many of these bombs fell in open spaces, and kindly nature has wiped out almost all traces of them, but very few of the towns and villages in the Island escaped damage and casualties.

---◆---

With the end of the war came local celebrations but they were decidedly lower key than those that had marked the end of World War I. In 1918 almost the entire County Press edition marking the end of the war was given over to the news whilst by contrast, the coverage of the end of the second war occupied just over one half of one page. While it is true, as this report makes abundantly clear, that there certainly were enthusiastic celebrations across the Island there was equally clearly a less muted response in some quarters.

"No organised celebrations were held at Freshwater or Totland"... "The celebrations in Sandown-Shanklin and the neighbouring area were remarkably restrained"... "Thanksgiving rather than boisterous merriment marked the celebrations in Ryde"... "At Godshill, apart from an evening service in the Church there were no celebrations"... "The day passed off very quietly at Bembridge... "

May 12th, 1945.

VE-DAY IN THE ISLAND.
THANKSGIVINGS AND REJOICINGS.

Not since November 11, 1918, when the Armistice ended the fighting in the last great War, have such scenes of public rejoicing and thanksgiving been seen in the Island as those which followed the announcement by the Prime Minister (Mr. Winston Churchill) on Tuesday afternoon of the total surrender of the

German armed forces. Repeated postponements of the historic announcement may have been a little disappointing and bewildering, that they at least gave the people time to prepare to celebrate the great news when it was eventually announced. By that time every old flag and piece of bunting had been found and displayed, and not only the towns and villages, but almost every little cottage in the country had its patriotic decorations.

Although, quite naturally, the young folk and the men and women of the Services let themselves go in rejoicing, more sober and thoughtful thanksgiving for final release from the anxieties and perils of nearly six long years of war, shared by civilians as never before, was the dominating feature of the public reaction to the end of hostilities in Europe. Thanksgiving services in the churches and other places of worship were everywhere largely attended, and many preferred to stay at home to hear on the wireless and moving speech in the evening from their King, and the broadcast descriptions of the wonderful scenes of rejoicing in London.

The ringing of bells, the crack of fireworks, the glow of bonfires, the flashing of searchlights (no longer concentrating on enemy raiders but waving joyously), the cheerful gleams from lightly-curtained windows all added to the memorable celebration of May 8th, 1945, which will be one of the most notable dates in history.

ISLAND NOTES.

SERVICE GRATUITIES. — The basis for gratuities is as follows:- Ordinary Seaman, Able Seaman, Private, Lance Corporal, for each month of service - 10/-

.... Warrant Officer (R.N.), Sub.-Lieut., Lieut. (Army), Flying Officer, for each month of service – 30/-.

... Admiral of the Fleet, Field-Marshal, Marshal of the RAF, for each month of service – 75/-.

For five years' service, therefore, gratuities range from a Private at £30 to a Field-Marshal at £220.

FAREWELL TO FREE FRENCH NAVY. — The French Chasseur Base established at Marvin's yard, Cowes, in the summer of 1941 is closing down. Shortly these valuable little ships with their gallant crews who have become familiar to the people of the yachting port during the past four years, will be returning to France, from which they escaped when the country fell in 1940. To mark their impending departure a full and final parade of the crews still remaining at the base took place on Monday.... (June 30)

AN ISLE OF WIGHT AMATEUR CINE SOCIETY for 8, 9.5, & 16mm. ENTHUSIASTS. Will owners of Cine Cameras or Projectors and others interested in the formation of the above, please communicate with L. W. Jennings, 6 Clarence Road, Newport, or R. E. Hannam, 1 Queen's Cottages, Old Rd., East Cowes.

ALVERSTONE SHOOTING TRAGEDY. Mr. Casswell, defending, accepted that William J— had shot Reginald H— during a violent struggle at Burnt House, Alverstone, but submitted that the case was a story of most lamentable accidents, and the shot was, as accused had said from the first, unintentional.... The jury were absent for half an hour and returned with a verdict of not guilty of murder, but guilty of manslaughter... Yesterday (Friday) his Lordship sentenced J— to six months' imprisonment, and said that but for his very good character it would have been longer.

Three Gates Road at Cowes had been closed since 1943 to enable the runways of Somerton aerodrome to be extended across the road into the fields on the other side.

Then, as now, it was a busy main road and the closure caused a great deal of inconvenience but along with many other hardships it had been tolerated since it was seen as being a vital part of the war effort.

But that was then, and now that the war was over the residents of Cowes wanted their road back...

July 21st, 1945.

COWES-YARMOUTH ROAD OBSTRUCTION.
PROTEST MEETING AT NORTHWOOD.

Arising out of a question put to Sir Peter Macdonald, MP, at Cowes during the recent election campaign as to the reopening of the Three Gates-Somerton road, a meeting of parishioners of Northwood was held in the School on Thursday, about 130 attending. The Chairman said that the road had been closed since 1943 under Defence Regulations in order to provide for the extension of Somerton Aerodrome. As the extension was intended for an emergency landing field for D-Day aircraft the necessity had passed. Very few aircraft landed there now, and all knew the inconveniences and unnecessary expenditure which had been caused and mainly affected residents of Pallance Road, Wyatts-lane, and the Horseshoe district. The bus fare from the Horseshoe to Cowes had been raised from 2d. to 4d., owing to the longer journey the buses had to make. The closed road was one of the most historic in the Island... Sir Peter had recently stated that if this road was not reopened an alternative road would be built. Mr. Nicholson (late of the Ward Estate) thought that that statement could be taken as a foregone conclusion that the road would not be reopened. The parish was being "umpired out." Somewhere, at some time, and by somebody, it had been decided that the road was not to be reopened... These official bodies had made their plans without consulting the inhabitants. The road was, for the people of Cowes, the main road to Yarmouth and the mainland. Residents in outlying districts were affected, especially farmers, many of whom still used horse and trap for milk delivery. The road was six miles long and it was just in the sight of its destination, when it petered out into a cul-de-sac... The whole of Northwood was penalised... A protest committee was formed and a petition of protest was to be sent to the Home Secretary...

Islanders had been well and truly in the front line during the last six years, suffering many hardships and now, quite reasonably, they were looking forward to enjoying the benefits of peace time. However, no sooner was the war over when there were complaints that visitors from the mainland were gathering up all the goods in local shops to take back home with them, leaving little on the shelves for the locals...

September 8th, 1945.

COMPLAINTS ABOUT VISITORS.

To the Editor of the IW County Press.

Sir, — I deny no one their right to a well-deserved holiday, but I do think it is very hard that we residents, many of whom have had no holiday and been in the front line for six years, should have to suffer for the influx of visitors who have flocked to the island. The food is stripped from the shops before we, who have homes to tidy, can queue at the shops. The worst offenders are those who come over for the day with empty baskets and go back laden. One man was heard openly to boast that he had taken buses round the Island and had collected 1000 cigarettes and three dozen eggs! and we can get none. Day visitors should not be allowed at this time. The best months of the year are ruined for us residents. If we are lucky enough even to get on a bus, more often than not we have to stand in great discomfort. We pay the rates, we support the shops during the quiet months, and we are pushed aside for visitors who are rough, rude, and many dishonest. Several shopkeepers have told me nothing lying about on show is safe. They, like us, admit they shall be very thankful when the holidays are over.

I am, Sir, yours faithfully, "THE RESIDENT WORM WHO TURNED."

The letter touched some raw nerves ...

September 15th, 1945.

MORE COMPLAINTS ABOUT VISITORS.

To the Editor of the IW County Press.

Sir, The complaint last week of "A Resident Worm Who Turned" will be endorsed by many other "worms," whether they turn or not. The locusts, as they are called by some of us, are both omnivorous and insatiable. They are not content with a share; they want it all— and grab it if they can. A well known lady resident, seeing on the counter in a grocery shop a dozen Cornish pasties, decided to purchase a couple, but immediately in front of her was a "locust," who told the assistant he would "take the lot." The complacent assistant took the money, he took the pasties, and went away no doubt pleased with himself... but Ryde is only now enduring for two or three months what many inland towns suffered all the year round for five or six years. Loud and bitter were the complaints of housekeepers in the towns that swarmed with evacuees at the rapacity of "visitors" who "took the lot" before other people could put on their outdoor clothes. There is no remedy except such as shopkeepers can apply. "Under the counter" may have its good points as a policy after all...

I am, Sir, yours faithfully, "ANOTHER RESIDENT WORM THAT TURNED."

To the Editor of the IW County Press.

Sir, I wish to endorse very heartily the sentiments of "The Resident Worm Who Turned." ... I learned this morning that visitors have been making parcels of foodstuffs bought in Ryde and elsewhere in the Island, and posting them away. They jostle one in the street, line up in queues outside the British Restaurant long before the local young ladies serving in shops can do so, and thereby get the choice of a hot lunch while the shop assistants have to put up with whatever is left. When a friend of mine remarked at the length of a sausage queue the other day, mentioning that there were obviously many visitors in it, a stranger turned round and said haughtily, "Well, we keep you all the winter." Who, may I ask, kept the shops going all through the war, then? I'm delighted to find that several of the shopkeepers I deal with are at last realising our position, and now tell these scrounging strangers that goods are for "residents only."... It is to be hoped that before they come here next summer they will have learned a little better manners and give a thought to the residents. They see the flowers in the Esplanade Gardens, and the streets lighted, and they seem to think there has been no war here... It seems dreadfully hard that as soon as the war is over and there are some signs of cheer in the town we can't have the place to ourselves for a brief space, instead of these "locusts" being allowed to overrun our little town, buying up everything, and pushing us about to get it. Like the "Resident Worm Who Turned," I, too, shall be very glad to see the back of the last visitor.

I am, Sir, yours faithfully, VERA PARKIN. 50 George-street, Ryde.

THE WEEK'S NEWS.

ISLAND C.O.'S ORDER RESENTED. — Yarmouth figured prominently in the national newspapers on Monday and Tuesday as the result of the disclosure that Lt. Col. Grove of the R.A.S.C. Unit stationed there had issued the order "NCOs and other ranks will not walk arm-in-arm with members of the opposite sex, whether they are in Service dress or otherwise." As quite a number of the 1600 men in the unit have brought their wives to the district, and they were "checked" by the regimental police for walking arm-in-arm even with them, the order has aroused great resentment. A "Daily Mail" correspondent alleged that incensed wives of the men tore down copies of the order which were posted in Yarmouth...

PRESS CENSORSHIP ENDS. — Censorship of newspaper material in this country and of Press cables abroad ended on Sunday. British Press censorship during the war was maintained on a voluntary system, under which editors agreed to submit for censorship at the Ministry of Information any matter they considered of possible value to the enemy. This system was set up by agreement between the newspaper organisations and the censorship authorities, and left to editors' discretion regarding publication subject to Defence Regulations and advice issued by censorship. (Sept 8)

"Can you really cure V.D., doctor?"

I'm often asked that question — and I'm very glad to have a chance of answering it, because there is still a widespread impression that venereal diseases are incurable.

The answer is fairly simple. If either syphilis or gonorrhœa is treated in its early stages by a doctor who is skilled in this branch of medicine, failure to cure is rare. Of course, if anyone puts off being treated for any length of time, cure may be more difficult, and irreparable damage may be done to various parts of the body before the disease is checked.

A V.D. case is rather like a fire. The fire brigade finds it much harder to put out a fire that is well alight before it arrives, and it certainly cannot repair the damage already done.

If gonorrhœa is allowed to run on unchecked, important tubes in the body may be narrowed or completely blocked, with serious effects on fertility in both sexes.

If syphilis is allowed to continue until the blood has become positive to certain tests it takes much longer to cure than it would under early treatment — and by early treatment I mean as soon as the first signs appear. However, even if syphilis is allowed to run on until the heart or the nervous system is affected, it is usually possible to stop the mischief from getting worse, though we cannot always repair the serious damage already done. We can't give people new hearts and nervous systems.

The most important thing about V.D. is to avoid the loose living that spreads it. For those who have the slightest suspicion that they have V.D., it is vital — both for their own sake and for that of their fellow human beings — to get advice (and treatment if necessary) right away.

Clean Living is the Real Safeguard

FREE CONFIDENTIAL ADVICE AND TREATMENT are available at clinics set up by County and County Borough Councils. (The addresses are given on local posters.) Further information can be obtained IN CONFIDENCE from the Health Department at your local Council's offices, or by writing to the Medical Adviser, Central Council for Health Education, Tavistock House, Tavistock Square, London, W.C.1. Please enclose a stamped addressed envelope.

Issued by the Ministry of Health and the Central Council for Health Education. (VD-40-2)

ARMS AND THE MEN. — It was announced on Wednesday that after calling for a report on the order regarding service men walking arm-in-arm with the opposite sex, Lt. Gen. Sir Charles Crocker (G.O.C., Southern Command), had cancelled the order.

AN ISLAND FILM. — The Island has been selected by the Federated Film Corporation as a subject for their third film in a series of entertainment documentaries... The film will give a general picture of life in the Island from day to day... As it is to be shown in the West End, throughout the country, and abroad, the Island will get widespread publicity. It will take about 50 minutes to show. By Thursday 120 different scenes had been taken. Bird's-eye views have been secured from a plane loaned by Saunders-Roe Ltd., and the Southern Railway placed a special train at the disposal of the camera man to obtain views from the railway line.... Local people are included in a great many of the shots and the filming will continue for about another 10 days. (October 6)

"LORD HAW-HAW" CAPTURED. — William Joyce ("Lord Haw Haw"), the traitor commentator in English on the German wireless for the greater part of the war, was captured on Tuesday by two officers of the British Second Army near the Danish frontier. He is to be brought to this country and will be tried for treason at the Old Bailey. Joyce was in the Island before the war. He paid several visits as a speaker for a Fascist organisation.

———————————————◆———————————————

For several weeks now, the County Press had published reports of plans to open a greyhound racing track at Westwood Park football ground in Cowes. It was an ambitious proposal with serious financial backers behind it but the scheme eventually foundered when planning permission was refused.
A Cowes resident suggested alternative forms of gambling for the disappointed punters....

October 20th, 1945.

"AMENITIES" AT COWES.

To the Editor of the IW County Press.

Sir, The discussion on the question of whether or not Cowes should have a greyhound track has hinged largely on the lack of amenities. I invite the attention of the disgruntled to the free amusements already provided. First, the floating bridge. It has been said that the present bridge was acquired after the Flood, when Noah had finished with it. Certainly its emulation of the Ark in frequently remaining perched high above the flood lends credence to the theory, and the amusement to be derived from being a passenger cannot be overestimated! Do our disgruntled population wish to "have a flutter?" Well, there is a ready-made source of a gamble on the number of minutes the Cowes-Southampton boat will be late in starting, in arriving, or by how many minutes you will miss your London or Newport train, or bus. Hunting is also provided. Amusement can be derived from "Find the policeman," or "Hunt the convict." Is life lacking in thrills? A wholesome amusement, very beneficial to health, is to board a bus at Osborne for East Cowes, or Cowes to Gurnard. With potholes scientifically spaced by leave of a considerate Council all the thrills of the switchback may be experienced. To get the greatest enjoyment the bus should be packed tight, and it is recommended that you stand next to a large lady, who carries a large shopping basket. If, however, amusement in more sober amenities is preferred, we have bombed sites. Nothing is quite so serenely satisfying as gazing on those areas which the Council have so thoughtfully left for time and weather to improve the devastation and dirt. Let us, therefore, not seek further worldly pleasures but remain content with the amenities which are at hand, and, for the most part, free.

I am, Sir, yours faithfully, P.A. HORWILL. Sarnia, Battery-road, Cowes.

---◆---

During the war years Britain was ruled by a national government, a coalition of the main parties led by Winston Churchill. Churchill's popularity was undeniable, with an approval rating that stood at 83%, and at the general election in May it was widely assumed that he would lead the Conservatives to victory but in one of the biggest political surprises of the last century, the Labour Party won a landslide victory with a majority of 145 seats.

One of the aspirations of the incoming government was to build millions of working-class homes but they took great care to see that it remained just that, an aspiration, not a pledge. They had no intention of repeating the unfulfilled promises of "Homes fit for heroes" that had been made at the end of the First World War. Their caution was not misplaced...

November 17th, 1945.

THE HOUSING SITUATION.

As far as we are aware not a single brick has been laid in the Island towards providing homes for those who badly need them, particularly the men and women returning from the Forces. Council meetings this week show that the blame cannot justly be laid on the public authorities. They are so hampered by Government restrictions on the one hand and by uneconomic prices and lack of labour on the other, that they simply cannot move... As to prices, there appears to be a state of deadlock; the position being that the builders are entirely in the dark as to costs and supplies of material, and the amount of labour likely to be available. We recently suggested that it might be wise if local authorities and builders put their heads together and agreed upon fair prices in order that a start might more quickly be made, but the Ryde Town Council have found that this course is unsatisfactory, as the prices suggested by the builders are too high. The council have therefore decided to invite tenders from individual builders...

---◆---

THE WEEK'S NEWS.

SUDDEN DEATH OF ANGLER AND INVENTOR. — We record with regret the sudden death on Wednesday of Mr. Percy Wadham of The Lindens, Carisbrook-road, Newport, aged 71... The sad event robs the Island of its foremost authority on matters piscatorial. In his early years he set up business in Holyrood-street, Newport, and became so well-known and skilful that he was appointed Island naturalist to both Queen Victoria and King Edward VII. Later he abandoned taxidermy for angling... He was the inventor of dozens of ingenious gadgets and the products of his firm have become popular throughout the world... He had also made valuable contributions to our columns from time to time. His record catch was a 43lb. conger eel taken off Atherfield. (November 17)

ARTIFICIAL INSEMINATION. — "Naturally Anon." writes: "May an old lady venture a protest against artificial insemination, not only because nature will exact a terrible retribution on our herds. It is as much an outrage on helpless animals (and felt to be such by them) as the similar German sadistic experiments on my sex at their camps. Are our decent minded humane farmers about to turn their farms into Auschwitzs? If so, thank God I have only a few years to live in such an England."

◆

Six weeks after the County Press editorial reflecting on the complete lack of building on the Isle of Wight, the signs were still not promising...

December 29th, 1945.

HOMELESS AMID VACANT HOMES.

To the Editor, IW County Press.

Sir, In April I applied to the Shanklin Council about housing for two adults. I received a form to fill in. Two weeks later a council meeting reported in the "County Press" stated that there were very few applicants for houses. I heard nothing further until September, when I applied again. I received another form to fill in. In December I received yet another form. There are numerous vacant houses in Shanklin which have been requisitioned by the council for months, and many are quite habitable. I was offered by an estate agent a requisitioned house to buy. When I pointed out that the council had taken it over, he replied "That is all right. Buy it and it's yours." This house has been requisitioned for months. I am a disabled ex-Service man of World War 2 with 24 years' service in HM Forces.

We are now in two unfurnished rooms, with no water, gas, electricity, or cooking or washing facilities, in a very overcrowded house, and on sufferance. Will the council explain their attitude?

Yours faithfully, R MURDOCH. 20 Atherley R., Shanklin, IW.

◆

1946.

ISLAND NOTES.

EMERGENCY "999" TELEPHONE CALLS AT RYDE. — From eight o'clock on Monday morning the Post Office will introduce the "999" scheme for emergency calls at the Ryde Exchange. This scheme enables a caller by dialling "999" to secure the attention of a special operator for calls for Fire, Police, or Ambulance services in an emergency. Where there is a coin box it will not be necessary to insert coins...

IW AMATEUR CINE SOCIETY. — An interesting talk on television was given by Mr. W. G. Sherratt, of Newport, one of the local pioneers of television before the war... Mr. Sherratt said that before the war England was far in advance of other countries, and stated that the BBC hoped to start transmitting still pictures for test purposes at the end of January to enable some 20,000 sets to be put in order. Although it was generally considered that a perfect picture could only be received within 20-30 miles of the station, on certain nights the reception on Arreton Down had been as strong as if transmission was only 12 miles away. He forecast colour television in the near future and thought television phoning was possible.

COWES-YARMOUTH ROAD OBSTRUCTION. — In connection with the closed Three Gates Road at Cowes ... the local Protest Committee had been informed by the Ministry of Aircraft Production that it was very much regretted that the continued use of the extension of the airfield was necessary, and that the reopening of the road was, at the moment, impracticable. Mr. G. Farrant said this reply had come as a shock to the Cowes Council. Several speakers mentioned that they had never seen more than about three planes on the extension at once. (January 19)

FARM WORKERS FEAR "PETTING" OF GERMANS. — The National Union of Agricultural Workers will not tolerate "petting" of German prisoners of war brought to the Island for work on the land. This was made clear at a meeting of the Island Branch on Saturday... Comment was made on the treatment of Italian prisoners engaged in a similar capacity in the past. Mr. Allcorn (county organiser) told members that if it were found that any agricultural worker or member of the Women's Land Army had been displaced by a prisoner then the prisoner concerned was immediately withdrawn and the ex-employee reinstated...

———————————◆———————————

The cinema film featuring the Island's attractions, now entitled "Chip off the Old Rock" was about to be released and was given a preview at Newport. The County Press, for the moment, was full of praise...

January 19th, 1946.

"CHIP OFF THE OLD ROCK."
NEW ISLAND FILM SHOWN AT NEWPORT.

The Federated Film Corporation's film depicting the attractions of the Island as a health and holiday resort, a pre-view of which was given at the Odeon Theatre, Newport, on Saturday, is a splendid production. The Island is very fortunate in having been selected to benefit from such a magnificent free advertisement, which should ensure its prosperity in the days, not far distant we hope, when, with the ravages of war repaired, Vectis is once more in a position to cater for a full quota of visitors.

About 400 Islanders ... including those who helped in making the film, saw the pre-view, and they were delighted with it. To adorn the beauty which nature has showered on the Island with lavish hand is, of course, impossible, but this film portrays that beauty in a way which invests it with enchanting emphasis... There are several unfortunate inaccuracies in the commentary, but the worst of them are to be corrected and, in any case, they do not spoil the film's high pictorial appeal and value as publicity for "The Garden Isle."... "Chip off the Old Rock" faithfully and beautifully depicts all the Island's most charming views from land, sea, and air, its well-known resorts, its unspoiled villages, its old churches, its agriculture, its sports and pastimes — in fact, almost everything that the proudest Vectensian would desire such a film to show... The Mayor of Newport said he feared that the film would be so effective an advertisement that, with present restricted resources, it would be impossible to accommodate all the visitors who would wish to come to the Island. It was time the Government departments concerned got a move on in restoring war damaged hotels and boarding-houses, and in building more houses (hear, hear).... Mr. Balm, (managing director of the corporation), who produced and directed the film, has authorised the preparation of a 16mm print of the film for local use. He said that the film had already been exhibited in London, and had been warmly praised by the technical Press. Bookings so far made for its release on March 4th ensured that it would be seen by at least 22 million people in this country. The film is 3300 feet long, and takes about 40 minutes to run. It is being offered as "a second feature, second to none" — a description which we think is fully justified.

◆

The end of the war did not mean an end to rationing, in fact the number of goods on ration actually increased. Bread, which throughout the war had been freely available, went on ration in 1946 and potatoes followed for a year in 1947.

Happily, a few things did become available once again...

January 19th, 1946.

WELCOME, SWEET STRANGER!

Islanders have this week given an enthusiastic welcome to the banana - a stranger since the early days of the war. Occasional specimens brought back by Service men returning from abroad found their way into a few homes, and were consumed with due solemnity in very small pieces to make them go further, but

READERS are reminded that, owing to the stringency of paper supplies, copies can only be printed for regular subscribers who order in advance,

to the vast majority the banana was just a memory, and to most children a mystery.

This week the first post-war allocation, totalling 11 tons, has been distributed by the Island Fresh Fruit Association, and we are informed that the bananas, which come from Jamaica, are in excellent condition. Long queues formed in Newport when sales began on Monday. The allocation is confined to those under 18 on the basis of a pound per ration book. We hope the time is not far distant when the shops will be able to advertise, in the words of a once popular song, "Yes, we have some" for all.

———————————◆———————————

Following the preview of "Chip off the Old Rock" the general public were able to watch the film. Not all of them shared the recent enthusiasm of the County Press...
April 13th, 1946.

THE ISLAND FILM.

To the Editor, I.W. County Press,

Sir, — May I express the disappointment felt by many Islanders over the film "Chip off the Old Rock." This Island, with its unique and beautiful scenery, made a very deep impression on our war-time American visitors. Surely something better, as a memento, could have been produced to send to them. Why was so much of historic interest omitted from the film? Many feet of the reel were devoted to Ryde Pier and the canoe lakes that might have been used to show things of greater interest... There are many writers on the Island. Why was none asked to write the script? There would not then have been the confusion of the Newport Grammar School history with the Secondary School. The flippancy of the commentators was inappropriate, and utterly boring.

Yours faithfully, (Mrs.) C. LILIAN CHATFIELD. Boadicea, Wootton Bridge.

[Several other letters expressing similar criticism have been received. — Editor, I.W.C.P.]

———————————◆———————————

THE WEEK'S NEWS.

NINE NEW HOUSES. — The official housing return of the Ministry of Health, giving the position of new house construction up to the end of February, shows that in the Island only nine new houses had been completed, and they were all erected by private enterprise. No Island public authority has yet completed a house.

QUAY-STREET POLICE STATION CLOSED. — The police station in Quay-street, the headquarters of the borough section of the police for many years, was closed yesterday (Friday), and in future the town police station will be at the County Police Headquarters in Fairlee-road. The premises in Quay-street have been used as a police station for about 70 years. Prior to that the police had an office and two cells under the Guildhall, behind the old market house. (April 20)

TOBY THE CROSSING KEEPER. — Toby, a remarkable dog, is a mongrel owned by Mr. and Mrs. A Everett, keepers of the Pan Mill railway crossing. Toby displays wonderful intelligence. When the bell sounds warning of approaching trains Toby is the first to go into action. He leaves whatever he happens to be doing, even if it is toothing a bone, and runs up and down the road on each side of the line barking warning to pedestrians. He has been known to stop cyclists by a warning tug at a trouser leg. Toby allows chickens to wander along the line in the intervals between trains but once the bell sounds he sends them packing with a flurry of barks. He is always on time in the morning to catch a newspaper thrown from the train, and collects any other small packets or letters dropped from the trains for his mistress.

VALUABLE COW KILLED BY AN ADDER. — A valuable Red Poll cow belonging to Sir Hanson Rowbotham JP, which was averaging 4½ gallons of milk a day, died on Monday as the result of being bitten in the udder while grazing in a field near Ridgeberry Copse between Wellow and Prospect.

Many residents in the Carisbrooke district and travellers on the Calbourne road knew of "Bun" the pet fox belonging to Mr. K Reed, of Hunters' Way, Carisbrooke. "Bun" and her master are great pals and Mr. Reed is mourning the loss of his pet, which died on Thursday week at the age of nine. He had had her since she was a cub, and she was so tame that she would take sweets and other tit-bits of food from the hands of children. Mr. Reed had taught her many tricks, which she delighted to perform to the last. "Bun" would spring on her master's back, take his pipe from his pocket, and pretend to smoke it. Although kept on the chain when Mr. Reed was not about, she several times broke loose, but always returned, sometimes after spending a night away from home. (April 27)

ISLAND NOTES.

EASTER TRAGEDY AT FRESHWATER - MOTHER OF SIX ON MURDER CHARGE.— People in the West Wight were profoundly shocked when it became known on Tuesday that the Bank-holiday had ended in tragedy for a Freshwater family. Mr. Stanley L—, aged 36, an ex-soldier and father of six children ranging in age from 3 to 11 years, was found dead in his home at Norton Green, with severe head injuries. His wife Eva L—, aged 31 was taken into custody at Yarmouth and charged with the murder.

ADDER EATS YOUNG BIRDS. — Mr. B. H. Scott of Woodbine Cottage, Cranmore, writes: "Chaffinches had built their nest in a thickly-grown may shrub, about 4 foot from the ground, and had recently hatched. One morning vehement protests started and the intensity of protest called for investigation. It was found that an adder had climbed up to the nest and had eaten the young birds. Three hours later the birds were still protesting, but within two days, however, the chaffinches were busy building a new nest in another part of the garden.

TELEVISED VICTORY PARADE SEEN IN THE ISLAND. — The televised broadcast of the London Victory Parade was watched by Mr. C. W. Launder on his set at his home at Castle-hill, Carisbrooke, in spite of the fact that he was using an improvised aerial suspended from the eaves of the house. Good reception was also secured by Mr. W. G. Sherratt at his experimental station on Arreton Down.

◆

There had been a series of escapes from the Island's prisons in recent years. The County Press, usually objective in other matters, invariably maintained an outspoken finger wagging attitude towards the prisons and they had plenty of time to do so in this instance as the prisoner involved remained at large for nearly 2 weeks, once again attracting the attention of the national Press...

June 22nd, 1946.

ANOTHER PARKHURST PRISON ESCAPE.
CONVICT GETS AWAY FROM PUNISHMENT CELLS.
TROOPS JOIN IN HUNT.

George Jackson, a 25-year-old convict serving a five-year sentence for housebreaking and larceny, escaped from the punishment cells at Parkhurst Prison on Sunday afternoon. In view of the nature of Jackson's escape it is highly probable that it will be the subject of a Home Office enquiry. Since his escape there have been a series of burglaries in the Newport, Ryde, and Northwood areas, culminating in the early hours of Thursday morning with an alarming incident at the Horseshoe Inn, Northwood, when an intruder, believed to be Jackson armed with a hatchet, attacked the licensee and his wife Mr. and Mrs. Harwood, inflicting serious injuries on them.... Jackson is noted for his determined character and was described at his trial as "a man who had lived in and around crime since he was 11 years of age." He is only 5 ft 4″ in height. The first of a series of burglaries occurred at the home of Mr. and Mrs. Taylor, of 86 Worsley-road, Parkhurst, at about midnight on Sunday, when someone entered by lifting a window... Alerted by a dog barking, Mr. Taylor came downstairs, by which time the intruder had escaped taking with him a bottle of port wine. Mr. Taylor found the gas stove full on, with a kettle of water steaming on one of the jets. On another jet was a pan, and eggs had been placed ready for cooking on the kitchen table... In the early hours of Tuesday morning there were two further burglaries in Fairlee-road... When Mrs. Bowen, of Clovelly, Fairlee-road, came downstairs she found that the house had been ransacked and about £15 in cash was missing, including the contents of her 10-year-old son's savings bank box. A pair of her husband's trousers, his shaving kit and some tinned foods had also gone. The burglar had remained in the house long enough to make himself some tea and have a meal, including soup, and a wash and shave in the kitchen... At 1.45 a.m. on Thursday morning an intruder, believed to be Jackson, broke into the Horseshoe Inn on the main Newport-Cowes Road. On hearing a sound downstairs Mrs. P. Richards woke her parents and Mr. Harwood grabbed a police truncheon which he always keeps by the side of his bed, and went downstairs. Apparently the intruder was waiting for him, for as he entered the kitchen he was struck on the head with an axe. Although blinded with blood Mr. Harwood made a gallant attack on his assailant, and managed to get in one blow with his truncheon. The attacker rained blow after blow on Mr. Harwood. The state of the room next morning gave evidence of the terrific struggle which had ensued. The walls and floor were spattered with blood, and smashed crockery littered the floor. Mrs. Harwood was also the victim of a brutal attack. She endeavoured to pull off the attacker, but she was struck three times on the head…. Mr. and Mrs. Harwood are both over 60 and were confined to bed with their injuries on Thursday, but yesterday Mrs. Harwood was considerably better and her husband was out of danger. After the struggle the intruder drove off in a car, which he is alleged to have stolen from Newport. He took with him a bottle of port wine, a quantity of cigarettes, Mrs. Richards's baby's sweets, rusks, powder and puff, flannel, and soap… Supt Stanley talked to Pressmen at the police headquarters, Fairlee, and said that it seemed obvious that the convict was using a hideout from which he was making his nightly raids…

The following week, the County Press were able to report Jackson's capture…

June 29th, 1946.

JACKSON RECAPTURED YESTERDAY.

George Jackson was recaptured in the early hours of yesterday (Friday)… Game to the last Jackson led his pursuers on a three-mile cross country dash in the direction of Combley Farm. He was eventually run to earth drenched to the skin and exhausted in a spinney at Downend, near Newport. Thus ended the chase which has gained nation-wide publicity, in which one man has been matched against a search organisation involving, at times, personnel running into hundreds. In addition to warders, troops, all available police, including reinforcements from the mainland were called in, bloodhounds were used, and aircraft co-operated with the ground searchers.

The finger wagging began…

PRISON ESCAPES.

The Island has been getting a good deal of unwanted publicity in the daily papers during the last few days, as a result of the hunt for a convict who recently escaped from Parkhurst Prison. The man has proved a veritable Scarlet Pimpernel in successfully evading for 11 days the combined operations of the Army, Royal Air Force, police, and prison authorities, to say nothing of a party of special correspondents from the national daily newspapers, who seem to have conducted a sensation mongering hunt of their own. Their flights of imagination are amusing up to a point…

Naturally Island people do not like dangerous convicts wandering about at night but they … are prepared to put up with what might be termed ordinary escapes. If our information is correct, however, this most recent escape was in no sense ordinary; it was extraordinary. We understand that the convict escaped from the punishment cells or compound, where prisoners are supposed to be under constant watch of officers. If this is so, serious neglect of duty is implied. If our facts are wrong we shall be pleased to publish any statement the Prison authorities may wish to make…

For nearly 40 years Mr. Langton and his family had looked after the lighthouse on St Helens Fort. Their unusual existence was coming to an end...

July 13th, 1946.

ST. HELENS FORT CARETAKER
RETIRES AFTER 39 YEARS SERVICE.

Behind the announcement that Mr. Maurice Langton has retired from the position of caretaker and lighthouse keeper on St. Helens Fort, lies a story of devotion to duty and physical endurance over the long period of 39 years.

Since his appointment in 1907, with the exception of the period from 1915 to 1918, when he was on active service in France, Mr. Langton and his wife and family have made their home on the fort and although it is only a mile from land they have led a remote existence. Apart from rowing ashore to Bembridge once or twice a week for provisions and mails their only contact with other people has been the visits of the War Department representatives to the fort or the occasional presence of Royal Engineers engaged on repairs or other work. At intervals local yachtsmen and watermen have brought papers and periodicals, but in the main they have been left to themselves. Some indication of the loneliness of their existence may be gauged from the fact that Mr. Langton was due to retire seven years ago, when he was 60, but no successor could be found, and he was forced to remain... During his 39 years' service, Mr. Langton has had only three days' leave. He was granted a week, but his relief could stand it no longer than three days' isolation so he had to return.

Sometimes, owing to stormy conditions, periods of a fortnight or more have elapsed before Mr. Langton has been able to put off from the fort. At these times, when food stocks have fallen, the family have experienced an unenviable degree of privation... It being impossible for their four children to attend school regularly their education was entirely in the hands of their parents, until they reached their teens, when they were sent to the village school for about 18 months, but very often their attendance there was interrupted for long intervals by the weather. Food supplies were always an anxiety, so a certain amount of livestock was kept on the fort, including ducks and chicken. At one time the family had as many as 16 rabbits... Their numerous friends wish Mr. and Mrs. Langton many years of happy and well earned retirement. The new caretaker is a Southampton waterman.

THE WEEK'S NEWS.

GERMAN P.O.W. ESCAPES. – Kans Franz, who absconded from the hostel in Watergate-road, Newport, on Wednesday afternoon, was recaptured on Thursday night. Sgt Gormley, NCO in charge of the hostel, was walking down Watergate-road at 9.45 pm when he met the missing prisoner, who said he was coming back to the hostel. Franz stated that he had spent the day with farmers.

NEW COUNCIL HOUSES. — Claiming to be the first builders in the Island, since the war, to complete brick-built houses erected by private enterprise, Messrs. A. W. Rose, Ltd., have now earned a similar distinction in respect of

houses erected for local authorities. Two new houses just completed by them in Manor-road, Lake, were handed over to the Council on Thursday... They are to be let at the modest rent of 10s. a week.

THE FRESHWATER MURDER CASE. — Mrs. Eva L—, Norton Green, Freshwater, mother of six children, was found "guilty, but insane," after a two day's trial at Winchester , for the murder of her husband Stanley L—. Giving judgement, Mr. Justice Morris stated: "On that verdict Eva L— will be detained until the pleasure of His Majesty be known."

SHANKLIN PIER AGAIN OPEN. — On completion of repairs to the promenade deck the pier was reopened to the public on Monday after the breach made in it early in the war. (July 27)

MUSHROOM GROWTH. — On the marshes near Sandown on Thursday week the Misses Anne Brotchie and Barbara Hart found a mushroom weighing 1lb. 14oz. and 16 inches in diameter.

AN OUTSIZE WASPS' NEST. — Over a period of years Mr. R. F. Wilson has helped to destroy hundreds of wasps' nests in the Binstead district, but last week he came across his largest so far in a loft over the garage of Binstead House. The wasps were seen coming from between the slates and Mr. Wilson discovered a nest about 5 foot in circumference. He destroyed the wasps by covering it with cotton wool and applying cyanide, and so preserved the nest intact.

—————————◆—————————

In the late 1890s someone lost something on the beach at Sandown...
August 3rd, 1946.
VISITOR'S STRANGE FIND.
Enjoying three weeks' holiday in Sandown, Mr. T. H. O'Brien, of Welwyn Garden City, made a strange find on the western beach at low tide on Monday afternoon. Noticing what appeared to be a bicycle pedal protruding from the sand he investigated further and assisted by his young twin daughters, brought a "penny-farthing" bicycle to light after half an hour's digging. The machine, which was minus its tyres, but otherwise in fairly good preservation, must have been in the sand for a considerable period, but how it came to be there is a matter for conjecture. It is about 50 years since such bicycles were on the roads, and younger visitors have shown great interest in the machine, on the view outside Messrs. Hooper's hut.

—————————◆—————————

Southern Vectis were regular advertisers with the County Press throughout the war years and like Dabells, their advertisements had appeared in virtually every issue during the war. They had also been a good friend to the public during that time; in the words of a journalist for the 'Bus and Coach' magazine, "The Vectis Company certainly pulled its weight during the war"...

August 10th, 1946.
"BATTLE OF THE PEAKS."
Under this heading - referring to the peaks of public transport demands - a well-deserved tribute to the service given by the Southern Vectis Omnibus Co. during the war and in the present difficult post-war period, is paid in an illustrated article in the July issue of 'Bus and Coach.' The writer says: "Post-war problems at their worst have to be contended with by the company... Approximately one third of the company's fleet was requisitioned during the war, and only two post-war vehicles have arrived in return, therefore the needs of workers, residents, and visitors have to be met by what is virtually the war-time fleet... It is a case of every bus on the road for the greater part of the time, yet all vehicles are brought in for top overhaul at 20,000 miles, and for a complete overhaul at 100,000 miles." In a reference to the conductresses, some of whom have over five years' service, he says: "They have enhanced the company's reputation for courtesy." ... The article ends as follows: "The Vectis Company certainly pulled its weight during the war, when important work was being done in the factories and shipyards around Cowes. As it serves a community which increases more than fourfold in summer, it cannot relax. It is facing up to its problems, and is confidently expecting that in 1947 it will at least have normal facilities to deal with abnormal peaks."

Pluto, or the "Pipe Line Under The Ocean" was the codename for a series of secret undersea pipelines. Linking the Island to Cherbourg, they were intended to provide a supply of oil products to allied forces as part of the D-Day invasion in June 1944.

Unfortunately D-Day had long since been and gone by the time the pipeline was ready and to add insult to injury, when Pluto finally did come into service, seabed friction caused leaks in the cables almost from day one and after just 10 months in service, and very little use, five of the expensive pipelines were out of action after an average life of only 56 days.

Of the 5 million tons of oil products eventually delivered to Europe, Pluto was responsible for just 380,000 tons, just over half the contents of a modern supertanker. In a final indignity, after little more than a year on the seabed the leaking cables became a hazard to shipping and were recovered to be consigned to the scrapheap...

August 24th, 1946.
PICKING UP "PLUTO."
Two cable ships, the Empire Taw and the Empire Ridley, are engaged in salvaging the Isle of Wight to Cherbourg section of the "Pluto" pipeline which was laid on the seabed to supply petrol to our invasion armies. The job is expected to last to the end of the year and, it is hoped, to yield a rich harvest of about 4000 tons of wire and lead, which will be a valuable addition to our housing materials, and is worth about £200,000 at present prices.

The Empire Taw put into Southampton during the weekend for repair damage caused by a fire on her fore-peak, which was caused by petrol remaining in the pipe igniting when the pipe was cut with acetylene welding apparatus! It was not expected to find petrol in the pipe*, but the fore-peak was drenched with it when the pipe was cut, and the crew had a desperate fight before the flames were subdued. Since then they have used hack-saws.

The Swainston Estate slowly went the way of most of the country's big estates. The owner, Sir John Simeon decided to retain the house itself (and devote a considerable amount of money to restoring the extensive war damage) but most of the surrounding holdings were auctioned...

August 31st, 1946.

SWAINSTON ESTATE SALE
A PRE-AUCTION PURCHASE.

A large portion of Sir John Simeon's Swainston Estate, which was to have been offered for sale by auction, was sold privately this week. The name of the purchaser has not been disclosed but we understand that he is a Sussex resident who has bought the estate as an investment and that existing tenancies will not be interfered with.

The large portion of the estate which would have come under the hammer comprised a total area of over 2000 acres of agricultural holdings and woodland, which was described as one of the finest sporting estates in the south.

The properties sold include 10 well-known agricultural holdings in the West Wight. These are Manor Farm, Shalfleet; Hebberdens, Calbourne, with its Elizabethan farmhouse; Wheatenbread; Lower Watchingwell; New Barn, Calbourne; Apes Down, Rowridge; Rowridge Top Barn; St Hubert's Lodge, Porchfield; and part of Fullholding, Calbourne.

Picturesque cottages in Winkle-street, Calbourne, much admired and photographed for their quiet old-world charm, also figured in the sale, including No. 6 Barrington Row, Winkle-street, one of the most delightful of the cottages. Other properties sold are two well-known licensed houses, the Sun Inn, Calbourne, and the New Inn, Shalfleet, both of which are let to Messrs. W.B. Mew Langton, and Co.

Sir John retains the residence and a considerable acreage of the immediately surrounding land...

TOWN AND COUNTY NOTES.

ISLAND BRICK FIRM'S ENTERPRISE. — Bricks are No. 1 news in these days of acute shortages in building materials. The gravity of the position is illustrated by the present importation of Belgian bricks... It is more than good news to be able to state that, thanks to the enterprise of an Island firm, the brick shortage will be definitely at an end here by the autumn of next year. Island Bricks, Ltd.,

------

* 75,000 gallons of petrol were eventually recoveredfrom the cable.

of Rookley, has commenced a £45,000 scheme for one of the most modern brickmaking plants in the South. When completed it will increase the company's total weekly output to nearly 350,000, sufficient to build 15 to 17 average-sized houses. (August 31)

AIR SERVICE OPENED AT COWES. — A new air service, which should prove of considerable benefit to the Island, was opened at Somerton Aerodrome, Cowes, on Sunday by Mr. Russell Gunton, of Nottingham, who has taken over the lease of the Aerodrome from Messrs. Saunders-Roe for use for charter services, flying instruction, and as headquarters of the Cowes Aero Club... London can be reached inside 40 minutes, and Portsmouth in approximately 10 minutes. (September 7)

COWES AIRPORT AND A CLOSED ROAD.
To the Editor of the IW County Press. Sir, - The closure (of Three Gates Road) was accepted as a wartime necessity but ... we feel that the retention of the extension to Somerton aerodrome is unnecessary. At the recent air display twin-engine aircraft landed and took off without using the extension... Some of the reasons for reopening are that the distance to Cowes for pedestrians and cyclists could be considerably reduced; that doctors, nurses, and tradesmen could improve their attendance; that the aerodrome is rapidly becoming the centre of a built-up area; and that the bus service would be improved. -
Yours Faithfully, W. J. SANDERS AND S. BUNDAY, Northwood Residents' and Ratepayers' Association. (November 23)

MOVE TO REOPEN CEMENT MILLS. — At a meeting of the Chamber of Commerce on Wednesday the Secretary (Mr. F.W. Bright), said there seemed little hope of the Medina Cement Mills being reopened. - Sir Vere Hobart said it was a monstrous thing that one of the major industries of the area should be restricted in this way. At one time the mills employed 100 men, many of whom, now returning from the Forces, were without employment...

1947.

The national housing shortage continued. Such was the scale of the problem locally and the distress it caused, that when a homeless reader wrote a letter of protest the County Press, in a rare departure, abandoned its usual impartiality and joined in the debate on the letters page...

January 4th, 1947.
THE HOUSING PROBLEM.
To the Editor, I.W. County Press.
Sir,—We are hearing constant rumours that the Ministry of Health, or some other authority, is at last making a move to commandeer surplus accommodation in houses of every size. I feel that the people generally, and

especially ex-Service folk, have up to now displayed wonderful patience. When they know many large houses have perhaps only one occupant, and a servant of sorts, it does seem pretty awful that thousands are living without reasonable amenities, crowded six or eight in one room. I suggest that the so-called "comfortable" classes should share houses, and leave the unshared houses for families, two or three together. This would work out much more comfortably than putting a dock labourer's family into the house of Mrs. "Vere de Vere." Something has to be done very quickly, otherwise there is going to be serious trouble.—Yours faithfully. " HOMELESS WORKER."

[This letter, though it contains a suggestion which may be impossible generally to adopt, emphasises the pathetic position of many who are without reasonable housing accommodation. Could not something far more immediately effective be done by housing people in the unoccupied military camps at Northwood and Whippingham? The only serious expense needed would be in adapting the sanitary arrangements. These two camps could quickly provide a solution to the problem at Cowes and East Cowes.—Editor.]

———————————◆———————————

The demands of war had kept J.S White's shipyard working at full capacity for five years and when the war came to an end, Britain's shipyards expected a recession. Instead, they experienced a long boom as maritime trade recovered and the world's merchant fleet set about replacing lost vessels ...

January 4th, 1947
THE COWES SHIPYARDS AND AIRCRAFT FACTORIES
PROMISING OUTLOOK FOR 1947.
Messrs. J. S. White and Co. have fortunately experienced a very comfortable and satisfactory changeover from war to peace production. Their yards at Cowes have been busy ever since the cessation of hostilities, and orders in hand ensure a busy time during 1947. At present the firm are building two destroyers and converting a frigate for the British Admiralty, and building two passenger-cargo boats for French owners, 10 petrol tankers for canal use for French owners, two 3400-ton refrigerated cargo motor ships for Argentine owners; and several lifeboats for the RNLI. It is noteworthy that 70 per cent, of their present production will be for export. In addition, the adaptation of the Somerton Aircraft Works for the production of domestic furniture is proving a great success...

———————————◆———————————

THE WEEK'S NEWS.
ORANGES SALVAGED FROM THE NEEDLES WRECK. — Working on behalf of Lloyd's Underwriters, Mr. H. Simmonds, of Yarmouth, and his four sons have saved a considerable portion of the cargo of tangerines on board the wreck of the abandoned Greek steamer Varvassi, ground on the Needles Bridge since January 5th. On Saturday, they brought 400 cases ashore. On the following

day, with the co-operation of the R.A.S.C., they loaded 3500 cases into a tank landing craft. So far it has been impossible to save any of the wine. The salvaged fruit is reported to be in good condition and it will probably be marketed locally. (Jan 25)

BOROUGH POLICE COURT. — There were no cases before the borough magistrates at the Guildhall on Monday.

BEMBRIDGE - A VETERAN CANARY. – Comdr. J. B. Craddock, R.N., informs us that a canary given to him by a Maltese boatman in December, 1929, and later given to Mrs. Rooke, of Milton-road, is still alive and singing. It must be about 17 ½ years old. He wonders if this is a record of canary longevity.

THE COLD SPELL CONTINUES. - The cold spell, now commencing its fourth week has produced another unwelcome dose of bad weather for Islanders. A cold sleety rain, which commenced on Saturday, turned to a blizzard during the afternoon and by morning the ground was once more under a white mantle, some 2 inches having fallen during the night...Most of the snow had disappeared by Tuesday and Wednesday temperatures dropped again and have remained in the vicinity of freezing point during the day, with biting north-east winds and sharp frosts at night. (Feb 15)

Escapes from the Island's prisons continued in alarming numbers. Most of the prisoners were captured within a short while but occasionally one would stay at large for a number of days, generating nationwide publicity...

January 25th, 1947.
DRAMATIC END OF PARKHURST ESCAPE.
AIRCRAFT AND DESTROYER IN SOLENT RESCUE.
The week-end brought a highly dramatic conclusion to the escape bid of Arthur Anderson, the 29-year-old Parkhurst convict, for whom police and warders had been searching continuously since he broke away shortly before dusk on Wednesday week. Anderson's period of liberty thus fell short of Arthur Conmy's 25-year-old record of 12 days freedom, and also of George Jackson's more highly publicised adventure in June last, when he remained at liberty for 11½ days. But if Anderson received less publicity while on the run, the circumstances of his recapture provided a climax more exciting than the end of any Parkhurst escape hitherto... The first indication that Anderson had tried to reach the mainland came in a message from Cowes early on Saturday morning that a 14ft. dinghy owned by Mr. G.W. Shepherd, of the Woodvale Hotel, Gurnard, had disappeared... and that a pair of oars was missing. The police acted quickly in organising a local search... While this search was proceeding a Fleet Air Arm pilot, Lt commander. T.H. Sargeant, on a flight over the Solent saw something on the cable buoy off Egypt Point, about half a mile from shore. Going lower he saw that it was a man clinging desperately to the upper portion of the buoy with his legs trailing in the water. While he circled overhead he sent

a radio message, which resulted in the diversion to the rescue of the destroyer Myngs, which was proceeding from Portsmouth to Portland. She lowered her boat and the marooned man, who proved to be Anderson, was taken on board suffering badly from the effects of his long exposure, and at Portland he was handed over to the police.

... Anderson was fit enough to be sent back to the Island and a police car brought him to Lymington. They crossed by the last ferry to Yarmouth, Anderson, whose feet were heavily bandaged, being carried from the car to the first-class refreshment room, from which the public were excluded. He was refreshed with tea during the crossing and at Yarmouth a waiting police car was backed onto the ferry and pulled up alongside the door of the refreshment room, while Anderson was lifted in. A small crowd saw him smile cheerfully in the glare of Press photographers' flashlights as he was being carried to the waiting vehicle by the two police officers... After a good meal at police headquarters, Newport, at about 9 p.m. he was brought before Mr. W.G. Sibbick, borough magistrate, on a charge of breaking and entering. In a small room into which representatives of London Press were crowded as well as local Press men, Anderson looked very cheerful as he sat on a chair facing the magistrate and smiled broadly throughout the brief proceedings. He is a small, mild looking man and his appearance is not by any means that of a desperate character... He spent the weekend in the cells at police headquarters.

———————————————◆———————————————

From its very first issue the County Press had been the natural home of the middle and upper classes. It is fair to say that while the working classes might well appear in its columns, they were definitely not among its natural readers. In recent years sales of the County Press had climbed from 13,000 at the turn of the century to over 28,000 in 1947 and an unmistakable change in the paper's attitudes over the last 30 years showed that not all these new readers shared the politics or lifestyle of the older ones.

Following the war more and more letters were published from working class readers who were unashamedly vocal and assertive. They protested about shortcomings in their lifestyle and had no qualms about challenging the status quo, something unthinkable in years gone by.

On the face of it, the next article is simply a report on whether Sunday cinema opening should continue in peacetime (it had been introduced as a wartime measure to entertain the thousands of troops on the Island), but reading between the lines it is plain to see that peoples' attitudes and expectations were rapidly changing...

February 15th, 1947.
SUNDAY CINEMA OPENING.
NEWPORT MEETING VOTES IN FAVOUR.

By a majority of 57 votes, a public meeting at the Guildhall, Newport, on Friday week, decided in favour of the continuance of the opening of cinemas in the borough on Sundays when the present emergency regulations expire at the end of this year. The voting was 211 in favour and 154 against... The meeting was so crowded that the doors had to be locked, and those who were outside

" THERE I WAS, AT THE BRIDGEHEAD, MA,—SURROUNDED BY THE ENEMY . . ."
(German P.O.W.s laying new gas main under Coppins Bridge, Newport).

repeatedly banged on the doors in the hope of gaining admission. The meeting was somewhat noisy. Speakers in favour of Sunday cinemas were given a quiet hearing, but as soon as opposition speakers began to emphasise the moral and religious side of the question they were often interrupted with ironic comments and laughter by a section of the audience, composed chiefly of young persons, who showed a sad lack of appreciation of the usual courtesies of debate... The discussion in favour was opened by Mrs. Sheaf, who said it was the right of the people to do what they wished with their freedom. They could live the Christian life every day and not save it up for Sundays. She had nothing to say against people going to the cinema on Sundays. It took the young people off the streets. People were living in overcrowded conditions, and there were hundreds of names on the Town Council's books for houses. She knew of instances where three or four families were living in one house, and in one case there were 11 people living in four rooms. The cinema was the only place that many such people could go to for relaxation on a Sunday evening. There was no outcry against people playing golf on Sundays. Speaking on behalf of cinema employees, Mr. A. Fry said there was no compulsion for any members of cinema staffs to work on Sundays. The employees favoured Sunday opening it was if the cinemas were closed on that day, that would be their day off ... Mr. G. Linington said he had seen people playing golf on the downs on Sunday morning and those same people going to church on Sunday nights. What right had those people to say that others should not be allowed to go to the cinema on Sunday? Men were working at the Jetty getting out coal on Sundays; was it wrong for them to be working? Mrs. Fry, the wife of a cinema employee, said she deeply resented that interference with her liberties. Let the people go to the cinema on Sundays if they wanted to. Those who were trying to close the cinemas on Sundays were no more than self-righteous tyrants; it was Nazi Germany all over again. She demanded the right to do what she liked on a Sunday...

Mr. S. V. Croucher, said he had heard nothing in the arguments to convince him that Sunday cinema performances were either necessary or advisable... What people needed was to be uplifted spiritually and intellectually (loud cries of dissent)...

———————————◆———————————

Pan-Am began transatlantic flights in 1939, a ticket for a single journey from Southampton to New York costing over £150, 30 weeks wages for most people. The flights were long, noisy and not for the faint hearted. Such was the rarity value of a flight to America that an account of a flight was still considered newsworthy...

Feb 22nd, 1947.

LOCAL LADY'S AIR TRIP TO AMERICA.

Mrs. J.A. Dixon has arrived in New York after her Atlantic flight on a business tour. She left Prestwick Airport on the evening of Friday week in a four-engined Skymaster plane and arrived at Gander Airport, Newfoundland, 12 hours later. Speaking to her husband on the transatlantic telephone on Saturday after her arrival in New York, Mrs. Dixon said that shortly after taking off from Gander trouble developed in one of the starboard engines, which finally stopped, and the plane was obliged to return for repairs causing two hours' delay. Mrs. Dixon said that the crossing was fairly smooth, but she had been unable to sleep owing to the noise of the engines, and she was extremely tired. Although she would not have missed the experience, she would not care to make such a long trip by air again unless it was absolutely necessary. New York, she said, has got everything that we have not - marvellous food, clothes, and shops. On Tuesday Mrs. Dixon left New York for Toronto, from which city she will go on to St. Paul, Montreal, Winnipeg, and Calgary, where she will have a 10 days' break from business with her sister, Mrs. Dorothy Webb. From Calgary she returns to Chicago and then south to Washington, Philadelphia, and Boston, and back to New York to join the Queen Elizabeth on April 9th.

———————————◆———————————

In an effort to reduce the amount of money spent on imports the government introduced the Exchange Control Act. Newsprint was singled out as a major contributor to the loss of foreign exchange and tough rationing was introduced for weekly and provincial newspapers.

It left the County Press in an even worse position than it had been in during the war...

March 22nd, 1947.
THE "COUNTY PRESS" AND NEWSPRINT SUPPLIES.

At the beginning of the fuel crisis all newspapers were deprived of the small additional allowance of newsprint which was granted a few months earlier, and which enabled the "County Press" to have 12 pages once a month. This week the Rationing Committee of the Newsprint Supply Company, an organisation set up by the industry during the war to allocate supplies, have restored the additional allowance to all newspapers except London and provincial weeklies and Sunday papers. This means that the "County Press," with the news of the whole Island to cover, cannot exceed eight pages, and will be in a much worse position to serve the public than during the war. Then numerous local societies were dormant, public activities necessarily largely curtailed, and there was a much reduced demand on our advertising space. Today most of the organisations which lapsed during the war have been revived and many new ones formed, greatly increasing the calls on our news space, while the demands of advertisers have at least trebled. In view of this unfortunate situation, we can only ask for the kind indulgence of our readers. Reports generally will have to be drastically condensed, and publication of advertisements may have to be delayed. We have had to refuse over 10 columns of advertisements for this issue. In an effort to conserve news space we have reluctantly decided that, until the situation improves, we cannot publish lists of private wreaths and private wedding presents.

———————————◆———————————

THE WEEK'S NEWS.

SUNDAY CINEMAS POLL AT RYDE. — By a majority of 1983 the electors of Ryde on Wednesday decided in favour of Sunday cinema opening... Despite a vigourous and intensive campaign by both sides only 5310 of the total electorate, about 35 per cent., took the trouble to vote, and this on a day when the weather was favourable.

EMPLOYMENT OF P.O.W. LABOUR. — Mr. W.A. Christy, referred to the concern of the council's water consulting engineers at the slow progress being made by the contractors laying the new main from Westridge to Brading owing to the shortage of labour. The weather had prevented much work being done and it was essential that the work should be completed before the summer. They were asking that 20 German prisoners should be employed for four months, which would increase the contract price by between £250 and £300.

WINE FROM THE VARVASSI - SAMPLED BY P.O.W.S. — Rough seas on Friday week tore a hole in the port side of the Greek Steamer Varvassi, wrecked on the Needles Bridge on January 6th, and her cargo is being washed out. During the weekend about 50 huge casks of Algerian wine from the ship were adrift in the Solent and the beaches were littered with Tangerine oranges and broken crates. A number of casks were recovered at Colwell Bay, Fort Victoria, and Yarmouth. A Customs official informed a "County Press" representative that the wine was in a raw state and unfit for human consumption, but the casks were worth £10 each. He added that there was a danger of dysentery if anyone drank the wine in its present form. These warnings have not prevented a number of people from sampling the wine, including a party of German P.O.W.S, who broke open a cask which they found on the shore near Colwell.

Mr. T. A. Cleaver told the following good story at the Island Farmers' Union dinner. George, a country lad, won a shoot pig at a village whist drive, and was taking it home under his arm when he met Bill, a friend, and the following conversation occurred: Bill: "Where did you get 'un, Garge? George: "I just won 'un at the whist drive." Bill: "Where you goin' to keep 'un; you 'ant got a sty?" George: "No, I'm goin' to put 'un in bed-room." Bill: "You can't do that. What about the smell? " George: "He'll have to put up with that."

————————————◆————————————

In 1947 Britain experienced the severest winter in living memory. Intense cold and snow affected much of England and Wales from December 1946 until the end of March the next year. It had been the coldest February on record with temperatures falling as low as -21°C. and the following month proved to be even worse, as this digest of articles from March makes clear...

ICEBERGS IN BEMBRIDGE HARBOUR. — The first signs of a thaw in Bembridge Harbour, where for the previous fortnight small vessels on their moorings and ships at St. Helens Quay had been hemmed in by ice, occurred with the change of wind on Saturday afternoon. At the St. Helens end, where the East Yar drains, the fresh water froze and during the cold spell large blocks of ice were seen floating on the sea water. These rapidly collected until a field of some 20 acres in extent was formed, and this eventually froze into a solid mass. Ice formed along high-water mark at the lower end of the harbour, and extended seawards in parts to 30 feet, but was only a few inches thick. From the main ice field pieces broke away on Sunday afternoon, forming miniature icebergs, some of them about 15 feet square and two feet high, which were carried seawards by the ebb tide. As they passed through the fairway towards St. Helens Fort swans could be seen perched on them, and they were still visible when a mile out to sea. On Monday morning when the temperature rose to 40 degrees, the amount of ice in the harbour had considerably diminished, and several boats had been freed. (Mar 1)

The toll which the severe weather is taking of old folk is shown in the list of deaths on page 1. It includes four over 90, twelve between 80 and 90, and nine between 70 and 80 years of age. (Mar 8)

Mr. John Dover of the Totland Bay Meteorological Station, writes: "This was the coldest February I have known here, the average temperature being 34.4 F. The nearest approach to it was 34.9 in February, 1895. The lowest maximum reading was 28.8 on February 17th, and the lowest minimum 17.1 (15 degrees of frost) on February 25th, when on the grass the thermometer fell to 6.1 (24 degrees of frost), the sea temperature was down to 36.0 on February 18th. It is rarely so cold. There were 20 completely sunless days. I have never registered so many in February before." (Mar 8)

COLD WEATHER RETURNS. – The mid-week forecast of a final end to the cold spell proved false and there has been a renewal of piercing winds and keen night frosts after two days of cold rain… Friday saw the welcome return of the sun. The fuel shortage remains and there is little prospect of a general improvement until the country is released from winter's grip…(March 8)

ELECTRICITY RESTRICTIONS. – We are asked by the I. W. Electric Light and Power Co. to point out that the statuary prohibition of the use of electricity in residential premises between the hours of 9 a.m. and 12 noon, and 2 p.m. and 4 p.m., remains in force…(Mar 15)

———————————————◆———————————————

Having escaped from a Newport farm, an enterprising pig spent six months at large in Parkhurst Forest defying capture until five months later when he was caught and returned to his owner.

Today, the plucky animal might well be adopted by the readers of a national newspaper or perhaps purchased by an anonymous benefactor in order to save it from the slaughterman.

Would there be such an uplifting end to the story in 1947…

April 26th, 1947.
LOST, A SHOOT* - FOUND, A PORKER!

Few of the bus passengers who frequently saw a fine white pig rooting contentedly amongst the undergrowth in Parkhurst Forest were aware that he was a runaway who had defied all attempts to recapture him since he escaped as a three weeks' old piglet last November from his owner, Mr. A. J. White, of Little Kitbridge Farm. The fugitive, now a porker of about seven score, was returned to his owner by Mr. A. Jacobs, of Parkhurst, whose two dogs found pig hunting an exciting change from rabbiting and seized their loudly protesting quarry by the ears. Mr. Jacobs rescued the pig from its tormentors, secured it with a rope, and the owner's son led the chastened truant back to the farmyard. Five months of freedom had failed to dim the porker's memory, and he headed straight for his former sty, violently resenting being quartered in an air raid shelter while his original home was being prepared for him. Mr. White and his son spent most of their Christmas holiday in the forest trying to trap the pig, and on one occasion, when a hunt by 20 men was organised, he charged through the cordon and escaped into the undergrowth. A trough placed in the forest by his owner was kept regularly replenished, but this sturdy animal generally scorned such soft living and thrived on a diet of fallen acorns and horse chestnuts. He did well on his chosen fare and will go the way of all good pigs this week-end.

◆

TOWN AND COUNTY NOTES.

WEMBLEY BY TELEVISION. — At the invitation of Mr. W. Clark, of Messrs. C. Clark and Sons, of High Street, a small company, among whom were Press representatives, assembled at his private residence, The Rondels, on Saturday to witness the televised broadcast of the FA Cup final at Wembley Stadium. Considering the fact that the receiver was well outside the prescribed range of the transmitting apparatus, and that there was considerable local electrical interference, the viewers received quite a good impression of the match. Those coming within close range of the cameras were clearly seen, including the Duke of Gloucester and Don Welsh, the Charlton captain, during the presentation of the cup.

PRISONERS OF WAR ENTERTAIN COMRADES. — At the Medina Cinema, Newport, on Sunday, the central camp of the P.O.W unit at Brockenhurst entertained Island POWs and a number of invited guests... About 550 P.O.Ws out of approximately 700 stationed on the Island were present... The programme concluded with the song "Lilli Marlene," in which the audience joined. (May 17)

BINSTEAD HOUSE ESTATE SOLD. — Col Stephenson Clarke, CB., who for over 50 years has been a prominent resident, has recently sold his Island home,

---

* A young pig just weaned from its mother.

"CAPITAL" COMPARISON in St. James,'s Square, Newport. (January 18th, 1947.)

KB
RADIO
in the
'Queen Elizabeth'

The radio broadcast receiving equipment installed in the world's greatest liner, "Queen Elizabeth," as in her sister ship "Queen Mary," was designed and built by K.B. exclusively, to the specifications of International Marine Radio Co. Ltd., who were responsible for its installation. This is unparalleled testimony to the efficiency and reliability of K.B. Radio—yet another sound reason why K.B. Radio should be your first choice.

KOLSTER-BRANDES LIMITED · FOOTSCRAY · KENT

The cartoon is referring to the use of the letter 'S', backwards, in a national advertising campaign.

Binstead House, near Ryde, and the adjoining estate comprising some 36 acres, which has a sea frontage of about three quarters of a mile. With one exception this is the last of the large houses in the neighbourhood ceasing to be a private residence and, although its future is not quite certain, it will probably be used as a convalescent home. Col Stephenson Clarke told our correspondent that the increasing heavy burden of taxation and the inability nowadays to obtain domestic staff have forced him to sell... (May 31)

A reader calls our attention to a letter recently published in the "Daily Herald," which reads as follows: "I have just returned from a holiday in the Isle of Wight, and while there I was struck by the Islanders' obvious dislike of visitors from the mainland. They do not hesitate to express their feelings either. This was my first holiday in the Island and I was rather surprised to find that our own people should feel this way towards us. – A. R. Reynolds, Hackney, London.

PUBLISHER'S ANNOUNCEMENT. – The Rationing Committee notified all newspapers on Tuesday that the present ration of paper would be reduced as from Monday next by 25 per cent... With the present size of the "County Press" (8 pages of 9 columns) we are already unable to meet the demand for news and advertisements... Although it means serious financial loss*, the proprietors have decided to take off one column from each page and to complete the required saving by making a five per cent. cut in the number of copies printed...(July 19)

———————————◆———————————

Mr Ross-Hime of Ryde wrote to protest about the numbers of trippers visiting his hometown and to share his thoughts on their "low tastes" and also the "cheap flashness" of the Council decor along the seafront...

Aug 23rd, 1947
RYDE – "A SORT OF CONEY ISLAND".
To the Editor, IW. County Press.
Sir,— Ryde, which used to be such a fine good-class little town, now appears to be nothing more than a sort of "Coney Island," catering only for low tastes. The town is packed to suffocation with trippers, who crowd the streets during the day till they are impassable, and who seem to spend the night going up and down the sea front singing bawdy songs and shouting to each other. The town is embellished by such atrocities as loudspeakers every few yards along the front that pump out canned music at high pressure and generally add to the

---

* Up to a point. Maurice Leppard in his history of the County Press, *"Black on Wight"* states "Being a shareholder in the company continued to be highly remunerative, as was shown in July 1947, when the directors recommended a final dividend of ten per cent, plus a bonus of 20 per cent, making, with an interim of 20 per cent, a total of 50 per cent for the year. The staff shared in the prosperity with a £700 bonus, which included £100 for the editor."

bedlam, and the whole is illuminated at night by high-power glaring greeny-white lights suspended on futuristic concrete pillars, which are thoroughly out of keeping with the main architecture of the town. For this cheap flashness we, the residents, are expected to pay incredibly high rates. I am under the impression that not a few of these residents, like myself, seek to move elsewhere, realising that Ryde, under the present regime, has had it.

Yours faithfully, G. L .ROSS-HIME. The Strand, Ryde

RURAL NOTES.

UNUSUAL SIGHT NEAR NEWPORT. — Much interest has been aroused lately by a three-acre field of giant sunflowers, belonging to Mr. G. A. Green, of Durton Farm. Staplers, which made a vivid landmark to people passing along the road between Newport and Arreton. The sunflowers, believed to be the first under mass cultivation on the Island, are being grown for the manufacture of oil for margarine.

CAT VERSUS ADDER. — Driving on the Brighstone Road near Pitt Place recently, Mr. J. Rendell saw a large tabby tomcat engaged in a battle royal with an adder, which he described as one of the largest he had seen. The cat was circling the reptile warily alternately pouncing and retreating out of range, while the adder reared its head and sought an opportunity to strike at its nimble opponent. Fearing that the cat might be fatally bitten if he allowed the fight to continue Mr. Rendell despatched the adder, which measured nearly two feet in length.

LABOUR WOMAN AND DANGEROUS FISH WRAPPINGS. — At a meeting of the Central Committee of women's sections of the Labour Party at Newport on Thursday concern was expressed at the practice of wrapping wet fish in newspaper, so running the risk of disease being spread. It was decided to forward a resolution to the Minister of Health asking for early action.

PRODUCER TO CONSUMER. — Rather than let his marrows and cucumbers rot on the ground, Mr. N. L. Ball, of Sainham Farm, Godshill, loaded them on a lorry and sold them in Shanklin on Saturday morning at 1d. each. Mr. Ball brought over three tons of cucumbers and a large number of marrows, but towards the end of the morning sales dropped and he gave a large number away. His total takings were only £5 17s., not enough to pay expenses. He was satisfied, however, as otherwise he would have received nothing and the crops would have been a complete waste.

LONGEVITY OF FEATHERED PETS. — A Newport lady informs us of a sad bereavement this week — a dove which had been her pet for 28 years has died. The dove, a wild one, was found in the garden with a damaged wing, and the lady rendered first-aid and secured a roomy cage for it. It refused to leave its new home. She wonders if 28 years is a record age for a dove.

It has already been noted how the ill-fated 'PLUTO' pipeline was full of petrol when it was recovered from the sea bed. A year later, appropriately enough just as severe petrol rationing brought leisure motoring to an end, a section of line buried under the Island provided a welcome bounty for the contractors engaged to recover it...

October 4th, 1947.
"PLUTO" OBLIGES ISLAND MOTORISTS.
Island motorists who are "in the know" have recently been able to obtain free and unrationed supplies of petrol which have been doubly welcome in view of the cancellation of the basic ration as from October 1st. This was due to the fact that the "Pluto" pipeline, installed during the war to supply the Forces which invaded the continent, traversed the Island from north to south, and is in process of being dismantled. Although the line was pumped out with water at the conclusion of its period of usefulness, pockets of petrol accumulated in dips and considerable quantities of petrol have either gone to waste or found their way into the tanks of motorists. These, however, have to take the risk of finding water in the fuel. We understand that the position has been examined by oil company experts who have decided that the quantities, although considerable, are insufficient to make the reclamation of the spirit and the separation of the water an economic proposition.

TOWN AND COUNTY NOTES.
POSTAL RELICS. — While dismantling a grate at his home, Gresham House, Mr. J. E. Rolf discovered some interesting old papers, which were probably lost during the time the premises were used as the Post Office. Among them was a 30s. money order issued on December 21st, 1880, payable at Wroxall to Rachael Nash; a letter posted on Ryde Esplanade on October 9th, 1886; and a programme advertising daily steamer excursions starting on June 13th, 1883... Mr. Rolf was removing the grate because of the noise caused by crickets.

GERMAN PRISONERS. — The recent cancellation of certain of the restrictions imposed on prisoners of war appears to have given rise to the impression that prisoners are now allowed complete freedom. Prisoners are permitted to have English currency, received in payment for work authorised by the camp commandant, but some have been supplementing their income by making and selling such things as toys and slippers. This practice is forbidden. Prisoners may enter shops, cinemas, restaurants, and other places of public resort, but they are not allowed to use licensed premises or any premises where liquor is sold. Prisoners are not issued with clothing coupons, nor are they allowed to be in possession of them. The use of public transport is permitted within a 5-mile radius of camp. All prisoners, including men billeted on farms, must be back in camp or billets by 10 p.m.

NORTHWOOD CAMP NOT AVAILABLE FOR HOUSING. — Cowes Council were told that Northwood Camp is to be handed over to the Ministry of Works for housing Polish workers engaged on agricultural and forestry work... The Ministry of Works made a bid to the War Department as long ago as 1945 for any accommodation becoming available at Northwood and Whippingham Camps or Albany Barracks... Mrs. Venner said there would be a lot of disappointment because some young people who had been unable to get one of the prefabs had been looking forward to getting a hut at Northwood Camp. Mr. L. J. Berryman said there was a camp at Rew Street which had been idle for a long time and was going to rack and ruin.

TWO ISLAND AIR ACCIDENTS - FATAL CRASHES AT BRIGHSTONE AND VENTNOR. — Two air crashes in the Island on successive days this week caused the loss of three lives. The aircraft involved were a Sunderland belonging to B.O.A.C., which crashed on Wednesday, with the loss of one life, and a British Air Transport Anson landplane on the daily newspaper run to Jersey from Croydon, which broke up after striking a mast at the Radar Station on St. Boniface Down, Ventnor, on Thursday. Both crashes occurred in thick fog.

———————————————◆———————————————

Freshwater Bay and its attractions, or rather, lack of them, came under the spotlight of a reader from Perthshire...

December 14th, 1947.
THE FUTURE OF FRESHWATER BAY.
To the Editor, IW. County Press.

Sir, — Before the war Freshwater Bay was sadly wanting attention. Visitors did not despise it, but many met with a rude disappointment when they arrived, not from the point of view of scenery or from lack of hospitality from the residents, but from the lack of general facilities. Complaints were lodged on all sides that the Bay was out of date, and particularly that there were no conveniences, but the war came and the matter had to be left. Now, after two years of peace, it is high time that these forgotten things were brought back to mind. The future of Freshwater Bay depends upon its being brought up to date and made comfortable for visitors*...

W. P. THOMSON. Pitlochrie, Perthshire, N.B.

---

* The letter may not have had the desired effect. Aubrey de Selincourt in his book *'Isle of Wight'*, published just a few months later, wrote: *"It is better to travel than to arrive. I wish the saying were not true of Freshwater Bay. This famous beauty spot is as tawdry and sluttish as an unswept room. The dismal hotels, the dreary eating-houses, the neglected shanties, the cracked concrete, the heaped stones, the patient charabancs, the pervading atmosphere of paper-baggery and crumbs, are disconcerting to say the least of it. Being hungry, I entered one of the eating houses - I hoped at least for a bean-paste sandwich or a sawdust bun. But there was nothing - sold out. I escaped as quickly as I could to Tennyson Down..."*

1948.

THE WEEK'S NEWS.

FRESHWATER. — Mr. C. Newbury, licensee of the Star Inn, Freshwater, took his gun and went to the River Yar marshes on Tuesday in the hope of getting a wild duck. He did not see one, but nevertheless took home a good supper for his family. Seeing something dark moving just below the surface of a shallow side stream he fired, and a fine huss, a species of dogfish, leaped four feet out of the water before falling back, dead. The fish was nearly three feet in length and weighed just under six pounds. Fishing with a sporting gun is certainly a novelty, but fishing in rivers with Mills bombs was a popular utility sport with our troops during the two great wars.

GURNARD HOLIDAY CAMP SOLD. — The Gurnard Pines Holiday Camp has recently been purchased by Mr. G. A. Preece (managing director of the Bramble Chine Holiday Camp, Freshwater). The camp was built just prior to the war and almost on completion was taken over by the War Department . It was reopened in 1946.

DEARER WATER — It was agreed that the charges of the Sandown water undertaking should be increased by 50 per cent, and that consideration of a proposed new scale of charges for the Shanklin undertaking be deferred.

———————————◆———————————

The new Labour government had come to power promising to nationalise Britain's key industries. Railways were next on the agenda and on the Island the changeover prompted reminiscences of times gone by...

January 3rd, 1948.

THE ISLAND RAILWAYS.
END OF 85 YEARS OF PRIVATE OWNERSHIP.

A new chapter in the history of the Island railways was opened on Thursday when, as part of the Southern Railway Co.'s system, they passed into public ownership. Since a railway was first opened in the Island in 1862 there have been many changes and the various companies of the early days had a hard struggle in establishing their then new form of transport. Under succeeding amalgamations the railways prospered and, since the final merger in 1923, the Island Railway has played an important part as one of the leading transport undertakings ... It is fitting at this time to pay tribute to its proud record of service to the travelling public, and to record appreciation of the courtesy shown by the officials at all times. It is difficult to-day to realise that when the suggestion was made that there should be a railway in the Island it met with the most determined opposition. The notice in Hampshire papers in 1845 that the company was in the course of formation raised a tremendous storm in the Island... In a short space of time the Island was divided into two camps. The landowners and gentry were practically unanimous in opposing the railway, while the trading classes and the working population were more more inclined to look favourably upon the scheme. The "nobility" argued that the Island should remain unspoiled, while the "common people" replied that they, too, wanted to see what Ventnor was like... Meetings were held at Newport and Cowes, at which there were many hard words. Eventually a resolution was passed at both meetings in favour of railways, but it was 14 years before the opposition of the landowners was finally overcome...

January 17th, 1948.

THE EARLY DAYS OF THE RAILWAY.

The recent reference to the end of the 85 years' private ownership of the Island railways, which have now been absorbed into public ownership under nationalisation, has brought me some interesting reminiscences of the early days of the various Island companies from Mr. W. H. Baker, of Clatterford Road, Carisbrooke, one of the original members of the "County Press" staff. He recalls that when the Cowes and Newport company ran their first train to Newport, the station comprised a wooden hut on the site opposite the present coal company offices at Station Approach. This hut was later burnt down, and the stationmaster at the time was a Mr. Thomas, who was also the landlord of the Sun Inn. When the Newport-Ryde line was commenced in 1870, Mr. Baker, as a boy, used to secure rides on the engine which pulled the trucks carrying the soil from the cutting above the Fairlee tunnel to make up the level of the track opposite Round House. He remembers a navvy, nicknamed "Mutton," being killed there by one of the tips. The first sod of the Newport-Sandown line was turned at Shide fields near the present station. It was a gala occasion, with the former I.W Volunteers on parade and a holiday for all the school children, who received a bun and an orange. When this line was first opened it only ran to Pan, where the station was situated, and the building of the viaduct over Coppins Bridge and the continuation of the track to Newport Station was completed in 1878.

Like J.S. White's shipyard, the Saunders-Roe factories at East Cowes were enjoying a post-war boom. Three huge flying boats were under construction for BOAC airlines and Saunders Roe 'predicted with confidence' that flying boats were the future...

January 17th, 1948.

THREE GIANT FLYING-BOATS BUILDING AT EAST COWES.

FIRST TO BE BEADY IN TWO YEARS.

At the invitation of Messrs. Saunders-Roe, Ltd. a party of London Pressmen, photographers, and representatives of aeronautical journals visited the firm's works at East Cowes on Wednesday to see the progress made in the construction of the three giant flying-boats known as the SR45. It was in May 1946 that the Ministry of Supply accepted the design and proposals made by Messrs. Saunders-Roe to build three flying-boats, which the firm feel confident will gain further fame for the British aircraft industry. The SR45 has been designed to meet the requirements of the most exacting routes in the world. It will have a wing span of 220 feet, and the range and speed required for a direct

England - New York service, flying at 350 miles an hour at a height of eight miles. It is to be powered with 10 Bristol Proteus engines, each of 3500-h.p. and can accommodate up to 100 passengers. The first aircraft is in an advanced stage of construction, and the others are fast taking shape. It is hoped that the first will make its initial flights late in 1949 or in the early part of 1950.*

In spite of its great size the SR 45 is undoubtedly a beautiful craft, shapely and elegant, and promises a high standard of speed and comfort. The decision of the Ministry to entrust Messrs. Saunders-Roe with the development of the SR45 has emphasised the importance attached to the part which flying-boats will play in future long-range air transport, and it is predicted with confidence that other countries will in due course follow the British example.

◆

RURAL NOTES.

ANCIENT VESSEL IN HARBOUR MUD. — Considerable interest has been aroused by the discovery of the remains of an ancient wooden vessel during dredging operations in Yarmouth harbour, and there is much speculation as to its age. The fact that it was found under 12 ft. of silt indicates that it is of great antiquity, but unfortunately it had to be broken up to remove it, and the timbers brought ashore give little indication of its original size or shape. No metal had been used in its construction, the massive oak timbers being pegged together with dowels of the same wood. The largest piece salvaged appears to be a portion of the stern, and a local boatbuilder (Mr. S. Smith), who has carried out a careful examination of the wreckage, ventures the opinion that it may possibly have been a Viking ship. (February 21)

BEAGLING BY BUS.— Passengers on the 8.33 p.m. bus from Newport to Freshwater on Friday week enjoyed the thrills of the chase. A hare, caught in the headlights near the Common, ran ahead in the middle of the road, keeping some 20 yards ahead. It obeyed the one-way traffic signal at the top of High Street and turned sharp left into Basket Lane. Ignoring the side turning into Ommanney Road and the entrance to the Recreation Ground, it led the bus round the corner into Tennyson Road. Again it took no notice of side turnings, and, following the correct traffic route, swung to the right at the school and into South Street. After passing the church, the hare decided that it had had enough, and it was last seen racing across the Square as the bus turned to the left for Freshwater.

---

*In the event, the first SR 45, later named the 'Princess', did not take to the air until August 1952. Engine design problems delayed delivery of the plane to the customer, BOAC, who in 1954 rejected the craft as "out of date technically." The three planes were each loaded with eight tons of silica gel and cocooned awaiting new buyers. Two were stored in hangars at Calshot while the third one was placed on a concrete hard at Medina Road, West Cowes, where it became a local landmark for many years. No buyers were forthcoming and the two planes at Calshot were scrapped in 1965, and the one at Cowes was sold for scrap in 1967.

ISLAND HOUSING RETURNS. — The returns of the Ministry of Health for January show that during that month 24 new houses were completed in the Island (20 by local housing authorities and four by private builders). (March 13)

HEN CHANGES SEX. — A Rhode Island Red hen now in its third year, has confounded its owner Mr. T. Boyes, of Norton Green, Freshwater, by changing its sex. As a pullet the bird laid exceptionally well and last year hatched a clutch of duck eggs, and proved a good mother to the offspring. Early this year it began to crow, developed a fine comb, wattles and tail, and is now the undisputed ruler of the roost.

Despite the war having been over for three years, the Island was still home to hundreds of German prisoners of war. So far there had been only one minor escape scare when an inmate at a Newport camp had returned home late one night but some German P.O.Ws in France, presumably less happy with their accommodation, made a more serious attempt at escape, eventually making their way to the Isle of Wight...

May 22nd, 1948.

GERMAN PRISONERS LAND AT SHANKLIN.
ESCAPE FROM FRENCH CAMP.

Observing what appeared to be a shirt flown as a distress signal from a 40ft. motor launch which drifted into Sandown Bay on Tuesday afternoon, Mr. Bert Kemp, of Shanklin, longshoreman and councillor, put out in his motor-boat to investigate. He found three young Germans on board. They were Gerhard Seelig, Helmut Homeyer, and Erich Schulze, three P.O.W.s who had escaped from a French camp at Le Havre. They had escaped on Monday and stolen the launch. After a fairly rough trip the motor had apparently broken down and they had been carried by the tide into the bay. All were very tired and very seasick. After securing the boat, Mr. Kemp left the young men on board and returned to the beach, where he contacted the local police. Later he took P.C. Wheeler out and they brought the three men ashore, with the suitcases and haversacks containing their belongings. They were met by Police Inspector Turnbull and Sergeant Fry, who took them to Newport Police Station for questioning, and they were later handed over to the military authorities. The three men could speak little English. On Wednesday coastguards, customs officers, and a representative of the French Consulate inspected the stolen launch, which was later towed to Bembridge harbour by Messrs. Wade, of Bembridge. She will remain there until the owners in France have been contacted.

THE WEEK'S NEWS.

ISLAND RAILWAY ENGINES' NEW LOOK. — During April the first engines on the Island Railway system to bear the words "British Railways," in place of the familiar "Southern" have been in service. The first of these was No. 15 (Cowes), which had been repainted and appeared on April 8th on the Ryde-Ventnor service, where she was joined on Saturday by No. 17 (Seaview). No. 33 (Bembridge) was out a few days beforehand and was the first engine with the "new look" to be stationed at Newport... Altogether, there are 28 locomotives on the Island. (May 1)

Monday's "Daily Graphic" contained some fine pictures taken on The Needles lighthouse. One showed lighthouse keeper Ernest Mills, of Cowes, signalling to the Board of Trade signal station on The Needles promontory with an Aldis lamp, which was the only means of communication between the lighthouse and the shore, and other pictures showed the keepers attending to the lamp and baking bread. The accompanying story disclosed a fact which was veiled in wartime secrecy, viz., that German airmen shot up the lantern in 1942, but a repair party from Cowes came out the same day and the light was burning again at night, as it has shone every night since 1858.

THE OLD SHIP. — A letter from the Timber Development Association stated that the association's technical director had examined a portion of the old ship discovered in the harbour during the dredging operations and considered it unlikely that it was a Viking ship because the timber was English oak. It was almost impossible to give any idea of its age as its condition could have been produced in a comparatively short time under the conditions.

YARMOUTH - JACK ASHORE. — The Clerk reported that he had ordered six metal seats for the pier in place of the wooden ones, which he considered would be more suitable for use on the quay. The reason was that when sailors or others came ashore they had sometimes thrown the seats into the sea. Wooden ones floated away and were lost, whereas metal seats sank and could be recovered.

BASIC PETROL IN EVIDENCE. — There was ample evidence of the popularity of petrol restoration on Tuesday. Union Street, the leading shopping centre, which has been a comparatively quiet thoroughfare since the autumn, regained much of its pre-war atmosphere. During the morning one of our reporters counted no fewer than 60 cars parked there, and the majority were privately owned. (June 5)

———————————————◆———————————————

Organised pigeon shoots across the Island were a common event during the thirties and forties, usually co-ordinated via advertisements in the County Press. Food shortages and rationing meant the destruction of pigeons had become even more important than ever and as a consequence the Government was subsidising the cost of shotgun cartridges by 50%. There had never been any opposition to the shoots in the past but this time the County Press received letters from several readers protesting about the event, in particular,"the barbarity of shooting the birds, some of whom may not be shot cleanly. It also seems hardly fair to destroy nesting birds and their fledgelings." The drive began...

May 15th, 1948

The County Agricultural Executive Committee's drive against young rooks is now in full swing. Up to yesterday (Friday) nearly 1200 birds had been marketed. Owing to the dense undergrowth in many of the rookeries, it is estimated that nearly half of the birds destroyed were not found.

◆

The following week saw no letup...

May 22nd, 1948.

ABOUT 7000 ROOKS DESTROYED - NOW FOR THE JACKDAWS.

The County Agricultural Executive Committee's blitz on young rooks came to an end on Thursday, and, although exact figures are not yet available, the pest officer (Mr. G.R.W. Dade) estimates that at least 7000 birds have been destroyed. As it is considered that jackdaws do as much, if not more, damage than rooks, attention is now being turned to thinning them out. The great increase in their numbers is due, largely to the high cost of ammunition. Gamekeepers are not shooting as many as in pre-war years, and more are nesting in high cliffs and the chimneys of buildings where central heating has been installed. Mr. Dade hopes to trap a great many in special 6ft. square cages, with a few of which he accounted for 160 birds last year. He also announced the interesting fact that in the last three years his department has destroyed more than 100,000 rabbits, which have been sold for human consumption.

◆

Life in Britain was about to change forever; the NHS was about to come into being and it was also the end of the line for the Workhouse...

July 3rd, 1948.

THE NEW NATIONAL HEALTH SERVICE.

The new social service, introducing many drastic changes in national health insurance and public health arrangements generally, comes into operation on Monday. In our last issue the new Executive Council for Health published an advertisement in our columns pointing out that there will be no more doctors, dentists, nurses, or hospital beds on the Island than before and that the new service will have to develop before everybody can obtain full benefit from it... Forty-eight doctors in the Island have agreed to cooperate in the scheme and their names can be seen at Post Offices. The Island dentists, too, have this week decided to enter the scheme for the time being and to reconsider their attitude in the light of events.

July 3rd, 1948.
PASSING OF THE POOR LAW.
... The first admissions to the workhouse occurred on August ninth 1774. Persons admitted by reason of "criminality or a loose morals" were entered in the Black Book, had no meat on "meat days,"and wore distinctive clothing "or other disgraceful badges." Stocks of "flax, hemp, wool, cotton thread, iron, stone and wood" were provided for the employment of the poor, and the Guardians were authorised to "set up, use and occupy any trade, mystery or occupation whatever in such house." Amongst the occupations carried on were spinning yarn, shoemaking, and brewing. The officers of the house were a governor, matron, surgeons, apothecaries, chaplain, secretary, and "chappel" clerk. The schoolmaster, nurses, etc, were selected from the poor themselves.

The "House of Industry" has become the Public Assistance Institution, which now includes a separate hospital... The Poor Law is finally and completely to be abolished to-morrow under the provisions of the National Assistance Act. On Monday the entire 440-bed Public Assistance Institution will be transferred to the Regional Hospital Board, to form the largest unit of the Island's free hospital accommodation under the National Health Service Act. The non-sick residents will remain there temporarily until separate hostels can be provided for them, but the atmosphere of "charity" will disappear. Every non-sick resident will pay an agreed fee for the accommodation subject to a minimum of 21s. per week. In the few cases where a State pension or other means are not available, the State, through a government department, will provide the resident with the necessary sum to meet the charge.

◆

The elegant Seaview Pier had been a part of the local landscape since the 1880s. In its heyday Seaview had been a port of departure for Portsmouth and Southsea and the pier had always managed to turn a profit but passenger services and pleasure cruises came to an end with the outbreak of war in 1914, when the Government closed all but necessary cross-Solent services. The pier never regained its custom after the war and in the 1920s, when the new Southern Railway began to sell through tickets from London to the Island using its own ships and routes, the writing was on the wall. The pier lingered on until it was sold just after the war to a mainland developer, Mr. Figgins, for £775.

Now in a sad and sorry state it's future seemed secure when Mr. Figgins declared his intention to renovate the pier. Within a short while, however, he had changed his mind...
July 17th, 1948.
SEAVIEW PIER PROBLEM
PUBLIC MEETING OPPOSE DEMOLITION
There was a packed attendance of ratepayers at a meeting in St Peter's Hall, Seaview, on Monday to discuss the future of the pier, the owner of which had given notice that he intended to demolish it. Col L.W. Lewer said the meeting had been called with regard to certain differences of opinion on the proposed demolition of this unique chain pier. The structure was private property and

had recently changed hands. It was considered to be unsafe. The owner had thought of repairing it and had applied to the Government department for permission to do so, but was inundated with so many forms that he got "fed up" and sent them back and the pier was now going to be pulled down. He had been approached by several people as to what could be done to save it. In whatever action they might take it should be remembered that they would be hampered by restrictions on the use of timber, steel, and concrete, and they would probably go round and round in Government officialdom and in the meantime the pier would fall down. He was told that at present the pier was being held up by barnacles.

Mr. S.L. Matthews, Town Councillor, said that the problem had been brought about by the inability, during the war, to maintain the pier. Its former owner, Mr. Andrew Maitland, had spoken two years ago about its bad condition and the great difficulty in repairing it. Its maintenance had been helped by the small steamers which landed passengers from the mainland during the season, and he said that they would have to face the fact that it would have to be demolished. A few weeks later a letter appeared in the "County Press," giving details of the technicalities involved in saving the pier and nothing more was heard until the sale of the Seagrove Estate, when, with the Esplanade, it was bought by Mr. Figgins, a gentleman in the building trade, of Bedhampton. He felt that it could be restored and set about doing so, but found the difficulties too great, abandoned the project, and came to the conclusion that it would have to go*. They had seen a notice in the "County Press" to that effect, and if there was no response to that announcement it would be demolished after July 14th... The Works Committee then communicated with the owner... So far there had been no reply.... It was proposed that expert advice be obtained to shore up the present pier ... and that the co-operation of Trinity House and Ryde Council be sought... Motion carried.

A sketch of Seaview Pier by our artist (Tom Smitch). Built in 1879 by an Island company, it is 1050 feet long and 40 feet wide at the head and up to a year or so before the war was regularly used by small passenger steamers. The architect was the late Mr. Frank Caws, of Seaview. The Spit, Horse Sands, and No Man's Forts can be seen between the arches.

---

*The following week, the County Press reported that Seaview ratepayers had decided not to offer any financial support for the repair of the pier, and that "on being informed of the committee's decision Mr. Figgins said he would carry on with his plans to demolish the pier entirely and that his 'demolition fleet' might now be expected at Seaview at any time." In the event, Mr. Figgins sold the pier the following month for £1000, realising a healthy profit for the short time he had owned it.

THE WEEK'S NEWS

MUSKET BALLS AT "THE CASTLE." — A new roof is being placed on the Castle Inn at the top of the High Street, which dates from 1684. While the old roof was being removed a small linen bag containing some musket balls (round, and about the size of an ordinary glass and marble) was discovered in an attic.

A HEDGEHOG HUNT. – After being apprehended by the police in the act of stealing lead from a derelict building at West Medina Mills, defendant, James W—, when asked why he was there, replied, "I came down to get a hedgehog, because my wife is not well."... At the Police Station W— made a statement in which he said that his wife fancied a hedgehog, and he had taken his lorry and gone down Stag Lane to get one. When he was turning, the wheel struck something in the road and he found it was a piece of lead. He picked it up and put it in the back of the lorry. Fined £2.

A NEW LIGHT INDUSTRY MAKES GOOD. – A successful business is being conducted at Moira House, Sun Hill, Cowes, by Readers Ltd. The firm have, for a little over 18 months, been engaged in the manufacture of plastic lampshades and are now producing, entirely by hand, artistic lampshades at the rate of about 6000 a week for the biggest retailers of these articles in the country... The company now has 35 full-time workers and over 120 fully paid out-workers, who assemble the shades in their spare time in their own homes and whose average earnings are about 30s. to £2 per week. There is no limit to what out-workers can earn...

ALLEGED IRREGULARITIES AT PARKHURST PRISON. – The Home Office is investigating a letter sent to the Governor, alleged to have been written by a former convict, purporting to show that prisoners' records, including those of IRA men, and other confidential papers were stolen from the Prison... We understand that investigations into other irregularities, including trafficking, are still being made and that five prison officers have been suspended. It is freely rumoured in Newport that Scotland Yard detectives are also enquiring into alleged expensive thefts of prison stores, including shoes and clothing... Among the suspended officers are some with long service.*

◆

In many areas of public life, especially matters of public health, what had gone before was no longer regarded as adequate. For the inhabitants of Arreton, who were still relying on dirty and contaminated wells, 'modern life' couldn't come quick enough...

December 11th, 1948.

WATER SUPPLY FOR ARRETON.

"The days of Rebecca at the well are long past, yet it is a sad commentary that inhabitants of a part of this famous Island have still to use the same methods

---

* Four Parkhurst warders were eventually charged with trafficking tobacco with inmates and stealing prison goods and materials, one being sent to jail for six months the other three being fined.

which were operated 2000 years ago," said Mr. R. F. Buckley (clerk of the Rural District Council) at the public enquiry into the council's request to be allowed to borrow £22,615 to supply the parish of Arreton with a piped water supply... In 1944 a scheme was prepared for water to be supplied by the Vectis Stone Company, who had agreed to let the council have between 10 and 20,000 gallons a day at one shilling a thousand. The company agreed to supply and maintain the pumping plant and were agreeable to the construction of a 50,000 gallon reservoir on St George's Down... A letter from the Parish Council stated that the lack of water very adversely affected the development of the parish. As more root crops were grown in the area, more men per acre were employed, and this labour force had to be imported. There were insufficient houses and more could not be built until there was a water supply. Water was carried from Newport for dairy purposes and the school had no supply at all... A letter from the Women's Institute spoke of nine houses being dependent on one well, which, for three months of the year, 'went dry.' After one family had been taken ill, the well was examined and two mice, one mole, and one frog, in a badly decomposed state were found. The water smelt badly... Doctor John Mills (medical officer of health) said South Arreton residents relied for their supplies upon shallow wells, which had been shown to be contaminated in the most undesirable way. The local school used rainwater collected from the roof and shallow well water. The position at the school had been aggravated by the provision of a new canteen, and, owing to water difficulties, the used crockery had to be taken into Newport to be washed. Mr. H.B. Cullin (sanitary inspector) said that at many times it was impossible to get samples of well water for analysis because of lowness of the level. He had seen many insects in the buckets of water, which smelt badly.There was no doubt that a piped water supply was urgently needed... There were no objectors.

TOWN AND COUNTY NOTES.

A RYDE HOUSE BEING MOVED TO CORNWALL. — "The Gates of St John," a large residence in Riboleau Street, Ryde, built in Italian style in 1911-13, at a cost of £20,000, is being pulled down on the instructions of its owner, Mrs. S.M. Locke, of Henley-on-Thames, and is to be re-erected at Perranarworthal, Cornwall*. The small chapel, orangery, and much ornamental stone and marble work in the grounds are also to be transferred. The property, at present value, is estimated to be worth nearly £100,000. The work is being carried out by J. Ball and Son, of Cowes, and needs much care as each stone has to be numbered.

According to a letter in the "Birmingham Evening Mail" there are some boarding-house keepers who fail to appreciate the value of a satisfied customer. They say: "Last year we spent our holidays in the Isle of Wight. We paid tip-top price and it was awful. The meal at six o'clock was a salad, no change whatsoever. We were glad to eat out, which suited the landlady. Although the

---

* The materials were taken to Perranarworthal but the house was never rebuilt. The stonework spent some years in storage before eventually being auctioned off.

wireless was in the room it was never put on, even on a wet day when we were expected to go out. Are we going again? — No! This year we're off to a holiday camp where we can get a cup of tea in bed, plenty of amusement, exercise, and rest, together with good food and a soft bed, and believe me, it won't cost as much."

RYDE BOAT SERVICE RADAR INSTALLATION MAKES HISTORY. — The Portsmouth-Ryde boat service, for the first time in its long history of well-nigh a century, was regularly maintained in dense and persistent fog during the early part of the week. This ... was the outcome of radar installation on the twin-screw vessel Southsea, which plied regularly in the worst fog experienced for many years... The Southsea carried out a two-hourly service similar to that provided on Sundays. The ship behaved admirably throughout this long period of duty...

───────────────◆───────────────

1949.

TOWN AND COUNTY NOTES.

"If you want to know the time (in Newport) ask a policeman." Do not rely on the clock on the Guildhall, which, in keeping with modern controls, is rendering its reports in triplicate. Two of its faces agree, but the other two differ by about three or four minutes.

NORTHWOOD CEMETERY. — Mrs. Wall asked if anything was being done to repair graves and tidy up Northwood Cemetery, as many people were very distressed at the state of the cemetery. Ald. Warrior said when they took into consideration what happened at the cemetery during the war* he thought they were getting it cleared up very well. He was surprised that people were complaining and would remind them of the big difference in the appearance of the cemetery now compared with three years ago. It all took time...

Following the warning published in the "County Press" of January 15th that a wireless license check was about to be made in the Island, 1346 new licences were taken out.

ANTIQUATED PICTURE POSTCARDS ON SALE. — Mr. Frank Hilton, of Wellfield, Wyatts Lane, Northwood, calls our attention to a matter which should receive immediate attention to preserve the Island's good name as a progressive pleasure resort. He sends a picture postcard of High Street, Newport, which he bought in a local shop this week. It is not only a very poor reproduction, but the type of motor-car and the dress of people in the street

---

* There had been an unpleasant incident in May 1941 when a bomb had fallen in the cemetery, disturbing graves and exposing bodies.

show that the photograph must be at least 40 years old. Mr. Hilton says that at the same time he bought a strip of views of Cowes, and "the Victorian dresses brought a lump to my throat!"...

———————————◆———————————

Austerity had become a way of life. Rationing and shortages were still very much the order of the day and some items would remain on ration until the early 1950s but luckily for children one form of rationing did come to an end...

April 30th, 1949.

OFF-RATION SWEETS.
VERY FEW ISLANDERS WERE GREEDY.

When sweets came off the ration on Sunday the few shops open were besieged, but the main rush came on Monday, when a brisk trade was experienced throughout the day, but no shop was sold out. Certain lines, especially milk chocolate, were soon cleared, but boiled sweets were and still are plentiful. One shop at Newport served over 1000 children in the course of the day, and the popular demand was chewing gum, licorice sticks, licorice "skipping ropes" and pipes and lollipops. Another shop, which normally does a very brisk business with ice-creams, did not sell one all day.

Most customers were reasonable in the amount they purchased, but there were a few instances of greediness. One woman entered a sweet shop carrying a deep wicker basket already filled with sweets, and purchased another three-quarters of a pound... It was a cheering spectacle in Newport on Monday morning to see the crowds of happy children in the streets, enjoying their sweets. Some were "smoking" licorice pipes, and many were to be seen with their cheeks bulging as they consumed their various purchases. Adults were obviously as delighted as the youngsters at this new found freedom; there were many in the queues.

———————————◆———————————

THE WEEK'S NEWS.

"GUEST HOUSES" FOR OLD PEOPLE — The homes for aged and infirm people at present accommodated at St Mary's Hospital, which it is hoped will be ready for occupation shortly, are to be known as "guest houses," and the occupants of the homes are to be known as "guests."... Three buildings in Shanklin and Ventnor were being acquired to house the 80 old people who were at present at St Mary's Hospital.

HOSPITAL STOPS FREE ISSUES OF SWEETS AND TOBACCO. — The Clerk of the County Council raised the question of the free issue of sweets and cigarettes, which had been the custom of the old people in their care to receive. It was stated that the practice was to be discontinued... Councillor Moody said he would not support the cutting off of the supply. It was the only comfort that some of the old people had... It was agreed unanimously to recommend the council to continue the issue of sweets and tobacco.

£15,000 FOR CATS' CLINIC - SHANKLIN WOMAN'S BEQUEST. — Miss
Constance Aston of Shanklin, who died in February, left £51,904... Miss Aston
bequeathed £15,000 to the Cats' Protection League for the endowment and
upkeep of a clinic for cats in the Island...

"THE OLD GREY MARE" - WROXALL VETERAN'S PASSING. — After
spending two years in contented and well earned retirement Snowball, the 35-
year-old grey mare owned by Mr. A.C. Morris of Redhill Lane, Wroxall, died
this week. Seven days a week for 28 years without ever missing a journey was
her proud record. She trotted to Sandown, first with vegetables and in later
years with milk and she was undeterred by snow or ice-bound roads, although
on one occasion her harness froze on her back. Her owner, who is naturally
grieved at the loss of such a good friend and faithful servant, says he does not
think there was another mare to equal her.

———————————◆———————————

Today a trip to London from the Island takes anywhere up to 2½ hours but in 1949 a
Sunday Times journalist on expenses could make the journey in just half an hour...

June 18th, 1949.
THIRTY MINUTES FROM LONDON.
In an article on suggestions for holidays at home and abroad in the "Sunday
Times" this week, Elizabeth Nicholas, the travel correspondent wrote:
"Determined last week-end to avoid train queues and train strikes, I booked
myself a seat on a plane leaving Croydon and flew to the Isle of Wight in 30
minutes. The return fare cost 78s. I had, I must confess, never visited the Isle of
Wight before, and I was most agreeably impressed by its charms. The Island
obviously, has been but lightly touched by the brutish hand of progress, and the
coastal towns have the authentic atmosphere of the old-fashioned seaside resort
which depends on sun and smooth sand and a safe sea for its living. There was
a most pleasing tranquillity about it all, and an excellent lunch at a small inn
was some compensation for the shrimp tea which I was unable to obtain. Last
week I wrote of the glories of Roman cuisine, but on reflection I think there is
much to be said for the country which can provide cold meats, garden-fresh
lettuce and cucumber and tomatoes, home-pickled onions, crusty bread and
butter, and a glass of bitter all for 3s. I stayed, by the way, in a house which was
for many years the home of Tennyson, and is now a hotel. It still has a good deal
of period atmosphere, and there is a most wonderful view across the downs to
the sea...

———————————◆———————————

Déjà vu. Again...

June 25th, 1949.

A BIG BILL TO FOOT FOR NEWPORT'S ROADS

BOROUGH SURVEYOR'S WARNING ABOUT STEADY DETERIORATION.

In the course of a "my job" talk at the luncheon of the Newport Rotary Club on Wednesday, Rotarian Mr. F. Rath, (borough engineer and surveyor) gave a warning that there would be a very big bill to foot with regard to Newport's 57 miles of roads if something were not soon done, because of the steady deterioration... Consideration was being given to a new scheme for utilising the cinders from household refuse, which should be a valuable asset in road-making in the Island...

In the speaker's 32 years in the profession the worst problem with which he had had to contend occurred just before the war, when it was found that sufficient arsenic to poison the entire population of a mainland township had somehow found its way into the water supply. The townspeople never knew of the danger, and the trouble was overcome. It had been caused by a member of the water authority illegally connecting to the water main an apparatus for spraying his fruit trees with an arsenic and nicotine solution. The machine had gone wrong and had pumped the solution into the mains.

TOWN AND COUNTY NOTES.

A 4ft. GRASS SNAKE. — Mr. Fred Short of Alderbury Road, Newport, killed a grass snake 4 foot long in his garden on Sunday. The snake was seen for the first time in the morning and in the evening it was again discovered in Mr. Short's garden and, not being recognised as a harmless snake, and because there were several very young children in the vicinity, it was killed with a blow from a spade.

17TH-CENTURY BARN BECOMES A BUNGALOW. — Travellers on the Carisbrooke-Shorwell road will have noticed with interest the demolition of the old barn at Cheverton and its re-erection as a modern bungalow by Messrs. A. Henton, of Loverstone.* The walls, which date from the 17th century, have been carefully preserved in the design... A keen interest in the change has been taken by Mr. R. Cheverton as one of his forbears, a Lord Mayor of London, first built the barn. The original date has been carefully preserved and the current date incorporated. The alterations give much improved visibility to road users at what was formerly a dangerous "blind" spot.

MICAH MOREY'S CAVE. A GRIM RELIC GOES. — It has been brought to our notice that Micah Morey's cave in the chalk pit on Arreton Down, near the Hare and Hounds Roadhouse, no longer exists. Enquiries have revealed that the cave was not destroyed as a result of excavations by the company operating the chalk pit, but that it was blown up during the war by the army during training. The cave used to extend some 30 feet into the down, but now only a few feet remain.

---

* Cheverton Bungalow opposite Cheverton Farm.

The survival rate of oiled seabirds is not high, few of them recovering despite the care and attention they receive. In the summer of 1949, the Davies children of Colwell Bay had found an oiled guillemot on the beach and taken it home where despite their best efforts, it could not be persuaded to eat...

July 9th, 1949

OIL POLLUTION OF THE SEA.

Further evidence of the cruelty inflicted on seabirds by such oil discharges comes in the following story from the West Wight. Walking along the beach at Colwell Bay nearly 3 weeks ago the young children of Mr. S. Davies of Burley, Colwell Common found a young guillemot lying helpless, smothered in oil. They carried the bird home to their father, who sacrificed his margarine ration to remove the oil, only to be faced with the bigger problem of how to keep the foundling alive. Fortunately one of his Light Sussex hens had hatched out four chicks the previous day, and as an experiment the little seabird was placed in the run with them. From the start the hen treated the newcomer as one of her family, and it quickly disappeared from sight under her protective wings. But for two days the guillemot refused to feed ... even disdaining to accept a sardine from the hand of Mr. Davies. At last Mr. Davies tossed a sardine to the hen and immediately she picked it up the guillemot ran forward with open beak to be fed. The hen carefully broke up the sardine and fed the youngster with tiny morsels. After devouring a second one it came boldly forward to take one direct from Mr. Davies's hand. Within a few minutes it had disposed of two tins of sardines, and Mr. Davies began to look around for a cheaper source of food supply. Fortunately he is in business as a fish and chip fryer, and the waste on fish tails is now put to good use. The bird, much to the horror of its foster mother, loves to swim in a bowl of water, and is now so tame that it has been taken down to the beach for a bathe. It is still too young to fly and presents a comical sight as it struts about among the chickens. Once it can fly Mr. Davies will make no attempt to restrain his novel pet from taking its freedom, but he believes that by that time it will be content to live in the garden.

THE WEEKS NEWS.

BONCHURCH CONVENT TO BE CLOSED - LARGE-SCALE EXHUMATION CARRIED OUT. — The Convent of the Sacred Heart at East Dene, Bonchurch, will be closing at the end of the summer... Consequently the private cemetery of the community will no longer be used. On Tuesday morning at 9.30 a.m what is believed to be one of the largest Home Office Exhumation Orders was carried out when 55 former residents who were buried in the cemetery between 1907 and 1948 were reinterred in a communal grave at Ventnor Cemetery. (July 9)

RADIO AND TELEVISION IN THE ISLAND - LOCAL EXPERT'S VIEWS. — Mr. W.G. Sherratt, of Newport, a pioneer of radio and television in the Island gave an address to Newport Rotary Club, in the course of which he ... had to answer a barrage of questions on the performance of television sets in the

Island. He said there were about 200 viewers in the Island at the moment. It was true that reception varied considerably, but one reason was that so many people used the wrong kind of aerial... Ideal sites for television receivers faced in the direction of London. Such ideal spots were to be found in Palmer's Road, Wootton, and high parts of Ryde. In the speaker's opinion anyone who possessed a house on such a site could add £1000 to its value! (laughter).

SWARMING BEES OUT NAVIGATION LIGHT. UNUSUAL OCCURRENCE. - During the recent spell of hot weather a report was received at Trinity House headquarters at Cowes that two adjacent buoys in the Western Solent were extinguished... On arrival at the first buoy there was a strong smell of gas and they found the light mechanism was working perfectly but the light was extinguished. On opening up the top cowl of the lantern the cause was found - it had been invaded by a swarm of bees. Entering through the air passage they had virtually starved the light of oxygen thereby extinguishing it, and as the gas mechanism was still working, the lantern was almost filled with gassed bees... On visiting the second buoy, the cause of failure was found to be exactly similar.

THE DROUGHT CONTINUES. TODAY WILL BE THE 60TH DAY. — Only just over one tenth of an inch of rain has been recorded at Newport since June 3rd, and the drought which, if no rain falls today, will have lasted for 60 days, is the longest on record... It has provided ideal holiday and harvesting weather but a gloomier "harvest" lies ahead in serious shortages of root and green crops... The parched meadows are worrying the dairy farmers, as the milk yield is falling rapidly... At Garrett's Farm on St. Georges Down, ponds have completely dried out and the Fire Brigade have been carrying water to the farm for the cattle. This has never happened before in the memory of the occupier, (Mr. T.H. Alexander), who has farmed there for 60 years.

OBNOXIOUS SMELL AT EAST COWES. — A petition bearing 73 signatures asking the council to remedy the unpleasant smell caused by the seaweed at East Cowes Front has been referred to the Harbour Commissioners for their observations.

◆

The housing shortage showed no signs of ending and letters like the following still made regular appearances in the letters column...

October 8th, 1949.
HOUSING SHORTAGE AT NEWPORT.
As one who has spent three and a half years living, sleeping, and eating in one room I would like to support the Newport and District Trades' Council's remarks on the housing shortage and Newport. Probably the first part of the Pan housing estate will take two years to complete; in the meantime, has anything else being planned? The Newport Council have done nothing so far as agricultural workers are concerned. Those unfortunate enough to be classed as

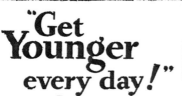

key workers (as I myself am classed, with four years' war service and two children) can only wait until the council decide to build in the areas in which they work. It is no relief to have someone say "Things will turn out all right in the end." When?

R.V.S. Dodnor

————————————◆————————————

TOWN AND COUNTY NOTES.

THE HISTORY OF DL 39. — Considerable interest has been aroused at the Devon Industries Fair this week by the exhibition of a 8 ½ hp. Humber car, a 1903 model, the property of Mr. A.F.J. Gibbs... The car has the Island registered number of DL 39, and its original owner was Dr C. Adkins, of Freshwater. It was the first car introduced to Freshwater and was later taken to Devonshire... and the car had travelled over 100,000 miles before being sold for scrap in 1917. It was a wreck when Mr. Gibbs rescued it after a 27 year sojourn on an open scrapheap.... The car now runs extremely well at a speed of 25-30 miles an hour, and does about 20 miles to the gallon, climbing all the steep Dartmoor hills with ease and arousing curiosity wherever it goes....

CENTRALISATION OF ISLAND GAS PRODUCTION. — The County Council have decided that the proposals of the Southern Gas Board to erect a gas manufacturing plant on a site at Kingston, East Cowes, to serve the whole Island, except, for the time being, the extreme western end, should be approved in principle... When the new works were completed, the manufacturing stations at Cowes, East Cowes, Newport, Ryde, and Shanklin would be closed down very soon afterwards.

A RAILWAY QUESTIONNAIRE. - WILL THE ST LAWRENCE LINE BE CLOSED? — At the recent Ventnor Town Council meeting a letter was read from the stationmaster (Mr. H.W. Harms) referring to a questionnaire he had received from British Railways regarding the future of the Ventnor West - St Lawrence line and in which he was instructed to obtain local views and reactions. He stated that the information was required in order that every aspect of the question could be assessed before further consideration was given to a proposal to close down the line.... Cllr. Worley said that on one occasion recently a good deal of road traffic had been held up at Dean Crossing for about five or six minutes while a train went by carrying only one passenger.

DOUBLE-DECKERS IN THE UNDERCLIFF. — Sir, Everyone who loves nature and finds joy in beauty will feel horrified at the thought of cutting down some of the grand old trees of the Undercliff in order to let double-decker buses pass along. I write as one who loves trees, who has known these trees and kept them in memory for over 70 years. They are the glory of one of England's most beautiful roads. To destroy some and mutilate others would be sacrilege. The Island has suffered much in the last few years. Surely this further outrage can be prevented? "TROUBLED."

Although BBC television had not officially arrived in the Isle of Wight, those with deep pockets and a suitable aerial had been able to pick up the transmissions for the London area since 1936. Reception of the broadcasts from the Alexandra Palace transmitter was erratic, depending on location and weather conditions, and the long-distance viewers on the Island, numbering some 200 by now, were awaiting the opening of a dedicated transmitter to serve the South of England. (It finally arrived in 1954 with the opening of the Rowridge transmitter, still in service today.) To bring the decade to a close, Mr. Sherratt, the Newport radio and TV dealer, spelt out the likely situation as he saw it...

December 24th, 1949.

THE ISLAND AND TELEVISION

Mr. W.G. Sherratt, of Newport, writes on this subject as follows : "On Saturday the new BBC television station near Birmingham was opened. When conditions are favourable it will be received with tremendous strength in the Isle of Wight, but a different television and aerial will be needed to receive it, as the wavelength is not the same as that used by the London transmitter .. By the end of 1952 about 70% of the United Kingdom will be brought into the service area. This leaves about 30%, including the Isle of Wight, out in the cold... Will the Isle of Wight be fortunate enough to ever receive television? I sincerely hope so... We shall have to wait until about 1954 to find out. The outlook is bleak indeed, yet the Island itself would be an ideal site for a television transmitter.... If only the BBC could be persuaded to make some tests they would find that an Island transmitter would serve a very large proportion of Southern England extremely well, including Brighton, Portsmouth, Southampton, and Bournemouth, who are all at present out in the cold...
